Exploring English Grammar

This engaging textbook bridges the gap between traditional and functional grammar. Starting with a traditional approach, students will develop a firm grasp of traditional tools for analysis and learn how Systemic Functional Grammar (SFG) can be used to enrich the traditional formal approach.

Using a problem-solving approach, readers explore how grammatical structures function in different contexts. Each chapter focuses on a real-world issue or problem that can be investigated linguistically – such as 'mis'-translation or problems arising from a communication disorder – using a wide variety of thought-provoking and engaging texts and activities, including adverts, cartoons, phone calls, and chatrooms. Through these activities, readers will become equipped to understand and analyse formal and functional grammar in different genres and styles.

With usable and accessible activities throughout, *Exploring English Grammar* is ideal for upper undergraduate and postgraduate students of English language and linguistics.

Caroline Coffin is Reader in Applied Linguistics at the Open University, UK. Prior to joining the Open University she was a lecturer at the University of Technology, Sydney, Australia.

Jim Donohue is currently Head of Open ELT, the English Language Teaching Unit of the Open University. He has been involved in the teaching of English for specific purposes for 20 years.

Sarah North is currently Senior Lecturer in Applied Language Studies at the Open University, UK. She has been involved in English language teaching and teacher training in a number of countries, including Indonesia, Tanzania, China, India, Malaysia, and Mexico.

Exploring English Grammar represents a bold and innovative attempt to present university level grammar from a functional perspective without losing sight of the formal conventions ... by the end of the book, through the careful staging of the many activities provided, along with the worked answers, students should have built up a broad range of skills for describing and analysing texts in terms of the various levels of meaning that they make.

Tom Bartlett, Centre for Language and
Communication Research,
Cardiff University, UK

This is the book we've been waiting for – a bridge between traditional grammar and the more functional approach to grammar, which focuses on 'language as a resource for meaning'. Full of practical activities and written in an accessible manner, this book will become an indispensable reference for those interested in how language works.

Beverly Derewianka, Professor of Language
Education, University of Wollongong, Australia

Exploring English Grammar

From formal to functional

**Caroline Coffin,
Jim Donohue, and
Sarah North**

Routledge
Taylor & Francis Group

LONDON AND NEW YORK

First published 2009
by Routledge
2 Park Square, Milton Park, Abingdon, Oxon OX14 4RN

Simultaneously published in the USA and Canada
by Routledge
270 Madison Ave, New York, NY 10016

Routledge is an imprint of the Taylor & Francis Group, an informa business

Typeset in Stone Serif and Stone Sans by
Florence Production Ltd, Stoodleigh, Devon

Printed and bound in Great Britain by
CPI Antony Rowe, Chippenham, Wiltshire

British Library Cataloguing in Publication Data
A catalogue record for this book is available from the British Library

Library of Congress Cataloging in Publication Data
Coffin, Caroline, 1958–.
  Exploring English grammar: from formal to functional/Caroline Coffin,
  Jim Donohue, and Sarah North.
      p. cm.
  1. English language – Grammar.   2. Systemic grammar.   3. Functionalism
  (Linguistics)   I. Donohue, Jim.   II. North, Sarah.   III. Title.
  PE1112.C578 2009
  425 – dc22   2008051500

ISBN10: 0–415–47815–4 (hbk)
ISBN10: 0–415–47816–2 (pbk)

ISBN13: 978–0–415–47815–1 (hbk)
ISBN13: 978–0–415–47816–8 (pbk)

Contents

Acknowledgements

Crystal, D., Fletcher, P. and Garman, M. (1989) *Grammatical Analysis of Language Disability*, 2nd edition, London: Whurr, pp. 153–4 (reproduced by kind permission of John Wiley & Sons Ltd).

Painter, C. (1984) *Into the Mother Tongue: A Case Study In Early Language Development* (reproduced by kind permission of Continuum International Publishing).

Kerl, S. (1867) *A Comprehensive Grammar of the English Language: for the Use of Schools,* New York: Ivison, Phinney, Blakeman & Co., pp. 4, 8.

Carter, R. (1992) 'Language in the National Curriculum. Materials for Professional Development', Nottingham University, p. 255 (reproduced by kind permission of the author).

Bradley, A. 'Adult conversation' from www.finslippy.com (reproduced by kind permission of the author).

Short extract of transcript from 'Food Advice Centres, 1941 trailer from Ministry of Food, Imperial War Museum, film reference NPC 1583, available from www.screenonline.org.uk/film/id/424904/index.html (reproduced by kind permission of the Imperial War Museum).

Acknowledgements

'Kitemaking' from http://zhidao.baidu.com/question/4197118.html?fr=qrl3

Pecan almond tart recipe from www.fooddownunder.com

Hickman, L. (2007) 'Call 999! With the midwives stuck in traffic and his wife going into labour', *The Guardian*, 15 September 2007, © Guardian News and Media Ltd 2007 (reproduced with kind permission).

'Making a potato battery', from www.doitpoms.ac.uk, © DoITPoMS, University of Cambridge (reproduced with kind permission of DoITPoMS).

'The Why Files – Biomass Energy Cycle', from http://whyfiles.org, © University of Wisconsin, Board of Regents (reproduced with kind permission).

Adams, C. (1995) 'If Teflon is non-sticky', from The Straight Dope, http://www.straightdope.com/classics/a4_173.html, © 1995 Creative Loafing Media Inc. (reproduced with kind permission).

Short extract from Patent 4395445, from www.FreePatentsOnline.com (reproduced with kind permission).

'Tempeh', from www.fao.org (reproduced with kind permission).

Riha, W.E. and Wendorf, W.L. (1993) Short extract from 'Evaluation of color in smoked cheese by sensory and objective methods', *Journal Of Dairy Science*, 76(6): 1491–7 (reproduced with kind permission).

'Kitemaking', from www.travelchinaguide.com/intro/arts/kites.htm (reproduced with kind permission).

Extract from http://en.wikipedia.org/wiki/Dog

Simpson, Rita C., Briggs, Sarah L., Ovens, J. and Swales, John M. (2002) *The Michigan Corpus of Academic Spoken English*, Ann Arbor, MI: The Regents of the University of Michigan (reproduced with kind permission).

Extract from www.articlesdashboard.com

Extract from http://www.vnstyle.vdc.com re T'rung.

Review of Odjo D'Agua Hotel, from www.thomson.co.uk. (reproduced with kind permission of TUI UK).

WGASA found at www.snopes.com

Short extract from www.historylearningsite.co.uk (reproduced with kind permission of Chris Trueman).

Short extract from Louis de Bernieres, *Captain Corelli's Mandolin*, Vintage (reproduced with kind permission of The Random House Group Limited and Random House Inc.).

Tannen, D. (2007) 'Talking Voices, Repetition, Dialogue, and Imagery' in *Conversational Discourse,* 2nd edition, Cambridge University Press, pp. 130–40 (reproduced with kind permission of Cambridge University Press).

Danks, K. (2007) 'Stricken ship poses threat', 9 June 2007 (reproduced with kind permission of Australian Associated Press).

Extract from Amitav Ghosh, *The Glass Palace,* © Amitav Ghosh, HarperCollins Publishers (reproduced with kind permission of HarperCollins Publishers).

Fawkes, C. (2007) Online weather report, BBC Online, 14.00 Friday 26 October 2007 (reproduced with kind permission of BBC Weather).

Brompton, S. (2007) Daily Horoscope extract. © Sally Brompton. As published in the *New York Post,* Friday 26 October 2007 (reproduced with kind permission).

Crown copyright material is reproduced with the permission of the Controller of HMSO.

Text 6 Committee meeting, from www.athel.com/sample.html Reprinted with kind permission.

Fernandez-Armestro, F. (1999) Extract from 'What if the Armada had landed?' *The New Statesman,* 20 December 1999 (reproduced with kind permission).

Corballis, Michael C. (1992) Extract from *Lopsided Ape: Evolution of the Generative Mind,* Oxford University Press (reproduced with kind permission of Oxford University Press).

Extract from http://en.wikipedia.org/wiki/spider

Wilson, J. (2005) 'Capitol cleared in plane alert', *The Guardian,* 12 May 2005, © Guardian News & Media Ltd 2005 (reproduced with kind permission).

Acknowledgements

We are grateful to the Universities of Warwick and Reading for permission to use an extract from the British Academic Spoken English (BASE) corpus (http://www2.warwick.ac.uk/fac/soc/al/research/projects/resources/base/). The corpus was developed at the Universities of Warwick and Reading under the directorship of Hilary Nesi and Paul Thompson. Corpus development was assisted by funding from the University of Warwick, the University of Reading, BALEAP, EURALEX, the British Academy, and the Arts and Humanities Research Council.

Beechener, C. and Jacob, A. (2004) Short extracts from *Think History: Modern Times*, Heinemann (reproduced with kind permission of Pearson Education Limited).

'John, I'm looking for a job, and I've heard . . .' Article provided by wikiHow, a collaborative writing project to build the world's largest, highest quality how-to manual. Please edit this article and find author credits at wikiHow.com. Content on wikiHow can be shared under a Creative Commons License.

Short extract from transcript 'Ireland v England' 30 March 2003, BBC Sport, © BBC (reproduced with kind permission).

Extract from 'Wilkinson throws doubts aside' Hayward, *The Daily Telegraph*, 31 March 2003 (reproduced with kind permission of Telegraph Media Group).

Sierra, K., (2008) image 'The elimination of wrinkles is achieved . . .', from http://headrush.typepad.com, © Kathy Sierra (reproduced with kind permission).

Short extract from www.zephyrus.co.uk about rock types (reproduced with kind permission).

Lake, R., extract from 'The Three Magic Arrows' by Rosemary Lake. © Rosemary Lake (reproduced with kind permission of the author, www.rosemarylake.com).

De Silva, Joyce and Burns, Anne (1999) *Focus on Grammar*, © Macquarie University (reproduced with kind permission from the National Centre for English Language Teaching and Research (NCELTR)).

Extract and image 'What causes a fallen star?' from http://starchild.gsfc.nasa.gov.

Pehrson, Marnie 'Everything I Needed to Know About Personality Types I Learned in Little League Baseball', www.marniepherson.com (reproduced with kind permission of the author).

Extract from 'Can you explain the basic difference between analog and digital technology?', from www.howstuffworks.com (reproduced with kind permission).

Extract from www.savvychicks.com (reproduced with kind permission).

Swinburn, K., Baker, G. and Howard, D. One figure from *CAT: The Comprehensive Aphasia Test*, Psychology Press (reproduced with kind permission of Taylor and Francis Books (UK)).

Figure 8.4 and Text 8.1 from www.animatedknots.com (reproduced with kind permission of Alan W. Grogono of Animated Knots by Grog).

Peanuts cartoon 'Father's Day strip', 18 June 1989 (reproduced with kind permission of Knight Features).

Ali, Mohammed N. (2004) 'How to get yourself on the door of a job: A Cross-cultural Contrastive Study of Arabic and English Job Application Letters', in *Journal of Multilingual and Multicultural Development*, 25(1): 1–23 (reproduced with kind permission of Taylor & Francis Journals UK).

Bennett, R.G. (1995) review of 'Spider Taxonomy', *Journal of Arachnology*, 23(1), (reproduced with kind permission of the author).

Extract from 'Spiders!' Exhibition, © Australian Museum (reproduced with kind permission).

'Hedge funds uncovered', *The Financial Times*, 1 April 2005, © Financial Times (reproduced with kind permission).

Nelson, M., extracts from 'The Business English Corpus (BE)' © Mike Nelson (reproduced with kind permission of the author).

Goodale, The Language of Meetings, 1E © 1987 Heinle/ELT, a part of Cengage Learning Inc. (reproduced with kind permission www.cengage.com/permissions).

Biber, D., Conrad, S. and Leech, G. (2002) *Longman Student Grammar of Spoken and Written English* (reproduced with kind permission of Pearson Education Limited).

Extracts from 'NatWest Markets, 'Global Economic Forecasts' Second Quarter, 1992' (reproduced with kind permission of Media Relations, Royal Bank Scotland).

Bateman, J., Train notice from 'An introduction to applying linguistics'.

Personal statement, Ms Chioma P. Ukaigwe, from www.studential.com (reproduced with the kind permission of the author).

Campbell, C. (1999) *The Lady in White,* Cambridge University Press, Cambridge English Readers, Level 4 (reproduced with kind permission of Cambridge University Press).

Dennett, D., extract from Professor Daniel Dennett's lecture on Consciousness (reproduced with the kind permission of Professor Daniel Dennett).

Fine, J. (2006) *Language in Psychiatry: A Handbook of Clinical Practice*, Equinox Publishing Ltd, p. 123, © Equinox Publishing Ltd 2006 (reproduced with kind permission).

With thanks to Clare Painter for permission to use the extracts from her research into child language acquisition.

We would like to thank our critical readers who commented on the first proof draft of this book and made invaluable suggestions for its improvement. In particular we would like to thank Judy Anderson, Mike Baynham, Kieran O'Halloran and Diane Phillips.

one

From formal to functional grammar

1.1 Introduction

This book sets out to show that it is useful to know about grammar. Each chapter aims to illustrate how knowledge about grammar can be used to achieve real-world goals and solve real-world communication problems. Although this may seem uncontroversial, it is not the way that grammar is always perceived. Not all those who write about grammar would make such a claim, and not all those who have studied grammar have experienced such benefits.

The grammar that will be presented here is functional grammar. Functional grammar focuses on how language is used – that is, on the functions of language. It is sometimes contrasted with formal grammar. Formal grammar focuses on how language is formed – that is, on the forms of language.

It would be possible to present formal and functional grammar as entirely different from each other. Instead this book seeks to explore the connections between formal and functional grammar. In order to start the process, you are asked to consider what it means to <u>know about grammar</u> and, in particular, what <u>you</u> know about grammar.

1

It could be said that grammar is something that everybody <u>knows</u> but not everybody <u>knows about</u>. To consider that distinction, read the following:

Mary in Glasgow work

If asked about this string of words, people who have been brought up speaking English – and many who haven't – would probably think there is 'something wrong' with it. If they have never been introduced to grammatical terminology, they might say something like:

You can't have work at the end. It has to go after Mary. And you need an s on the end of work.

They can impose grammatical order on these words because they <u>know grammar</u> intuitively as <u>language users</u> – having been immersed in English all their lives.

The comments above can be contrasted with the following:

If this is a sentence, the verb should come directly after the subject.
And because the subject of the verb is the third person singular, the form
of the verb should agree with the subject and have an s on the end.

For the moment, it is not important to understand fully the terminology used in this response. What should be clear is that it is a different kind of explanation to the previous one and shows some of what we have called 'knowledge about grammar' – the grammatical principles and grammatical terminology of a <u>language observer</u>. These are the comments of someone who has not just learned to use the grammar of the language, but also how to talk about it.

Scenario

The scenario that follows is designed to focus your awareness on yourself as an observer of language. It is based on a real-world issue – problems in a child's language development. The child, who is three years, five months old, has been diagnosed as having the language level of a child of eighteen months and is undergoing a period of speech therapy. The extract below comes from a session near the beginning of that period of therapy.

Activity 1.1

Describe the difficulties that the child (Paul) has in this extract and what the speech therapist (T) seems to be doing in order to deal with these difficulties.

Text 1.1 Speech therapy

Speech therapist (T); Child (P); Child's father (D)

T:	The horse is/(pause)
P:	jumping
T:	yes/you say it
P:	jumping
T:	no/say the whole thing
P:	whole thing/ – horse is jumping

. . .

T:	the big horse is jumping/you can say that one for me
P:	no
T:	yes/go on/
P:	can't say it/
D:	you can say it/
T:	you can
P:	okay
T:	go on/
P:	horse is – jumping/
T:	good boy/the horse is jumping/the big horse is jumping/
P:	big horse jumping/

. . .

(Crystal, D., Fletcher, P. and Garman, M. (1989 2nd edition) *Grammatical analysis of language disability*, pp. 153–4, London: Whurr)

In order to explain what is happening in this therapy session, it would – just about – be possible to give an explanation that simply used the language from the transcript. You could say:

The therapist is trying to teach Paul to say *the big horse is jumping.* Paul has difficulty doing this and at different times leaves out *the horse is, the,* and *is.* In the end, Paul almost says *the big horse is jumping* but he leaves out *is.*

However, this is a limited explanation. It is highly specific to this session. Why is the therapist trying to do this? What does Paul achieve by the end of the session? To talk about the language in Text 1.1 in a more general way, some grammatical terminology is useful. Think back to your own explanation and notice which grammatical terminology you used in it.

Your terminology may have been more, or less, specialised. A certain amount of grammatical terminology is in common, everyday use: *word* and *sentence* are examples. Some other grammatical terms are probably less commonly used, but have some kind of meaning for many people: *verb, noun, adjective, subject,* and *clause* are examples that may have occurred in your explanation. Other grammatical terms can be seen as more specialised and less commonly used: *structure, noun phrase, determiner, verb phrase, auxiliary,* and *aspect* are examples of less common terms that could be used to explain what is happening in this session.

Activity 1.2

The explanation that follows was given by the speech and language specialists who organised the therapy session. Read their explanation and notice which grammatical terms they use. Compare these with your own. Do they use any terms that you did not? Did you use any they do not? If you used the same grammatical terms, are you able to tell whether they use them with the same meaning that you do? Are these specialists using the same grammatical principles as you?

Text 1.2 The therapists' explanation

The session was concerned with expanding noun phrases in Subject (S) position in SVO (subject–verb–object) clause structures. The noun phrase was expanded by inserting an adjective between the determiner and the noun. The model structure was of the type *The big horse is jumping the fence.* We built up to the first model in stages – *the horse is jumping*, *the big horse is jumping* – because we knew that P was variably imitating auxiliaries and that he reduced structures too long for him rather unpredictably. The first excerpt shows him with the shortest structure, *the horse is jumping*.

T: The horse is/(pause)
P: jumping
T: yes/you say it
P: jumping
T: no/say the whole thing
P: whole thing/ – horse is jumping

Apart from P's little joke of literal repetition, it seems that the only item in this sequence he has difficulty with is the determiner. The next excerpt from the same session comes when T increases the number of items in the model by adding an adjective, *big*, in the noun phrase, the horse.

> Note that noun phrases are mainly referred to as nominal groups in this book.

T: the big horse is jumping/you can say that one for me
P: no
T: yes/go on/
P: can't say it/
D: you can say it/
T: you can
P: okay
T: go on/
P: horse is – jumping/
T: good boy/the horse is jumping/the big horse is jumping/
P: big horse jumping/

As soon as another item is added, P cuts out one of the items he is already producing, usually the auxiliary (*is* in *is jumping*). The only way T could get him to include the auxiliary was to emphasise it, and then P would omit the adjective from the noun phrase . . . It is interesting to see P's own reaction to the model given him, in the excerpt quoted. He was obviously well aware of the problem on a conscious level.

(Crystal, D., Fletcher, P. and Garman, M. (1989, 2nd edition), *Grammatical analysis of language disability*, pp. 153–4, London: Whurr)

By using grammatical terminology in their explanation, the specialists are able to show how this particular instance of language use fits into the overall development of a child's language. Without the grammatical terms, it would be possible to say that the goal of the activity was to help Paul produce 'longer strings of words'. And in fact, 'mean length of utterance' is one of the features that speech therapists do measure as part of their diagnosis of language development. However, the terminology shows that the activity in this session does more than develop the length of the utterance; it develops the child's grammar.

For the moment, it is not the purpose of the activity to explain the grammatical terms used by the speech therapists. The purpose is to put you in the role of language observer and for you to reflect on your current knowledge about grammar. The therapists describe Paul's language by using their knowledge of formal grammar and focusing on the forms of Paul's language. The terms they use in this formal description will be explained more thoroughly throughout this book.

1.2 A functional approach

The speech therapists in the extract above are using their knowledge of formal grammar to describe what is happening in the therapy session. The next activity contrasts that formal description with a different description of a child's language, derived from functional grammar.

Activity 1.3

Each of the following interactions is a short exchange between a two-year-old child (Hal, H) and his mother (M). For each exchange, decide how you could describe what the child is doing. For example, in exchange (v), Hal is *giving information*. What grammatical terms could you use to describe these exchanges?

Text 1.3 A child's interactions with his mother

(i) H: Some Mummy? (holding up biscuit)
     M: Thank you darling.

(ii) H: Mummy fix car (thrusting toy car in her hands)
      M: Alright, I'll have a go

(iii) H: Little girl crying
       M: Yes, she must have hurt herself.

(iv) H: Where's the lid?
      M: Don't know love

(v) M: What did you do today?
     H: Throw frisbee.

(vi) M: You are a baby, Hal
      H: Not baby; that's Hal (pointing at self)

(Painter, C. (1984) *Into the mother tongue: A case study in early language development*, pp. 236–7, London and Dover, NH: Pinter)

The Answer key provides only the first part of the answer to this activity. Labels such as *demanding a service* or *requesting information* identify what Hal does in each of the exchanges. They are usually referred to as **communicative functions**. They do not appear in a formal approach to grammar and, from a formal point of view, may not be regarded as part of grammar at all. However, what people do and mean through language is important in a functional approach to language.

In Activity 1.3, it is unlikely that you based your labelling of these utterances explicitly on their grammar. Instead, you probably focused on their meaning. But in order to make himself understood Hal is using grammar – and, in fact, developing grammar for that purpose. To explain more fully what Hal is doing and how he is doing it, an approach is needed that can relate form to function. That is the approach to language that this book adopts. By the end of this first chapter, some answers will have been provided for the second question in Activity 1.3.

1.3 Perspectives on grammar

For the purposes of this book, we categorise grammar into three types, according to the focus of attention in each: (i) formal, (ii) communicative, and (iii) systemic functional. The first half of the book presents a communicative approach to formal grammar. It focuses on grammatical forms but explores what these forms are used for. The second half of the book presents a systemic functional approach. It reconsiders grammatical forms in terms of which forms we use, in which contexts, for which purposes. The book thus constitutes a journey from the more formal end of the grammatical spectrum towards a more functional one.

In actual language use, form and function cannot exist separately. But in formal grammar, form is treated separately from function. Communicative approaches, and, still more, systemic functional ones, seek to describe language in ways that bring form and function together. The question for a language observer is where grammar sits along the spectrum from form to function – closer to the form end, or closer to the function end?

Our intention is to demonstrate that a combined form- and function-focused grammar provides important practical insights into the achievement of real-world goals and the solution of real-world problems.

GRAMMAR?

FORM ———————————————————— FUNCTION

1.4 Formal grammar

Traditional grammar can be traced back to the study of rhetoric in ancient Greece. This was concerned with how to create speeches that would inform, persuade, or entertain listeners and with the arrangements of words designed to achieve this. In this way, grammar was related to meaning and function. The relationship between rhetoric and grammar was preserved as the use of writing spread through the middle ages and the classical rhetorical tradition was applied to written texts.

However, the connection between grammar, meaning, and function began to be lost in the 'school grammars' developed to teach the growing school populations of the seventeenth and eighteenth centuries. Increasingly, the study of grammar in school came to focus on isolated words and sentences and the applications of grammatical 'rules' derived from the long-dead languages of Greek and Latin. A sample from one of these school grammars can be seen in the next activity.

Activity 1.4

Text 1.4 shows two pages from *A Comprehensive Grammar of the English language: For the use of schools*, by Simon Kerl A.M., 1861. Bearing in mind the grammatical features highlighted in the speech therapy session in the opening scenario of this chapter, look through the extract and consider whether and how such grammatical information can be related to the therapy session.

Text 1.4 Nouns and pronouns

4   NOUNS AND PRONOUNS.

2. NOUNS AND PRONOUNS.

What is a noun?

A noun is a name.

EXAMPLES: God, Mary, man, men, George Washington, instructor, sky, sun, stars, clouds, town, St. Louis, street, flock, flower, soul, feeling, sense, motion, behavior.

Names are given to persons, to spiritual beings, to brute animals, and to things. The word *objects* may be used as a general term for all these classes.

Tell me which are the nouns in the following sentences :—

Lions and ostriches are found in Africa.

John and Joseph drove the horses to the pasture.

Pinks and roses are blooming in the garden.

Apples, peaches, melons, corn, and potatoes, are brought to market.

A proper noun is the name given to a particular object, to distinguish it from other objects of the same kind.

Ex.—George, Susan, William Shakespeare, London, New York, Mississippi, Monday, January; the *Robert Fulton*; the *Intelligencer*; the *Azores.*

A common noun is a name that can be applied to every object of the same kind.

Ex.—Boy, tree, house, city, river, road, horse, chair, ink, bird, blackbird.

Briefly: A *common* noun is a *gener'ic* name; and a *proper* noun, an *individ'ual* name. The former rather tells *what* the object is; and the latter, *who* or *which* it is.

Generic means belonging to a class; and *individual*, belonging to one object or group only, as distinguished from others of the same kind. All the objects in the world may be divided into a limited number of classes; as, rivers, valleys, hills, cities, leaves, flowers. A few of these classes—namely, persons, places, months, days, ships, boats, horses, oxen, rivers, mountains, and some others—are of so much importance to us in our daily affairs, that we have an extra name for each object of the class; as, *Thomas, Smith, Chicago, Missouri*. The names of the former kind are *common* nouns; those of the latter, *proper* nouns. A proper noun begins with a capital letter.

How many kinds of nouns are there, and what are they?

What is a pronoun?

A **pronoun** is a word that supplies the place of a noun.

Ex.—" William promised Mary that William would lend Mary William's grammar, that Mary might study the grammar," is expressed with greater facility and more agreeably, by saying, " William promised Mary that *he* would lend *her his* grammar, that *she* might study *it.*"

Pro means *for*, or *in stead of*; hence *pronoun* means *for a noun*. The word *substantive* is often used as a general term to denote either a noun or a pronoun, or whatever is used in the sense of a noun.

What is a personal pronoun?

A **personal** pronoun is one of that class of pronouns which are used to distinguish the three grammatical persons.

Ex.—" *I* told *you he* was not at home." " *We* told *him you* were not at home."

Persons, in grammar, are properties of words to distinguish the speaker, what is spoken to, and what is spoken of, from one another.

Which are the personal pronouns?

I, my, mine, myself, me; we, our, ours, (ourself,) ourselves, us;—thou, thy, thine, thyself, thee; you, ye, your, yours, yourself, yourselves;—he, his, him, himself; she, her, hers, herself; it, its, itself; they, their, theirs, them, and *themselves*

8   NOUNS AND PRONOUNS.

When must a noun or pronoun agree in case with another noun or pronoun?

When it is but a repetition of the other, or when it denotes, by way of explanation, the same thing.

Ex.—" I, *I* am the *man*." " Friends, false *friends*, have ruined me." " Smith is a *barber*." "Smith the *barber* is my *neighbor*."

How can the different cases of nouns be distinguished?

By their meanings: or, the *nominative* may be found by asking a question with *who* or *what* before the verb; the *objective*, with *whom* or *what* after the verb; and the *possessive* is known by the apostrophe.

Ex.—"Mary plucked flowers for John's sister." Who plucked?—plucked what?—for whom?

C. Having now shown you what properties nouns and pronouns have, I shall next show you, briefly and regularly, how the different nouns and pronouns are written to express these properties. This process is called *declension*.

What, then, is it, to decline a noun or pronoun?

To **decline** a noun or pronoun, is to show, in some regular way, what forms it has to express its grammatical properties.

Observe that nouns sometimes remain unchanged, and that pronouns are sometimes wholly changed, to express their properties.

DECLENSION OF NOUNS AND PRONOUNS.

Nouns.

	SINGULAR.			PLURAL.	
Nominative.	Possessive.	Objective.	Nominative.	Possessive	Objective.
Boy,	boy's,	boy;	boys,	boys',	boys.
Man,	man's,	man;	men,	men's,	men.
Lady,	lady's,	lady;	ladies,	ladies'	ladies.
Fox,	fox's,	fox;	foxes,	foxes',	foxes.
John,	John's,	John.			

Pronouns.

	SINGULAR.			PLURAL		
	Nom.	Poss.	Obj.	Nom.	Poss.	Obj.
1st Pers.	I,	my or mine,	me;	we,	our or ours,	us.
2d Pers.	Thou or you,	thy or thine, your or yours,	thee or you;	ye or you,	your or yours,	you.
3d Pers.	Mas. He,	his,	him;			
	Fem. She,	her or hers,	her;	they,	their or theirs,	them.
	Neut. It,	its,	It;			

	Nom. or Obj.		Nom. or Obj.
1.	Myself (or ourself);		ourselves.
2.	Thyself or yourself;		yourselves.
3.	Himself, herself, itself;		themselves.

Nom.	Poss.	Obj.	Nom.	Poss.	Obj.
One,	one's,	one;	ones,	ones',	ones.
Other,	other's,	other;	others,	others',	others

(Kerl, S., A.M. (1861), *A Comprehensive Grammar of the English language. For the use of schools,* Iveson, Blakeman, Taylor & Co.: New York; available from http://books.google.com/books?id=Hg8BAAAAYAAJ &dq=editions:099ZspPe68mSlSyc8o3MP)

It is difficult to relate the contents of this school grammar book to the therapists' work in a practical way, other than to notice that it refers to a *noun* as one of the 'parts of speech'. However, although the 'declension of nouns', for example, seems very remote from what a child does when they communicate in English, in fact, there is much in this school grammar that remains useable today.

School grammar books have traditionally recognised eight parts of speech. Each 'part of speech' is a **word-class** – a term that can be used for classifying words as 'nouns', 'verbs', 'adjectives', and so on. You have already seen the therapists using some of these word-class labels, for example, in their reference to *inserting an adjective between the determiner and the noun.* In order to teach the parts of speech, school grammar lessons introduced word-classes with simple definitions and illustrations.

For example, definitions of word-classes based on meanings:

> a **noun** is 'the name of a person, place, or thing';
> a **verb** is a 'doing, being, or having word'.

Definitions of word-classes based on relationships between words:

> an **adjective** 'describes a noun';
> an **adverb** 'modifies a verb'.

Although these four word-class definitions are very limited, they are sufficient for basic school grammar activities.

Activity 1.5

Using the simple definitions given above, identify the parts of speech in each of the sentences below, which, apart from the first one, come from *A Comprehensive Grammar of the English language*. Mark them with the following abbreviations:

n (noun), v (verb), adj (adjective), and adv (adverb)

The first one has been done as an example. Some words belong to other word-classes and cannot be labelled with these abbreviations.

         adj **n**   **v v**   **n**

1   The big horse is jumping the fence.

2   Mary plucked flowers for John's sister.

3   Lions and ostriches are found in Africa.

4   To think always accurately is a great accomplishment.

5   William promised Mary that he would lend her his grammar.

(Kerl, S., A.M. (1861), *A Comprehensive Grammar of the English language. For the use of schools*, Iveson, Blakeman, Taylor & Co.: New York; available from http://books.google.com/books?id=Hg8BAAAAYAA J&dq=editions:099ZspPe68mSlSyc8o3MP)

Even for these relatively simple sentences, not all the classifications are straightforward. Why isn't *John's* an adjective? How far is the noun, *accomplishment*, 'a thing'? Nonetheless, the limited 'definitions' above provide an everyday sense of the meanings of these four word-classes.

The four remaining word-classes are, perhaps, generally less well known and less easy to define.

Activity 1.6

Four more word-classes are presented below, with illustrations taken from the sentences in Activity 1.5. Using the definitions provided for Activity 1.5 as examples, write basic school grammar definitions for these.

Conjunction	and, that
Preposition	for, in
Determiner[1]	the, a, her, his
Pronoun	he

As the somewhat unsatisfactory definitions in the Answer key demonstrate, defining word-classes is not easy, and perhaps the best way to learn them is through exposure to examples. However, the question remains: what is the practical value of labelling words by their class? By reproducing isolated school grammar sentences, Activity 1.5 offered little opportunity to consider this question. The next activity provides a more authentic language sample in order to consider the question further.

Activity 1.7

The text below is the beginning of a report based on a school field trip, written by a nine-year-old boy. Label each of the words using the following word-class abbreviations:

det, v, n, pron, adj, adv, conj, prep

Then decide whether or how such labelling might be useful to either the boy or his teacher.

Text 1.5 Hedges

Hedges are valuable to the wild creatures of the country because they

provide homes, food, shelter, warmth, and protection for them.

This gives rise to birds and animals having their own territories.

We have heard two robins quarrelling over territories. We saw the

footprints of rabbits spreading from their hold near the hedges and then

we saw the footprints all over their territories and returning back to the

hedges.

(Carter, R. (1992), *Language in the National Curriculum*, Materials for Professional Development, p. 255, Nottingham University)

This writing was regarded as successful for a nine-year-old boy. Simply labelling the words provides limited insight into his success. However, the purpose of word-class labelling is to name and classify words and, so, is the beginning of analysis. In this case, it would be possible to congratulate the writer for having used a wide range of suitable <u>nouns</u> (*food, shelter, warmth, protection, territories*) and raise with him the question whether the <u>noun</u> he has spelt as *hold* is actually the noun *holt* or *hole*. We might want to draw his attention to the formation of the <u>verb</u> *have heard* and discuss possible alternatives. The word-class labels provide a vocabulary for this discussion and a way of organising it.

However, if grammar is to repay the effort involved in learning these labels – as well as many more – it might be expected to provide more insights than this. Identifying the word-class of words is a beginning, but its real value depends on what the labelling is used for.

A second school grammar activity popular up until the 1960s, which appears to go further than ascribing classes to words, was 'sentence parsing'. Sentence parsing is quite similar to what the therapists do in Text 1.2 when they say:

> *This session was concerned with expanding noun groups in Subject (S) position in SVO clause structures . . . The model structure was of the type The big horse is jumping the fence.*

The therapists do not refer to *sentence* or *parsing* but talk about *clause* and *structure*. (We will consider later why they do not speak about sentences.)

Presented as a parsed sentence, the therapists' 'model structure' looks like this:

Subject	Verb	Object
The big horse	*is jumping*	*the fence.*

The speech therapists' analysis identifies three main elements in the sentence above: subject, verb, and object. Expressed in simple school grammar terms, we could define these elements and their relationships as follows:

> *The subject is the person or thing that does the verb. The verb is the doing word. The object is the person or thing that the subject does the verb to.*

Although this is an oversimplified definition, it is adequate for the next activity.

A second important feature of sentence parsing is that, while word-classes only apply to individual words (e.g. *horse*, *big*, *the*), the terms subject, verb, and object can apply to groups of words as well, as demonstrated below.

Subject	Verb	Object
Noun	Verb	Noun
horses	*eat*	*grass*

15

Subject			Verb		Object	
Determiner	Adjective	Noun	Verb	Verb	Determiner	Noun
The	big	horse	is	jumping	the	fence.

Recognising how individual words are grouped to make up elements of a sentence is an important advance on simply labelling words according to their word-class. In modern grammar, even in sentences where each element is only one word, words are seen as parts of groups. When there is more than one word in a group, a particular word is treated as the main word, and the group is named after that word. This is illustrated below.

Subject			Verb		Object	
Nominal group			Verbal group		Nominal group	
Determiner	Adjective	Noun	Verb	Verb	Determiner	Noun
The	big	horse	is	jumping	the	fence.

Subject	Verb	Object
Nominal group	Verbal group	Nominal group
Noun	Verb	Noun
horses	eat	grass

As the tables show, a group is named after the main word in the group. Where the main word is a verb, the group is known as a **verbal group** (is _jumping_, _eat_ – main word underlined). Where the main word is a noun, the group is known as a **nominal group** (the big _horse_, _horses_). (Alternative terms are 'verb phrase' and 'noun phrase'.) By placing an emphasis on groups, these analyses go beyond sentence parsing as carried out in school grammars. This format will be used for clause analysis throughout this book.

Activity 1.8

Referring to the analysis above for guidance, identify the subject, verb, and object elements of each of the following sentences from *A Comprehensive Grammar*. Use the tables underneath the sentences for the analysis. If any part of a sentence does not seem to function as subject, verb, or object, leave it out of the analysis.

Subject–verb–object analysis

1   The soil produces cotton, rice, and sugar.
2   Mary plucked flowers for John's sister.
3   Give John the book
4   To think always accurately is a great accomplishment.

1

Clause element							
Group							
Word-class							
	The	*soil*	*produces*	*cotton,*	*rice,*	*and*	*sugar.*

2

Clause element						
Group						
Word-class						
	Mary	*plucked*	*flowers*	*for*	*John's*	*sister.*

3

Clause element				
Group				
Word-class				
	Give	*John*	*the*	*book.*

4

Clause element							
Group							
Word-class							
	To think	*always*	*accurately*	*is*	*a*	*great*	*accomplishment.*

As the verbs in the first two sentences are a particular type of 'doing' word, the school grammar definitions of subject, verb, and object fit well, although there is one part of Sentence 2 that is not accounted for by the SVO pattern – *for John's sister*.

Sentences 3 and 4 do not fit the SVO pattern so well. The verb in Sentence 3 is a 'doing word' but it is an **imperative form**, so has no subject. Sentence 3, therefore, has a VO pattern rather than an SVO one. In Sentence 4, the main verbal group is not a 'doing' word but a 'being' word (*is*). This means that the nominal group that follows (*a great accomplishment*) is not an object but something else. Finally, Sentence 4 has a second verbal group – *to think*. To parse this sentence, some kind of test for identifying which verb is the main verb is needed.

The complexities of even quite simple sentence parsing and the multitude of abstract rules required to carry it out led to increasing doubts about the value of teaching school grammar of this kind. By the second half of the twentieth century, it had been abandoned in the UK, US, and Australia. It continues in school English teaching in other parts of the world.

1.5 Communicative approaches to language

Another profession with an interest in grammar is teaching English for speakers of other languages (ESOL). For many years, ESOL teaching depended on a traditional account of grammar. However, the ESOL profession developed this account to be more appropriate to learners who are acquiring a new language, as opposed to developing an understanding of their own one. The focus was on incremental accumulation of language structures, with learners moving from 'easier' structures towards 'more difficult' ones.

By the 1970s, disappointment with ESOL learners' frequent incapacity to transfer knowledge of grammar structures in the classroom to actual communication outside led to the introduction of the apparently revolutionary 'communicative approach'. This challenged the traditional ESOL grammar-based syllabus and began to build syllabuses around 'communicative functions'.

Some examples of communicative functions were introduced in Activity 1.3 (*A child's interactions with his mother*). They included demanding a service, requesting and giving information, offering something, and contradicting. These, and many more communicative functions, became the basis of syllabuses designed to be more communicative than traditional grammar-based syllabuses.

Although some English language education professionals argued that grammatical knowledge served no useful purpose in the learning of such communicative functions or communication generally, in practice the English language education profession has since been at the forefront of attempting to relate grammar to communicative functions.

1.6 Clauses

Before considering how communicative functions and grammar may be related, we need to consider two different terms that have been used interchangeably so far – sentence and clause. Because school grammars focused on written language, the basic unit of analysis was a **sentence**, which 'begins with a capital letter and ends with a full stop'. New technology and the 'communicative turn' encouraged analysts to pay more attention to the streams of sound that constitute spoken language – where capital letters and full stops don't exist. As a result, the basic unit of analysis in contemporary grammar is the **clause**. This term existed in traditional grammar but was overshadowed by the emphasis on sentences. A clause in traditional grammar either constituted all or part of a sentence. This will be considered further in the course of the next activity, which practises identifying clauses in the absence of capital letters and full stops.

Activity 1.9

Text 1.6 is the beginning of the transcript of a telephone conversation (you will read the second half in Activity 1.10). In the telephone call a wife informs her husband of a disturbing discovery she has made at home. It has been transcribed with no punctuation (except apostrophes) or capital letters.

Identify each of the <u>complete</u> clauses in the text. First underline all the verbs in the text. Remember that a verb can be a 'doing, being or having word'. Since all complete clauses must have a verb, this will help you to decide where a clause begins and ends. Mark off the clause using double lines ||. You will find a number of incomplete clauses or single words. Put brackets round these and leave them out of the analysis. The first line has been done as an example.

Text 1.6 Crisis at home – part one

W:	|| i called the exterminator || there's a thing in our garage ||
M:	why are you out of breath
W:	i'm running in circles so anyway this thing must go the exterminator is coming
M:	like an insect thing
W:	OH NO NO NO like a big fuzzy gray thing big very big
M:	can you stop talking in exclamations
W:	no it's very big way up high in the rafters where it can drop on me i'm never going in there again
M:	is it like a
W:	probably a raccoon or a possum or a mutant raccoon possum hybrid i asked him if it was rabid and he laughed at me i think that means no
M:	okay honey i'm sure it's fine

(http://www.finslippy.com/finslippy/2007/05/transcript_of_p.html)

This transcript does not contain any information about pauses, intonation, or other non-verbal cues, so some of the clause boundaries are open to interpretation. However, it is likely that you noticed there are a number of complete clauses and a number of obviously incomplete ones. All but four of the complete clauses could be represented as sentences in a written text; that is, they contain a subject and a verb and could begin with a capital letter and end with a full stop. This means they are **independent clauses**, which can stand by themselves.

In the following examples, the subject and verb are shown separated off by single lines. Like the double lines for separating off clauses, this is a convention we will use throughout this book.

|| i | called | the exterminator ||
  S   V

there | 's | a thing in our garage ||
  S   V

Text 1.6 includes some clauses that are not able to stand by themselves. Look at the following three, which are connected by the conjunctions *if* and *and*.

|| i asked him || if it was rabid || and he laughed at me ||

In writing, these three clauses would be presented as a single sentence. Although they are all connected, they are not all connected in the same way. Whereas two clauses are independent, one is **dependent**.

|| i asked him || if it was rabid ||

are connected by the conjunction *if*.

The conjunction *if* is a **subordinating conjunction**. It makes the clause it begins dependent on another clause. *if it was rabid* cannot stand on its own: it is a **dependent clause**.

The conjunction *and*, which joins the first two clauses to the third clause, is a **coordinating conjunction**.

|| and he laughed at me ||

Coordinating conjunctions do not create a dependency relationship between the clauses they combine. The clause above is an independent clause.

Coordinating and subordinating conjunctions constitute a small, fixed set of words that play a particularly significant role in communication as a result of the connections they create between clauses.

where it can drop on me is similar to *if it was rabid*, in that *it can drop on me* is a complete clause, but the word *where* is a subordinating conjunction. *where it can drop on me* is therefore a dependent clause. What the wife says previously, *way up high in the rafters*, is not an independent clause, as it doesn't have a verb. It is common in spoken language to find grammar operating in ways like this that would be regarded as incorrect in written language.

Despite some of the complexities of analysing the stream of sounds that make up a conversation, such analysis shows how communication is achieved by manipulating the building blocks of language. These blocks – or **units** as they are called – are words, groups, and clauses. The study of grammar is the study of how these are combined – and, although formal grammar does not always make this clear, they are combined for communicative purposes.

1.7 Clause elements

Using only simple definitions, three clause elements have been identified so far: subject, verb, and object. As suggested in Activity 1.8, this does not account for all the elements of clauses. There are two further ones that will be identified in the next activity.

Activity 1.10

This activity presents the remainder of the dialogue you started work on in Activity 1.9.

(a) Continue marking off the clauses with double lines || as you did in Activity 1.9. Look out for subject–verb patterns to help you identify the beginnings and ends of clauses. Once again, there are some combinations of dependent and independent clauses. As in the previous activity, there are a number of single words or groups of words that do not constitute clauses. Put brackets round these and leave them out of the analysis.

(b) Using the subject–verb–object pattern that was introduced earlier, label the elements of the clauses listed on pp. 23–5, extracted from the dialogue below. Leave blank any parts that you cannot identify. Do not look at the answer until you have read the commentary at the end of the activity.

Text 1.7 Crisis at home – part two

W: ||he said||it was $185||

M: what's a 185

W: no, $185

M: oh, i thought that was like a code like we got a 185 up here we got a 324 situation in the garage like that (laugh)

W: (silence)

M: honey

W: i never wanted to live here i hate nature

M: i think it was your decision actually

W: he's going to set a trap that means we have to call back when the trap is filled it's going to be in the trap i'm never going near the trap never never never ever

M: no one said you had to

W: i'm going back outside to get my stuff if the raccoon eats me you have to marry again henry needs a mom

M: i think i'll marry the raccoon then there will always be a little bit of you around

(http://www.finslippy.com/finslippy/2007/05/transcript_of_p.html)

Clause element				
Group				
Word-class				
	I	*called*	*the*	*exterminator*

Clause element				
Group				
Word-class				
	there	*'s*	*a*	*thing*

23

Clause element					
Group					
Word-class					
	i	*'m*	*running*	*in*	*circles*

Clause element				
Group				
Word-class				
	this	*thing*	*must*	*go*

Clause element				
Group				
Word-class				
	it	*'s*	*very*	*big*

Clause element								
Group								
Word-class								
	so	*i*	*'m*	*never*	*going*	*in*	*there*	*again*

Clause element			
Group			
Word-class			
	i	*hate*	*nature*

Clause element							
Group							
Word-class							
	it	*'s*	*going*	*to be*	*in*	*the*	*trap*

Clause element							
Group							
Word-class							
	i	*'m*	*never*	*going*	*near*	*the*	*trap*

In fact, only three of these clauses can be labelled fully using subject, verb, and object labels. Two other labels are needed to complete the analysis. These are complement and adjunct.

Objects were previously defined in school grammar terms as 'the person or thing that the subject does the verb to'. This definition is only effective when the verb is a particular kind of 'doing word', known as a **transitive verb**, that can take an object (*called, asked, got, eats, needs, marry* are examples in the 'Crisis' text). Of the many verbs that are not transitive, *to be* is one of the most common. The information following *to be* is not an object but is often a **complement**.

|| It | 's | very big ||
   S   V   C

|| Then | there | will always be | a little bit of you around ||
         S   V   C

Complements can be **adjectival groups** (that is, a group built around an adjective, such as *very big*), or nominal groups (that is, groups built around a noun, such as *a little bit of you around*). Other kinds of complement exist with other verbs, but these illustrations are sufficient for this chapter.

The second element that has not been identified yet is the **adjunct**.[2] It is illustrated by this clause:

I | 'm never going | in there | again
S V   A   A   A

As this example shows, an adjunct can be either an **adverbial group** (that is, a group built around an adverb, such as *again*), or a **prepositional phrase** (that is, a group built around a preposition, such as *in there*). Adjuncts are less central to the grammar of a clause than the other four clause elements and, if they are omitted, the clause can often still make sense.

Before looking at the answer for this activity, fill in any of the blanks you left in the tables above.

1.8 The finite

Having established that there are five clause elements and labelled them subject, verb, object, complement, and adjunct (SVOCA), we will now focus on the verb part of this clause structure. As you saw in the last two activities, the essential unit in any clause is the verb or verbal group. No clause can be complete without at least a verb. However, for a clause to be <u>independent</u>, it is not sufficient that it has a verb; the verb also has to be **finite**. The next activity begins to explore why.

Activity 1.11

Imagine you're a student who is writing a school project on nutrition in the twentieth century. You have discovered the text below, written in 1941 to announce the establishment of Food Advice Centres, and are planning to plagiarise it. You will need to end up with a historical account of Food Advice Centres rather than a contemporary description of them. After changing the opening to read *In 1941, the Ministry of Food,* what are the minimum changes you'd have to make to the text below so as to locate it in the past?

Text 1.8 Food Advice Centres

In 1941, the Ministry of Food . . . has opened Food Advice Centres all over the country and more are being set up. Their advice is free whether you want to know about buying food or cooking it. Some Food Advice Centres answer 2000 questions a week. There are Food Advisors in marketplaces and Food Advisors in the streets. They'll give you all the help you care to ask for. The people who work at the Food Advice Centres can advise you how best to use the food you buy or the things you grow for yourself. In some places Food Advisors will help you with your shopping so that you can buy the best cheaply. If you ask them, they'll come back to your kitchen and suggest new and appetising dishes. In this way everyone can make sure that their wartime meals are as healthy and economical as possible.

(Food Advice Centres. 1941 trailer from Ministry of Food. IWM Film and Video Archive Loans Catalogue; available from http://www.screenonline.org.uk/film/id/424904/index.html)

The minimum that an intending plagiarist would have to do would be to change the verbs to past tense. This would probably not fool a teacher, as there are other aspects of the text that would give the game away – but at least the grammatical form would be suitable.

You may have noticed that not all the verbs need to be changed. For example, of all the verb forms in the sentences below, only those under-lined are affected when the tense of the sentence is changed from present to past.

Their advice <u>was</u> free whether you <u>wanted</u> to know about buying food or cooking it.

They <u>would</u> give you all the help you <u>cared</u> to ask for.

To know, buying, cooking, give, to ask are not marked for tense.

In changing the tense from present to past, you had to pick out just the finite verbs. A **finite verb** is a verb that is marked for tense (present or past).* Verb forms such as *to know* and *buying* are **non-finite**.

The importance of Activity 1.11 is that it demonstrates that not all verbs in a clause are equal. For a clause to be <u>independent</u>, there must be a **finite element** in the verbal group – a verb that is marked for tense.

In some cases, the finite element is the only verb in the verbal group. These verbs are known as **lexical verbs**.

<u>answered</u> questions; <u>was</u> free

In other cases, there is an **auxiliary verb** before the lexical verb in the group. An auxiliary verb is a 'helping verb' that carries a meaning related to the main lexical verb which cannot be signalled by the main lexical verb. Often there is only one auxiliary verb, although there may be more than one, as in the example below, where the lexical verb is *set up* and the two auxiliary verbs are *were* and *being*.

were being set up

Whether there is one lexical verb, one auxiliary verb and a lexical verb, or more than one auxiliary and a lexical verb, the finite element is always the first verb in the verbal group. In the example above, *were* is the finite element – it is the verb that is marked for tense.

In some cases, there are two lexical verbs. Again, it is the first one that is the finite element.

started to say; stopped talking

The finite element locates the clause in time. This is the minimum requirement for a clause to be independent. If the only verb in a clause is

---

* It is also marked for number (singular or plural) to agree with the subject.

not finite, then the clause cannot be independent. It will depend on another clause to locate it in time.

Converting a text from present to past tense, or from past to present, can be used as a test for identifying the finite element in a clause. As will be seen in this and subsequent chapters, locating the clause in time is only one of a number of significant roles the finite element plays in communication.

1.9 Subject–verb patterns in clauses

It is now time to begin answering the question that was left unanswered at the end of Activity 1.3, *A child's interactions with his mother*: how can formal grammar be related to the communicative functions identified in that activity. In the last four activities you have looked mostly at clauses with a particular pattern of subject and verb.

```
|| I | called | the exterminator ||
   S      V

|| It | 's | very big ||
   S     V
```

Such a sequence – subject followed by verb (SV) – is a defining feature of one of three major clause structures. This clause structure is known as the **declarative**. If you consider the communicative functions from Activity 1.3 and look at the two clauses above, you will probably identify their communicative function as giving information. There is a close connection between a declarative clause structure and this communicative function. We will return to the connection below.

There are two other structures to be considered.

Activity 1.12

(a) Look back at Text 1.8 and underline some examples of full clauses that have a different subject–verb pattern to the declarative one. Look at both the man's and woman's words.

(b) Use the tables below to analyse these clauses from Text 1.8.

Clause element						
Group						
Word-class						
	why	are	you	out	of	breath

Clause element						
Group						
Word-class						
	can	you	stop	talking	in	exclamations

Clause element				
Group				
Word-class				
	what	's	a	185

Clause element				
Group				
Word-class				
	is	it	an	insect

The verb–subject pattern (VS) in these clause structures distinguishes them from declaratives. These are **interrogative** clauses. There are two main types of interrogative: those that begin with a *wh-* word and those that don't. Interrogatives that don't begin with *wh*-words usually invite a *yes* or *no* answer and are known as **polar interrogatives**. Except for the verbs *to be*, which is the main verb in three of these examples, and *to have*, which is not exemplified here, forming an interrogative requires the use of an auxiliary verb. This can be seen in the second example, where the auxiliary verb *can* is used to create the verb–subject pattern. Very commonly, the verbs *do* and *be* are the auxiliaries in interrogative clauses.

<u>Do</u> you want me to come up there?

What <u>were</u> you thinking about?

As pointed out in Activity 1.11, these finite auxiliaries are marked for tense. We can now see a second role they perform – to construct interrogatives. As with the declarative clause structure, there is a connection between the interrogative clause structure and the communicative functions in Activity 1.3, particularly that of requesting information.

The final one of the three main clause structures is not actually used in the telephone conversation. The next activity looks at some constructed examples that could have been.

Activity 1.13

Analyse the following three clauses.

Clause element				
Group				
Word-class				
	Take	*this*	*thing*	*away.*

Clause element			
Group			
Word-class			
	Marry	*someone*	*else.*

Clause element			
Group			
Word-class			
	Come	*here*	*quickly.*

These clauses are examples of the imperative. The pattern begins with a verb, and no subject is necessary. This clause structure can be connected with the communicative function of demanding a service introduced in Activity 1.3.

The following table summarises the relationship between the subject–verb pattern and the type of clause.

Subject–verb pattern		Clause type
Subject–Verb	*I called the exterminator.*	Declarative
Verb–Subject	*Why are you out of breath?*	Interrogative
Verb	*Marry someone else.*	Imperative

These three main clause types underlie all the communication of the children and adults observed so far in this chapter. Through their organisation of language into these patterns, they achieve their communicative goals with greater or less success. In children who are developing language, the relationship is a direct one. We see Hal demanding a service with the imperative clause, *Mummy, fix car.* For adults, the relationship between form and function is not so direct. Demanding the same service in a garage is likely to be by means of the interrogative, *Could you fix the car?* Developing the main clause structures and then manipulating them for communicative effectiveness is the process that we see Hal embarked on. For the time being, *Mummy, fix car* is effective. But he still has much language to learn.

1.10 Clause patterns and communicative functions

We are now in a position to consider some of what Hal does have to learn in order to develop adult wordings for the communicative functions he needs to perform. To focus attention on how his grammar is developing, the next activity compares Hal's actual words with some possible adult versions of the clauses he produces.

Activity 1.14

Hal's version is given first, and a 'more adult' version is given in the table following. Use the tables to carry out an analysis of the rewritten versions. Then compare Hal's original utterance with the rewritten ones. Which word-classes does Hal leave out?

  H: Little girl crying

Clause element					
Group					
Word-class					
	That	*little*	*girl*	*is*	*crying.*

33

H: Where's the lid?

Clause element				
Group				
Word-class				
	Where	's	the	lid?

H: Some Mummy? (holding up biscuit)

Clause element					
Group					
Word-class					
	Do	you	want	some	Mummy?

H: Mummy fix car.

Clause element			
Group			
Word-class			
	fix	the	car

H: Throw frisbee.

Clause element				
Group				
Word-class				
	I	*threw*	*a*	*frisbee.*

H: Not baby

Clause element					
Group					
Word-class					
	I	*'m*	*not*	*a*	*baby.*

In four of the six utterances, Hal leaves out words that affect the subject–verb part of the clause – in particular, the finite element of the verbal group. The significance of the finite element was considered in Section 1.8. In adult situations, where Hal is not surrounded by such supportive listeners as his parents, who are able to use the context and the close familiarity they share with him to make sense of his utterances, his manipulation of the grammar of this part of the clause will be critical for his communication success.

There is clearly a connection between the language forms that Hal is developing and the communicative functions he seeks to perform. Communicative grammar descriptions are designed to demonstrate what these connections are. The first half of *Exploring English Language* provides such an account of communicative grammar. It is an account that is grounded completely in the familiar terminology and categories of formal grammar, but framed in terms of communicative functions. It focuses on grammatical forms and explores what these forms are used for.

However, such a communicative grammar can only go part of the way towards explaining communication. The complexity of describing and explaining communication arises from the vastness of the resource represented by the English language on the one hand and the great range of language users, purposes, and contexts for communication on the other. It is this complexity that the second half of the book seeks to engage with through the theory of language provided by systemic functional grammar.

Like the first part of the book, the second half is functional in its orientation. It is distinguished by its attention to the systems of language forms and functions. To conclude this introductory chapter, we will provide an indication of how this approach applies to Hal's developing grammar.

The table below summarises the grammatical forms that Hal is developing. As it is a formal account, it does not specifically refer to the communicative functions of his utterances.

Clause type	Example	Pattern
Declaratives:	*That little girl is crying*	SV
Interrogatives:	**(i)** *Where's the lid?*	VS
	(ii) *Do you want some Mummy?*	VS[3]
Imperatives:	*Fix the car*	V

Hal's communicative functions were identified in Activity 1.3 as demanding a service, requesting information, giving information, offering something, and contradicting. To systematise the relationship between the clause forms above and these communicative functions, systemic functional grammar proposes that there are a number of fundamental **speech functions** which underlie the much wider range of communicative functions that Hal will grow up to perform. The speech functions and communicative functions are included in the next version of the table. It should be noted that the communicative functions column only includes the five functions from Activity 1.3, and these lists can all be considerably extended to include a far wider range of functions.

Speech functions will be explained more fully in Chapter 9.

Clause types	Patterns	Speech functions	Communicative functions
Declaratives:	SV	to make statements	giving information; contradicting
Interrogatives:	(i) VS	to ask questions	requesting information
	(ii) VS	to make offers	offering something
Imperatives:	V	to make commands	demanding a service

The table shows there is a direct relationship between the form and the function of Hal's language. It will also become clear throughout this book that, as Hal's language matures, the correlation between the clause types and the speech and communicative functions represented in the table will be broken, for deliberate communicative purposes. The difference in grammatical forms used by Hal and an adult to demand a service to their cars, which was referred to above, is an example of this. That so much hinges on the subject–finite verb pattern, and, within this, the use of auxiliary verbs, explains why the therapists in the opening scenario were concerned at Paul's variable and unpredictable use of auxiliaries.

1.11 Conclusion: from formal to functional grammar

As children grow, their language develops in interaction with the people around them. It is the same for adults as they move into different situations, encounter different texts, and take on new responsibilities, or for people from different language backgrounds learning English as an additional language. All learn how to mean more and how to do more through language

Dissatisfaction with the capacity of formal grammar descriptions to contribute to these communicative challenges has led to different responses. One response has been to turn the formal accounts of grammar into prescriptions of what language users ought to do. A contrasting response has been to do no more than formally describe grammatical forms and to make no claims about what language users actually do through the language so described. Another response has been to presume that grammar is of no value or interest and to give it no attention whatsoever.

Functional grammar is an attempt to take the formal accounts of grammar seriously, but at the same time relate these grammatical forms to what language users do and mean through language as they seek to communicate with those around them. The rest of this book sets out to do this. Chapters 2–5 will continue to build a description of grammatical forms, focusing on their role across a number of communicative functions. Chapters 6–10 will re-contextualise grammatical forms and communicative functions in a framework provided by systemic functional grammar. It is hoped that, in total, the book will provide professionals from a wide range of backgrounds with tools and insights that will enable them to develop their own or others' communicative effectiveness.

1.12 Summary

Grammar is a description of language users' practice by language observers. Early grammars were concerned with effective communication, but by the twentieth century many grammars, particularly 'school grammars', were focused on grammatical form.

Word-class labels and the SVOCA clause patterns developed in traditional grammar remain important elements of modern formal grammar and also communicative and functional grammars. However, apparent tensions between the formal and communicative or functional approaches have tended to obscure their compatibility.

Formal grammar is an account of the units constituting language and the systematic ways they are combined to create larger units. Words are combined to make groups, groups are combined to create clauses, and these in turn create clause combinations. Within clauses, groups constitute the elements of the clause, and the pattern of elements determines whether the clause is declarative, interrogative, or imperative.

Clauses can be independent or dependent. If they are independent, they have a finite verb. Finite verbs are marked for tense and play a number of important roles in the clause. Two or more independent clauses can be combined by a coordinating conjunction. If a clause does not have a finite verb or is combined with another clause by a subordinating conjunction, it is a dependent clause.

The form of the clause underlies the speech function that the clause performs, and this in turn underlies the communicative function of the clause. In this way form and function are related. Systemic functional grammar is a theory of language that seeks to represent the complex language systems that connect form and function.

1.13 Answer key

Activity 1.3

(i) Offering something

(ii) Demanding a service

(iii) Giving information

(iv) Requesting information

(v) Giving information

(vi) Contradicting

Activity 1.5: Parts of speech

	adj	n	v	v		n	
1	The big horse is jumping the fence.

	n	v	n		n	n
2	Mary plucked flowers for John's sister.

	n		n	v	v		n
3	Lions and ostriches are found in Africa.

	v	adv	adv	v	adj		n
4	To think always accurately is a great accomplishment.

	n	v	n		v	v		n
5	William promised Mary that he would lend her his grammar.

Activity 1.6

These very rough definitions are adapted from *A Comprehensive Grammar of the English language: For the use of schools.*

A **conjunction** is a word used to connect other words and show the sense in which they are connected.

A **preposition** is placed before a noun or pronoun and establishes a relationship between it and other nouns or pronouns.

A **determiner** is a word placed before a noun to specify its range of reference.

A **pronoun** stands in as a substitute for a noun.

Activity 1.7

```
     n    v   adj  prep   adj   n   prep    n     conj  pron
Hedges are valuable to the wild creatures of the country because they
                      det                 det

     v      n     n     n      n   conj   n    prep pron
provide homes, food, shelter, warmth, and protection for them.

        pron  v    n     n conj   n     v   det det    n
        This gives rise to birds and animals having their own territories.
              prep

pron v    v   det  n     v      prep   n    pron v  det
We have heard two robins quarrelling over territories. We saw the

     n   prep  n     v    prep det  n  prep     n   conj
footprints of rabbits spreading from their hold near the hedges and then
                                              det         adv

pron det  n    adv    det   n   conj  v   prep det
we saw the footprints all over their territories and returning back to the
     v              prep                        prep

    n
hedges.
```

Activity 1.8

1

Clause element	Subject		Verb	Object			
Group	Nominal		Verbal	Nominal			
Word-class	Determiner	Noun	Verb	Noun	Noun	Conjunction	Noun
	The	soil	produces	cotton,	rice,	and	sugar.

2

Clause element	Subject	Verb	Object			
Group	Nominal	Verbal	Nominal			
Word-class	Noun	Verb	Noun	Prep	Noun	Noun
	Mary	plucked	flowers	for	John's	sister.

3

Clause element	Verb	Object	Object	
Group	Verbal	Nominal	Nominal	
Word-class	Verb	Noun	Determiner	Noun
	Give	John	the	book.

4

Clause element	Subject			Verb	Object		
Group	Verbal			Verbal	Nominal		
Word-class	Verb	Adj	Adj	Verb	Det	Adj	Noun
	To think	always	accurately	is	a	great	accomplishment.

Activity 1.9

W:	|| i called the exterminator || there's a thing in our garage ||
M:	|| why are you out of breath ||
W:	|| i'm running in circles || so anyway this thing must go || the exterminator is coming ||
M:	(like an insect thing)
W:	(OH NO NO NO like a big fuzzy grey thing big very big)
M:	|| can you stop talking in exclamations ||
W:	(no) || it's very big || (way up high in the rafters) || where it can drop on me || i'm never going in there again ||
M:	|| is it like a (Note that this is an unfinished clause because of interruption by W)
W:	(probably a raccoon or a possum or a mutant raccoon possum hybrid) || i asked him || if it was rabid || and he laughed at me || i think || that means no ||
M:	(okay honey) || i'm sure || it's fine ||

Activity 1.10

(a)

W:	|| he said || it was $185 ||
M:	|| what's a 185 ||
W:	(no, $185)
M:	|| oh, i thought || that was like a code || like we got a 185 up here || we got a 324 situation in the garage || (like that) (laugh)
W:	(silence)
M:	(honey)
W:	|| i never wanted to live here* || i hate nature ||
M:	i think || it was your decision actually ||
W:	|| he's going to set a trap || that means || we have to call back || when the trap is filled || it's going to be in the trap || i'm never going near the trap || (never never never ever)

M: || no one said || you had to ||

W: || i'm going back outside to get my stuff || if the raccoon eats me || you have to marry again || henry needs a mom ||

M: || i think || i'll marry the raccoon || then there will always be a little bit of you around ||

* Note that although there are two verbs here – *wanted* and *to live* – we are not analysing them as two clauses. We will come back to this point in Chapter 2 in the context of non-finite clauses.

(b)

I | called | the exterminator
S   V   O

There|'s | a thing
　 S   V   C

I |'m running | in circles
S   V   A

This thing | must go
　 S   V

It |'s | very big
S V   C

I |'m | never | going | in there | again
S V   A   V*   A   A

I | hate | nature
S   V   O

It |'s going to be | in the trap
S   V   A

I|'m | never | going | near the trap
S V   A   V*   A

* The verbal group is made up of two verbs with an adjunct separating them.

Activity 1.11

opened, were being set up, was, wanted to know, answered, were, would give, cared, worked, could advise, bought, grew, would help, could buy, asked, would come back, could make sure, were.

Activity 1.12

(a) See clauses in step (b)

(b)

Why | are | you out of breath
     V   S

Can | you | stop talking in exclamations
 V   S   V

What |'s | a 185*
   S   V

Is | it | an insect
V S

Activity 1.13

Take | this thing away
 V

Marry | someone else
 V

Come | here quickly
 V

Activity 1.14

H: Little girl crying.

Clause element	Subject			Verb	
Group	Nominal			Verbal	
Word-class	Determiner	Adjective	Noun	Verb	Verb
	That	little	girl	is	crying.

---

* The word *What* functions as subject and creates an exception to the V–S pattern.

H: Where's the lid?

Clause element	Verb		Subject	
Group		Verbal	Nominal	
Word-class	Adverb	Verb	Determiner	Noun
	Where	's	the	lid?

H: Some Mummy? (holding up biscuit)

Clause element	Verb	Subject	Verb	Object	Subject
Group	Verbal	Nominal	Verbal	Nominal	Nominal
Word-class	Verb	Pronoun	Verb	Determiner	Noun
	Do	you	want	some	Mummy?

H: Mummy fix car.

Clause element	Verb	Object	
Group	Verbal	Nominal	
Word-class	Verb	Det	Noun
	fix	the	car

H: Throw frisbee.

Clause element	Subject	Verb	Object	
Group	Nominal	Verbal	Nominal	
Word-class	Pronoun	Verb	Determiner	Noun
	I	threw	a	frisbee.

H: Not baby.

Clause element	Subject	Verb		Complement	
Group	Nominal	Verbal		Nominal	
Word-class	Pronoun	Verb		Determiner	Noun
	I	'm	not	a	baby.

		missing words	clause elements affected
(i)	*Do you want some Mummy?*	verb/pronoun/verb	V S V
(ii)	Fix *the* car?	determiner	O
(iii)	*That* little girl *is* crying	determiner/verb	S V
(iv)	Where's the lid?	none	
(v)	*I* Throw *[threw]* *a* frisbee.	pronoun/verb/det	S V O
(vi)	*I'm* not *a* baby; that's Hal	pronoun/verb/det	S V C

Notes

1   Determiner is the word-class that is used in contemporary grammars. This class did not exist in traditional grammar, and the word-class 'article' was used instead. In contemporary grammar, article is a subset of determiner. This is examined further in Chapter 3.

2   In some grammars, the A in the SVOCA pattern stands for adverbial.

3   It is the finite element that creates the VS polar interrogative pattern. The entire verbal group is made up of the finite element, *do*, and the lexical verb, *want*, with the subject, *you*, coming between. This is still referred to as a VS pattern in recognition of the particular significance of the finite verb, which in this case is the auxiliary.

two

Talking about procedures

2.1 Introduction

Despite the different approaches to grammar that have been outlined in Chapter 1, there is a certain amount of common ground among linguists concerning basic concepts such as clause, subject, verb, finite, and so on. The next four chapters explore relatively uncontentious ways of analysing English grammar, which are useful no matter which approach to grammar you take. This does not mean that we avoid controversy entirely, but on the whole the grammatical concepts and terminology in this part of the book have widespread currency, and where there are alternatives in common use, these will be indicated in the text.

The approach we take in these four chapters draws on traditional, formal grammar and involves analysing the structure of clauses and phrases. Unlike a traditional grammar, however, we aim to show how grammatical categories are put into use, paying attention not just to grammatical forms, but also to the way these forms contribute to meaning. The approach we take, then, is broadly communicative, and involves examining grammar, not in isolated sentences, but in the context of authentic written or spoken texts. The texts are taken from a wide range of sources across the English-speaking world. Although they have not been specially constructed for teaching purposes, we have selected them in order to illustrate particular grammatical features. Some grammatical features are more likely to occur in certain types of text (for example, you might expect to find past tense verbs in a newspaper report, but not in a recipe). For this reason, each chapter is organised around texts that have a broadly similar communicative function and allow us to explore particular areas of grammar. These areas of grammar will be revisited and built on in the systemic functional approach to grammar set out in the second half of the book. Indeed, one of the main purposes of Chapters 2–5 is to provide the foundational grammatical terms and concepts necessary for understanding and exploring a systemic functional approach.

Scenario

The text below was posted to a Chinese website in answer to a question about the procedure for making a kite. There are obvious problems here with the use of English grammar. If you were teaching this writer English, what would you focus on as your first priority in order to improve their ability to write this sort of text?

Text 2.1 Kitemaking

Procedure:

1   First immerses the thin bamboo strip, Make thin bamboo strip soft body, Again uses the knife to break the thin bamboo strip, Approximately three coarseness, Then repairs half shape, Because later must paste the thin bamboo strip on Ma Lazhi,[1] If too is thick, The thin bamboo strip can pull the broken paper, At the same time the thin bamboo strip too is thick, The gauze paper pastes is not steady Will fix the thin bamboo strip will plan and bring to completion two lengths suitable lengths [. . .][2]

(http://zhidao.baidu.com/question/4197118.html?fr=qrl3)

Text 2.1 sets out to give instructions on how to make a kite, but most readers would find them very difficult to follow. The writer appears to have control of appropriate vocabulary for the task, and to be able to construct nominal groups such as *the thin bamboo strip*, *the broken paper*, and *the gauze paper pastes* with reasonable accuracy. So we have some idea of the things that are needed for this procedure – the problem is that we can't tell what is supposed to be done to these things. To improve the text, the main priority would be to sort out clause structure.

Chapter 1 outlined the basic difference between declarative clauses, typically used to make statements, and imperative clauses, typically used to give instructions. In this text, however, imperative clauses do not always have imperative verb forms (e.g. *First <u>immerses</u> the thin bamboo strip*, rather than *immerse*), and clauses that appear to be statements do not always have subjects (e.g. *Will fix the thin bamboo strip*). As a result, it is hard to make out which clauses are meant to provide instruction, and which are meant to be a description of what happens. The text would appear to be written by someone with limited English proficiency, or perhaps to have been machine-translated from Chinese. Whatever the case, it does not succeed in providing readers with clear information about the procedure of kitemaking.

This chapter examines the grammatical structures that typically occur in texts about <u>procedure</u>, which can be defined as 'the established or prescribed way of doing something' (OED 1989). A procedure involves a sequence of steps taken to achieve a particular goal, such as making a kite. Notice that this definition doesn't tell us anything about the communicative function of such a text – it indicates the subject matter, but doesn't tell us why a speaker or writer would want to produce such a text. As we will see, a writer may want to instruct, to describe, to recommend, or to report a procedure, and the overall function affects the grammatical structures that are likely to occur. By the end of this chapter you will be able to identify the grammatical structures associated with procedure, and to understand the ways in which these may vary depending on the communicative function of the text and the context in which it is used.

Activity 2.1

The passage below appears on several Internet sites. What do you think are its ostensible function and its real function? How can you tell?

Text 2.2 How to give a cat a pill

1   Pick cat up and cradle it in the crook of your left arm as if holding a baby. Position right forefinger and thumb on either side of cat's mouth and gently apply pressure to cheeks while holding pill in right hand. As cat opens mouth, pop pill into mouth. Allow cat to close mouth and swallow.

2   Retrieve pill from floor and cat from behind sofa. Cradle cat in left arm and repeat process.

3   Retrieve cat from bedroom, and throw soggy pill away.

4   Take new pill from foil wrap, cradle cat in left arm holding rear paws tightly with left hand. Force jaws open and push pill to back of mouth with right forefinger. Hold mouth shut for a count of ten.

5   Retrieve pill from goldfish bowl and cat from top of wardrobe. Call spouse from garden.

6   Kneel on floor with cat wedged firmly between knees, hold front and rear paws. Ignore low growls emitted by cat. Get spouse to hold head firmly with one hand while forcing wooden ruler into mouth. Drop pill down ruler and rub cat's throat vigorously.

7   Retrieve cat from curtain rail, get another pill from foil wrap. Make note to buy new ruler and repair curtains. Carefully sweep shattered Doulton figurines from hearth and set to one side for gluing later.

8   Wrap cat in large towel and get spouse to lie on cat with head just visible from below armpit. Put pill in end of drinking straw, force mouth open with pencil and blow down drinking straw.

9   Check label to make sure pill not harmful to humans, drink glass of water to take taste away. Apply Band–Aid to spouse's forearm and remove blood from carpet with cold water and soap.

(http://videoforcats.com/cathumorpill.htm)

This passage takes the form of a set of instructions, with a numbered list of actions, each in the form of an imperative clause with a verb in its base (uninflected) form: *pick up*, *position*, *apply*, *pop*, *allow*, and so on. The grammatical features of the text allow us to recognise its ostensible function – to give instructions. It is, however, parodying genuine instructions, and its real purpose is to entertain. The joke only works, of course, because the reader can recognise the mismatch between the typical grammatical features of instruction, and the actual content of the text. Genuine instructions indicate the steps to be taken in order to achieve some desired outcome, but these instructions presuppose repeated failure and suggest repeated futile attempts to succeed. Genuine instructions are written so that they can apply in a range of different contexts. These instructions, however, specify particular objects and actions that would be unlikely to recur. In step 5, for example *Retrieve pill from goldfish bowl* cannot function as a real instruction unless there really is a goldfish bowl in the room, and the pill actually lands inside the goldfish bowl.

The fact that Text 2.2 has been very popular on the Internet suggests that most people get the joke – they can identify the grammatical features of instructions and recognise when they are being used inappropriately, even though they may have little conscious knowledge of grammatical rules. The next activity focuses on making the grammatical rules explicit. By analysing the grammatical features of genuine instructions, we can see more clearly how the spoof instructions work.

Activity 2.2

Compare Text 2.3, which gives genuine instructions, with the humorous instructions in Text 2.2 (*How to give a cat a pill*). What grammatical features are shared by both texts?

Text 2.3 Pecan almond tart

Ingredients:

1 crust for a 9-inch pie pan

3/4 cup light Karo syrup

1/2 cup sugar

3 tbl unsalted butter, cold

3 eggs

1 tsp vanilla

1 cup pecans, chopped and toasted

1/3 cup sliced almonds

Method:

Preheat the oven to 375 degrees.

In a medium saucepan over medium heat, stir the syrup and sugar together and bring to a boil. Continue cooking about 2 minutes to dissolve the sugar. Remove from heat and stir in the cold butter. Cool the syrup for 5 minutes.

Whip the eggs in a bowl with a whisk to break the yolks, then whisk in the syrup and vanilla. Pour through a sieve (to catch any bit of crystallised sugar) into the shell. Sprinkle with pecans then finally with almonds and bake to 30 minutes.

Place a sheet pan on the shelf below the pie to catch any drips. Cool before serving.

(http://fooddownunder.com/cgi-bin/recipe.cgi?r=191361)

The table below summarises the main grammatical features of the two instruction texts, and gives examples of each feature. At this stage, it's not too important whether you used the grammatical terminology (which was introduced in Chapter 1); instead, focus on the features themselves – did you spot these similarities between the texts?

	Examples from Text 2.2	Examples from Text 2.3
Mainly VOA structure (verb–object–adjunct)	*retrieve cat from bedroom*	*whip the eggs in a bowl*
Action verbs in imperative form	*pick up, pop, throw, force*	*stir, remove, whisk*
Omission of articles (a and the)	*wrap <the> cat in <a> large towel*	***only one example:*** *remove from <the> heat*
Adjuncts indicating circumstances	*in left arm, with right forefinger, vigorously*	*into the shell, with a whisk, for 5 minutes*
Non-finite clauses indicating reason/ purpose	*for gluing later, to take taste away*	*to dissolve the sugar, to break the yolks*

The two texts are broadly similar in terms of clause structure and verbal groups. You may have noticed, though, that there are some differences in the way nominal groups are used. Text 2.3 (*Pecan almond tart*) pays more attention to the materials used – obviously an important factor in cooking. The ingredients are listed in advance, and the equipment is mentioned as it is needed. Because of the step-by-step procedure, it is often easy to predict which materials are involved in each action. As a result, the object of a particular clause can often be omitted without causing comprehension problems for the reader. This makes it possible to avoid repetition; for example:

> *stir <u>the syrup and sugar</u> together and bring <u><the mixture></u> to a boil. Continue cooking <u><the mixture></u> about 2 minutes to dissolve the sugar. Remove <u><the mixture></u> from heat*

In Text 2.2 (*How to give a cat a pill*), the 'ingredients' are less predictable, but there is still a tendency to underspecify them by omitting the article:

> *Retrieve <the> pill from <the> goldfish bowl and <the> cat from <the> top of <the> wardrobe.*

Omitting the article, like omitting the object, suggests that the reader will have no problem in identifying these items. Part of the humorous effect of

Text 2.2 is the way it takes for granted that the reader can identify items that are not in fact obvious – the *goldfish bowl*, the *curtain rail*, the *Doulton figurines*. As a result, the reader is forced to imagine a scenario in which all these items play a part in the procedure of giving a cat a pill.

Nominal groups will be examined in more detail in Chapter 3, but in the rest of this chapter the focus will be on other aspects of clause structure that are particularly significant in texts dealing with procedures: imperative clauses, passive voice, and adjuncts.

2.2 Imperative clauses

A characteristic feature of Texts 2.2 and 2.3 is the use of imperative clauses to give instructions. As explained in Chapter 1, English clauses can be classified as imperative, declarative, and interrogative, and this choice is known as the **mood** of the clause. Notice the position of the subject and the verb in each type of clause:

Imperative			Verb	Object	Adjunct
			whip	*the eggs*	*in a bowl*
Declarative		**Subject**	**Verb**	**Object**	**Adjunct**
		he	*whipped*	*the eggs*	*in a bowl*
Interrogative	**Verb**	**. . .** **Subject**	**Verb**	**Object**	**Adjunct**
	did	*he*	*whip*	*the eggs*	*in a bowl?*

In interrogative clauses, the finite element of the verb comes before the subject, but any other words in the verbal group come after the subject. As a result, the verb in an interrogative clause is often discontinuous, as in the example (*did . . . whip*).

Activity 2.3

The text below is taken from the transcript of an emergency telephone call made by a prospective father (Leo) whose wife (Jane) is having a baby. Look at the subject and verb of each clause and classify it as declarative, imperative, or interrogative. If you find any clauses that are difficult to classify, think about what the problem might be.

Text 2.4 Call 999!

Operator:	Is the baby crying or breathing?
Leo:	Yes, it's crying.
Operator:	Right, what I want you to do is gently wipe off the baby's mouth and nose. And dry the baby off with a clean towel. Then wrap the baby in a clean, dry towel, OK.
Leo:	OK.
Operator:	Just wipe the baby's mouth and nose first. Yeah?
Leo:	(*Shouting downstairs*) Margaret! Quick!
Jane:	Lift him up!
Operator:	Have you got a boy or a girl?
Leo:	(*Shouting downstairs*) I need a clean towel! Quick!
Operator:	You need a couple, OK. One to dry the baby off with, and one to wrap him up with. Is it a boy or a girl?
Leo:	(*Laughing*) Er, I don't know yet. (*Pause*) A little boy.
Operator:	Congratulations.

(*The Guardian*, Saturday 15 September 2007; available at http://www.guardian.co.uk/family/story/ 0,,2169187,00.html)

As explained above, mood depends on the subject and the finite element of the verb:

Declarative (SV . . .)	*I have got a clean towel.*	*The baby isn't crying.*
Interrogative (VS . . .)	*Have you got a clean towel?*	*Is the baby crying?*
Imperative (V . . .)	*Get a clean towel!*	*Don't cry!*

However, some of the clauses do not have a subject and finite element; for example, *Quick!* and *A little boy*. Such **minor clauses** are common in casual conversation (and, given the emergency situation, you would not expect the speakers in Text 2.4 to use formal language!). In some cases, it is possible to reconstruct the elements that have been omitted, such as <*Be*> *quick!* and <*It's*> *a little boy*, and if you do this you can then identify *Be quick!* as imperative and *It's a little boy* as declarative. However, utterances such as *Right, OK,* and *Congratulations!* cannot be reconstructed in this way, so they cannot be classified as declarative, imperative, or interrogative.

Another feature that may cause difficulty is that the grammatical form of a clause does not necessarily match its function, as explained in Chapter 1. For example, when the operator says *what I want you to do is gently wipe off the baby's mouth and nose*, she is obviously giving Leo directions on what to do. But the grammatical form of the clause is declarative, not imperative:

Subject	Verb	Complement
what I want you to do	*is*	*gently wipe off the baby's mouth and nose*

Similarly, when Leo says *I need a clean towel!*, the clause is declarative in form, but functions as a command.

Mood is defined in terms of the subject and the finite element of the verb. The finite element is the first item in a finite verbal group, and in Chapter 1 a finite verb was defined as a verb that is marked for tense (present or past) and for number (singular or plural). This definition, however, doesn't seem to apply to imperatives. For pragmatic reasons, you can't tell somebody to do something in the past, so imperative clauses can't appear in the past tense:

*Please washed the dishes yesterday!
(*The asterisk indicates an ungrammatical form.)

The presumed subject of most imperatives is *you*, which is neutral between singular and plural. Although in some languages there are different imperative verb forms depending on whether the command is addressed to one person or several, this distinction is not made in English, where imperative verbs do not change to show singular or plural. So the tense and number markings associated with finite verbs do not apply to imperative verbs. Nevertheless, most linguists regard the imperative as a finite verb form. Can you think of any arguments to justify this decision?

The main argument is that of syntactic consistency; in other words, imperative verbs enter into many of the same patterns as finite verbal groups. Overwhelmingly, an independent clause in English requires a finite verbal group. Imperatives appear regularly in independent clauses and, conversely, cannot appear in dependent (subordinate) clauses:

Independent clause	Dependent clause	
gently <u>apply</u> pressure to cheeks	while	holding pill in right hand. *hold!

Independent clause	Dependent clause	
<u>cool</u>	before	serving. *serve!

Like other finite verbs, the imperative can also be the focus of a question tag, for example:

Get another pill, <u>will you</u>?
Let's try again, <u>shall we</u>?
Whip the eggs, <u>can you</u>?

Although imperatives have a very restricted range of grammatical possibilities, an imperative clause still behaves like a finite clause: it can stand as a complete sentence, may contain objects, complements, and adjuncts, and may have other clauses dependent on it.

The anomalous behaviour of the imperative arises in part from the nature of the directive function that it's associated with. Giving instructions can be a face-threatening behaviour, and speakers and writers often use other grammatical resources for this function to avoid sounding over-assertive.

When we read or listen to instructions, we do not always intend to carry out the actions ourselves, and may simply be interested in finding out in general how something is done. Imperative verbs are associated in particular with instructions, but a speaker or writer may choose to describe a procedure rather than give instructions about it. For this communicative function, they will need to draw on different grammatical resources.

2.3 Passive voice

Activity 2.4

Compare the two texts below, both dealing with procedures for producing energy. In what ways are they different and what do you think might account for these differences?

Text 2.5 How to make a potato battery

Equipment:

A potato

A clean copper coin (If necessary, clean it by placing it in a fizzy drink for a few minutes, or clean with steel wool.)

Some aluminium foil

Crocodile clips

Wires

A voltmeter or multimeter

Instructions:

Cut the potato in half and place the flat end on the foil. Push the copper coin into the potato. Attach crocodile clips to the coin and the foil, then wires to the crocodile clips. Now attach these wires to the voltmeter. The voltmeter should give a reading, showing that the stored energy is available and a current can flow, and that you have produced a battery!

(http://www.doitpoms.ac.uk/tlplib/batteries/potato_battery.php)

Text 2.6 Biomass energy cycle

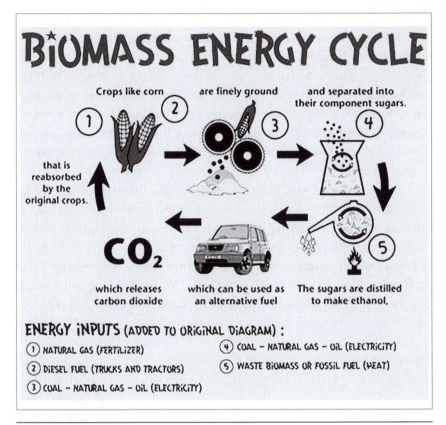

Figure 2.1 Biomass energy cycle (©University of Wisconsin, Board of Regents; available at http://whyfiles.org/253ethanol/index.php?g=2.txt)

Both texts are about a procedure, but this is treated in very different ways. Perhaps the most noticeable difference is that the biomass energy cycle is presented with the use of a diagram and labels. The diagram is an integral part of the text, which would be harder to understand without the visual elements. But in these texts, the choice of whether or not to use the visual mode does not seem to be determined by the topic itself. We could envisage a purely verbal version of 'Biomass energy cycle', or a verbal and visual version of 'How to make a potato battery'. (In fact you'll have a chance to explore some lemon batteries which are both verbal and visual later in this chapter.) The deciding factor may be the producers' judgements about who is likely to read the text, and how much impact they want to have on the readers.

The grammatical differences between the two texts are shown in the table below. These differences can be clearly related to the communicative function of each text. The instructions on how to make a potato battery are written with the assumption that a reader might wish to carry them out. Imperative verb forms imply that the subject is *you*, and in the final sentence this becomes explicit: *showing that . . . you have produced a battery*. Equipment is listed with a rough indication of the quantities required, and the nominal groups are indefinite – it doesn't matter which particular potato or foil you use.

In the case of the biomass energy cycle, however, there is no assumption that this is a process to be carried out by the reader. Instead of imperatives, present passive verb forms are used, providing a general description of the process rather than a set of instructions on how to do it. **Passive** verbal groups consist of a form of the verb BE followed by a past **participle** (normally ending in *-ed* or *-en*). Occasionally, a passive verbal group is formed using GET instead of BE. Examples of passive verbal groups are:

is washed

have been taken

being reviewed

got broken

Text 2.5: How to make a potato battery	Text 2.6: Biomass energy cycle
Indefinite nominal groups (*a potato*; *some aluminium foil*)	Generic nominal groups (*corn*; *trucks and tractors*)
Mainly VOA clause structure (verb–object–adjunct)	Mainly SV(A) clause structure (subject–verb–adjunct)
Verbs mainly imperative	Verbs mainly present passive

The difference between generic, definite, and indefinite nominal groups will be discussed in Chapter 3.

These two texts present a clear contrast between instructions (using imperative verbs) and description of a process (using present passive verbs).

Often, though, the distinction is blurred and both imperatives and passives may be used in the same text.

For example, several people have posted videos on YouTube demonstrating how to make a battery from a potato or a lemon. (You can find these multimodal texts by going to the YouTube website and typing 'potato battery' or 'lemon battery' in the search box.) The set-up is much the same in each video – a demonstrator carries out the procedure on camera while explaining the steps involved – but the language varies considerably. Here are some of the utterances used by speakers on different videos. Can you identify the clause pattern involved in each case?

Stab something metal into one side of your lemon . . .

If we insert this we should have . . .

You need to connect the negative end to the anode . . .

I am now using my voltmeter to prove that this lemon . . .

You turn the voltmeter on . . .

Let's add two more lemons . . .

A key issue here is **agency** – who is being represented as carrying out the actions? In a demonstration, the speaker may provide a running commentary on their own actions (*I am now using my voltmeter*) or give direct instructions to the listener, with *you* as the implicit subject of the verb (*Stab something metal into one side of your lemon*), or represent both speaker and listener(s) as cooperatively engaged in the actions (*Let's add two more lemons*).

If the subject *you* is explicitly used, however, it is potentially ambiguous. In *You turn the voltmeter on*, is the speaker simply adding a pronoun to an imperative sentence (such as *You stand over there please* or *Don't you look at me like that!*), or is this a description of a process that anyone may carry out (such as *First you connect the batteries, then you . . .*)? This sort of structure can be seen as intermediate between a set of instructions, such as Text 2.5 (*How to make a potato battery*), and a description of a process, such as Text 2.6 (*Biomass energy cycle*).

Connect the batteries	instruction
You connect the batteries	↕
The batteries are connected	description of a process

61

Both imperative and passive verb forms make it possible to leave unspoken the identity of the person who carries out the actions (the **agent**). In imperative clauses, there is no subject at all. In passive clauses, what would normally be the object of the verb is instead used as the subject:

Verb	Object
connect	the batteries

Subject	Verb
the batteries	are connected

In a passive clause, the agent may be mentioned in a **by-phrase**, but it is far more common to leave it unstated. The sentence below, for example, involves two passive clauses; the first one includes the agent (*by a rabid dog*), but the second is agentless:

In 1885, a young boy, Joseph Meister, had been bitten by a rabid dog, and was brought to Pasteur.

Subject	Verb	Object
a rabid dog	had bitten	Joseph Meister

Subject	Verb	Adjunct
Joseph Meister	had been bitten	by a rabid dog

	Verb	Object	Adjunct
?	brought	Joseph Meister	to Pasteur

Subject	Verb		Adjunct
Joseph Meister	was brought	?	to Pasteur

Style guides often pay particular attention to the passive voice. Traditionally, students have been advised to use the passive in academic writing, presenting a view of knowledge, especially scientific knowledge, as impersonal and objective. So, instead of writing, for example, *We put the seedlings in a dark cupboard*, they would be advised to write *The seedlings were put in a dark cupboard*. Nowadays, however, the pendulum seems to have swung the other way. For example, when I wrote the sentences above, the word processor flagged two verbs with the message 'Passive Voice (consider revising)', and when I called up the explanation, the grammar checker provided the text shown below. Is this advice likely to be helpful to a novice writer? Read through and consider how far you agree with the general statements and the examples:

Figure 2.2

Passive Voice
For a livelier and more persuasive sentence, consider rewriting your sentence using an active verb (the subject performs the action, as in 'The ball hit Catherine') rather than a passive verb (the subject receives the action, as in 'Catherine was hit by the ball'). If you rewrite with an active verb, consider what the appropriate subject is – 'they,' 'we,' or a more specific noun or pronoun.

• Instead of: <u>Juanita was delighted by Michelle</u>.
• Consider: Michelle delighted Juanita.

• Instead of: Eric <u>was given</u> more work.
• Consider: The boss gave Eric more work.

• Instead of: The garbage needs to <u>be taken out</u>.
• Consider: You need to take the garbage out.

Although the style advice claims that the active voice is 'livelier and more persuasive', it doesn't explain why this should be the case. The examples are not particularly helpful in this respect. The first one represents a rather unusual use of *delighted*, which occurs more commonly with *with* than *by*. You can confirm this yourself by typing *delighted with* and *delighted by* into an Internet search engine, and checking which produces most hits.

In the second example from the style guide, the choice of active or passive would depend on the overall context, and, if *Eric* is the topic, switching the subject to *the boss* might be clumsy. Consider the sentence quoted earlier: *In 1885, a young boy, Joseph Meister, had been bitten by a rabid dog, and was brought to Pasteur.* If you change it so that both clauses are active, you will need to bring in two different subjects, for example: *In 1885, a rabid dog had bitten a young boy, Joseph Meister, and some people brought him to Pasteur.* Does this really improve the sentence? In this context, use of the passive enables the writer to present the information coherently by focusing on the main participant.

Another example is the sign often seen on escalators that says *Dogs must be carried.* What would be the effect of rewriting this in the active as *People must carry dogs*? Changing the subject of the clause from *dogs* to *people* produces a bizarre change of meaning. Whereas the first clause is about *dogs* (if you have a dog, you must carry it), the second is about *people*, and apparently says that they cannot ride on the escalator unless they are carrying a dog.

The third example from the style guide (*The garbage needs to be taken out/You need to take the garbage out*) illustrates another factor that may influence the choice of active or passive: the assignment of responsibility. Using the passive allows the speaker to avoid mentioning the agent, perhaps as a way of evading blame. For example, *The carpet's been stained* could be a rather underhand way of obscuring the fact that you yourself caused the staining. But there are also occasions where we might avoid assigning responsibility in order to spare other people's feelings. In these circumstances, a passive sentence such as *The carpet's been stained* might be preferable to an active version that baldly states *You've stained the carpet.* Similarly, there may be occasions when the active clause *You need to take the garbage out* would be a very undiplomatic thing to say.

Passive voice, like any other grammatical feature, may be used appropriately or inappropriately, and blanket advice to avoid the passive is just as misleading as blanket advice to favour it. The choice of whether to use active or passive voice depends not only on what the speaker or writer is talking about, but also on various contextual factors. One of the weaknesses of traditional, formal grammars is that they often exemplify grammatical features in isolated sentences. This is sufficient to indicate what is or is not a grammatically correct form, but it is inadequate to account for the way the grammatical item is used to make meaning in context.

Activity 2.5

Look at the two texts below, which describe the same kind of procedure, but in two very different contexts. The first one comes from a website that answers questions sent in by the public. The other is an extract from a US patent – an official document that confers legal rights on the patent holder.

(a)   Identify which of the finite verbs are active and which are passive.

(b)   How would you account for the grammatical differences between the two texts?

Text 2.7 If Teflon is non-sticky, how do they get it to stick to the pan?

[. . .] Teflon, known to science as polytetrafluoroethylene, is a pain to work with because it's nonsticky in all directions, the pan side (the bottom) as well as the food side (the top). [. . .]

So how do they get Teflon to stick to the pan? First they sandblast the pan to create a lot of micro-scratches on its surface. Then they spray on a coat of Teflon primer. This primer, like most primers, is thin, enabling it to flow into the micro-scratches. The primed surface is then baked at high heat, causing the Teflon to solidify and get a reasonably secure mechanical grip. Next you spray on a finish coat and bake that. (The Teflon finish coat will stick to the Teflon primer coat just fine.)

(http://www.straightdope.com/classics/a4_173.html)

Text 2.8 Coating and primer formulation on the basis of a copolymer of tetrafluoroethylene and a perfluoro-(alkylvinyl) ether, and use thereof

[...] Aluminum plates are sandblasted with corundum (grain size 100 to 120 µm) to obtain a microinch finish of from 5 to 10 µm. The above primer dispersion is then applied to the surface so pretreated by means of a spray gun in a thickness of from 5 to 10 µm. The aluminum plates so coated are abandoned for 10 minutes at room temperature, and subsequently, a polytetrafluoroethylene dispersion containing 60 weight % of solids is applied. The two layers are then dried first for 10 minutes at 90 degrees C, then for 10 minutes at 250 degrees C, and finally sintered for 10 minutes at 400 degrees C.

(United States Patent 4395445. 1983; available at http://www.freepatentsonline.com/4395445.html)

In Text 2.7 the finite verbs are predominantly active in form. The passage starts as a description of how *they get Teflon to stick to the pan*, but a passive clause occurs midway through (*The primed surface is then baked at high heat*). The writer then reverts to active clauses, but now with the subject *you* rather than *they*. Grammatically, this feels a little inconsistent, but it's in line with the overall style, which mixes technical and everyday language in a tongue-in-cheek way. On the one hand, the writer uses technical terms, such as *polytetrafluoroethylene* and *mechanical grip,* and structures that are more common in writing than in speech, such as *The primed surface is then baked at high heat,* or *enabling it to flow into the micro-scratches.* On the other hand, the writer also uses colloquial language that is more typical of speech, such as *a pain to work with, it's nonsticky,* or *just fine.* This mixed style arises from the website's aim to explain technical issues in a way that makes them both entertaining and clear for the general public.

In Text 2.8, however, there is no need to appeal to the general public. The key point of a patent is to describe an invention in a precise way so that the inventor can establish his claim to it. Precision is important, so the terminology is technical, and specific details are included; for example, *a polytetrafluoroethylene dispersion containing 60 weight % of solids.* The question of who carries out the procedure is irrelevant. Presumably the inventor has performed all the actions, but a patent is concerned more with all the potential future users (who will of course be liable to pay for the privilege of following the procedure). Passive clauses are a natural choice in this context, precisely because they do not require any mention of an agent. In this text, every single finite verb is passive (regardless of the grammar-checker's disapproval). This is fairly typical of technical writing.

Activity 2.6

Text 2.9 comes from the 'Letters to the Editor' section of a secondary school magazine, and was written by a third form student. The writer uses a number of passive verb forms.

(a) Focusing on the finite verbs, identify the passive and active forms.
(b) Do you think the passive forms are used appropriately or not? If you think any are used inappropriately, suggest a more appropriate active version.
(c) How does the use of passive verbs in this text compare with Texts 2.7 and 2.8?

Text 2.9 Letter to the Editor

Sir, I was interested to read the article about proposed drug testing in our schools. I generally support the idea of drug testing in schools. However it is important that it is carried out the right way, not with 'sniffer dogs'. A more subtle approach is necessary, for example randomly selecting a whole class for testing. Children should be informed that random tests are regularly carried out, so acting as a deterrent. My concern is that it is adding to a teacher's burden of responsibility. I feel the testing should be done by an outside body as expressed by J.G. Children who are found to have a positive test should be offered help and advice. Their parents should be notified and a discrete watch should be kept over the pupil during break times.

Yours faithfully,

The writer is discussing the procedure for drug testing in schools, and most of the steps that he proposes are presented in passive clauses. The subjects of these clauses tend to refer either to testing/tests (*is carried out, are regularly carried out, should be done*), or to children (*should be informed, are found to have, should be offered*). The exceptions are *Their parents should be notified* and *a discrete watch should be kept*.

Our own view is that the passive is used effectively in this text to focus on the writer's chosen topic. The writer has focused on the steps he would like to see, not on the individuals who might carry them out. In most cases, trying to change the passive clauses to the active voice will produce a clumsy result. One of the problems is that it is not entirely clear who the agents should be (and this is something the writer addresses in his suggestion that *an outside body* should take responsibility). You could use a vague term such as 'the authorities' as the subject of each clause, but if you try this, you will find that it tends to deflect the reader's attention away from the key topic, which is the <u>procedure</u> for drugs testing.

Grammar reference books often suggest that the passive voice is used when the agent is unknown or unimportant. These are not the only factors involved, but they are certainly significant. When people are talking in general terms about a procedure, they tend to be more interested in the actions involved than in the agents that carry them out, so passive verbs are common in such texts, particularly if they are formal, written texts. Text 2.7 dealt with a general procedure, but because the context was informal it tended to use active verbs with a non-specific pronoun as the subject (e.g. <u>*they*</u> *sandblast the pan*, <u>*you*</u> *spray on a finish coat*). Text 2.8, on the other hand, was a formal, technical text that favoured the passive voice (e.g. *Aluminum plates are sandblasted, The two layers are then dried*). The student's letter is similar to Text 2.7 in that it deals with a general procedure and uses the passive voice. The style is quite formal, though not technical. The two texts differ, though, in their particular function. The patent applicant is describing a procedure that he has developed and is specifying this procedure in order to protect his legal rights. The student is talking about a procedure that does not yet exist; his aim is to propose what he sees as a desirable procedure to be carried out by someone else. Compare:

Connect the batteries.	giving instructions for a procedure
Aluminum plates <u>are sandblasted</u>.	describing a procedure
Their parents <u>should be notified</u>.	recommending a procedure

2.4 Adjuncts

So far in this chapter, the focus has been on finite verbs and their subjects. In the final section, we turn to other clause elements that frequently occur in texts dealing with procedures. This will provide more opportunity for you to practise working with the SVOCA clause structure introduced in Chapter 1.

Activity 2.7

Text 2.10 is from a bulletin on soybean technology that is distributed by the Food and Agriculture Organization of the United Nations.

(a)   Read the text and identify any finite verb forms in the passive voice.

(b)   What clause element typically occurs after the passive verbs in these clauses? Why is this?

Text 2.10 Tempeh

Tempeh is a fermented soybean product of Indonesian origin. It consists of cooked, dehulled whole soybeans which have been fermented by *Rhizopus* moulds. It is a moist solid cake with a mild, pleasant taste. It is usually sliced, dipped into a salt solution and deep-fried in oil. The traditional product is highly perishable and is usually consumed the day it is made. In industrial production, it can be preserved by drying or freezing (after blanching to inactivate the mould and its enzymes.)

Production methods vary as with most traditional foods. In a typical process, soybeans are soaked in water, dehulled and then cooked in boiling water for one hour. After draining the soybeans are spread out for air-drying of the superficial moisture. Tempeh from the previous day is used as a starter. The prepared soybeans are thoroughly mixed with the starter, wrapped in banana leaves and left to ferment for one to two days. Mould growth is vigorous and the whole mass is soon covered and bound together by Rhizopus mycelium.

(http://www.fao.org/docrep/t0532e/t0532e10.htm#9.4)

One feature to notice is that very often two or three passive clauses have been conjoined in a single sentence. When this happens, the finite element of the verb is often ellipted (omitted); for example:

The whole mass is soon covered and <is> bound together.

There was a similar example in Text 2.8 (*Coating and primer formulation*):

*The two layers are then dried . . . and <are> finally sintered for
10 minutes.*

In Text 2.10 (*Tempeh*), almost all the passive verbs are followed by clause elements that indicate some of the circumstances involved. You may have recognised that these clause elements are adjuncts (as described in Chapter 1). The most common type of adjunct in Text 2.10 is an adjunct of place, such as *in the water*. There are also adjuncts of time (*for one hour*), manner (*by drying*), purpose (*for air-drying*), and means (*by Rhizopus moulds*).

Adjuncts are often used when talking about procedures; they provide relevant information about the way the procedure is carried out, both in texts that give a description, such as Text 2.8 (*Coating and primer formulation*) and Text 2.10 (*Tempeh*), and those that give instructions, such as Text 2.2 (*How to give a cat a pill*) and Text 2.3 (*Pecan almond tart*).

One feature that distinguishes adjuncts from other clause elements is that, from a grammatical point of view, they are optional. In the sentence below, if you omit the underlined elements, the result is still a grammatical sentence:

*<u>After draining</u> the soybeans are spread out <u>for air-drying of the superficial
moisture</u>*

On the other hand, if you omit the subject (*the soybeans*) or the verb (*are spread out*), the sentence is ungrammatical. Adjuncts also tend to be more mobile than other clause elements; it is often possible for an adjunct to appear in several different positions in the clause. For example:

After draining the soybeans are spread out.

The soybeans, after draining, are spread out.

The soybeans are spread out after draining.

Look at the clauses below from Text 2.3 (*Pecan almond tart*). Experiment with omitting groups of words or moving them around in the clause. Can you identify the adjuncts?

> *In a medium saucepan over medium heat, stir the syrup and sugar together.*
>
> *Continue cooking about 2 minutes to dissolve the sugar.*
>
> *Cool the syrup for 5 minutes.*

The adjuncts in these clauses are: *in a medium saucepan, over medium heat, about 2 minutes, to dissolve the sugar,* and *for 5 minutes.* The tests also help you to recognise where there are two or more adjuncts in one clause, as each adjunct can be omitted or moved separately; e.g.

> *Continue cooking about 2 minutes to dissolve the sugar.*
>
> *To dissolve the sugar, continue cooking about 2 minutes.*
>
> *<For> about 2 minutes, continue cooking to dissolve the sugar.*
>
> *Continue cooking about 2 minutes.*
>
> *Continue cooking to dissolve the sugar.*

Activity 2.8

The following text comes from the 'Materials and Methods' section of an academic article, and reports the procedure used to evaluate smoked cheese on the basis of its colour.

(a) The finite verbal groups have been removed from this text. Using the lexical verb shown in brackets, decide what form you would use, bearing in mind the choice of active or passive voice.

(b) When you have finished, look again at these finite clauses and identify any adjuncts (do not worry about adjuncts that occur in non-finite clauses).

Text 2.11 Evaluation of smoked cheese

The visual descriptive sensory analysis of the smoked cheese samples (PERFORM) _____ by the University of Wisconsin Sensory Analysis Laboratory under conditions prescribed for sensory analyses. Three separate sensory panels (CONDUCT) _____: Cheddar, Swiss, and Cheddar and Swiss sampled together. For each panel, 28 volunteers consisting of University of Wisconsin Dairy Store customers and graduate students (SELECT) _____.

Each panelist, situated in a Macbeth lighted viewing booth, (PRESENT) _____ with four smoked cheese samples on a 15-cm plastic plate. The samples (SLICE) _____ about 1 cm thick perpendicularly to the smoked surface so that the panelists (SEE) _____ the smoked exterior and unsmoked interior of the samples. Each sample (CODE) _____ with a different three-digit numerical code. The panelists (ASK) _____ to rate the products visually and then to place a mark along a 15.24-cm semistructured line scale. Descriptors (PLACE) _____ 1.0 cm from each end of the scale. Panelists (MARK) _____ the line where they (THINK) _____ that each sample (FIT) _____ best. Scores (DETERMINE) _____ by measuring the distance of the mark from the left end of the scale with a template coded on a seven-point basis.

(Riha, W.E. and Wendorff, W.L. (1993) 'Evaluation of color in smoked cheese by sensory and objective methods'. *Journal of Dairy Science*, 76/6, pp. 1491–7)

As you might expect in a piece of scientific writing, most of the finite forms occur in the passive, and the agents are not stated. In this way, the scientists who conducted the experiment remain invisible in the text; the focus is on the objects of investigation rather than the investigator. Occasionally, the agent of a finite verb is not the scientists themselves, but another participant, and in these cases the active voice is used; for example, *the panellists could see*, *they thought*. In this extract, the passive is used in a similar way to Text 2.8 (*Coating and primer formulation*) and Text 2.10 (*Tempeh*), which are also examples of scientific writing. You may have noticed, however, a major difference in the use of tense in Text 2.11, which is reporting rather than describing a procedure, and therefore uses past tense forms throughout.

Activity 2.9

The table below shows some of the adjuncts from Text 2.10 and Text 2.11 arranged in three different categories according to their form.

(a) Can you identify what distinguishes each category?
(b) When you have decided, consider the additional adjuncts, taken from Text 2.2 (*How to give a cat a pill*), and decide which category each one belongs to.

Category 1	Category 2
by Rhizopus moulds	*usually*
in oil	*thoroughly*
in boiling water	*perpendicularly to the smoked surface*
as a starter	*visually*
in banana leaves	*best*
for one to two days	**Category 3**
under conditions prescribed for sensory analyses	*by drying or freezing*
	after blanching
with a different three-digit numerical code	*after draining*
	by measuring the distance
1.0 cm from each end of the scale	*of the mark*

Additional adjuncts		
tightly	*with left hand*	*from goldfish bowl*
vigorously	*for gluing later*	*in large towel*
to take taste away	*with cold water and soap*	

Prepositional
phrases and
adverbial groups
were introduced
in Chapter 1.

The classification in the table is based simply on the form of the different adjuncts. The first category consists of prepositional phrases; other examples are: *with left hand, from goldfish bowl, in large towel,* and *with cold water and soap.* The second category consists of adverbial groups; other examples are *tightly* and *vigorously.* The third category involves non-finite verbs, either the *to-***infinitive** or *–ing* form; other examples are *for gluing later* and *to take taste away.*

Items in the third category could be analysed in two different ways. One way is to see the non-finite clause as a component of the larger clause:

Subject	Verb	Adjunct
|| *scores*	*were determined*	*by measuring the distance of the mark . . .* ||

Alternatively, you can treat the non-finite clause as a separate clause with its own structure; for example:

Subject	Verb
|| *scores*	*were determined* ||

Verb	Object
|| *by measuring the distance of the mark* ||	

In general, we will usually analyse grammar at the level of the finite clause, without worrying about the internal structure of non-finite clauses. But whenever it becomes necessary to go into more detail in order to understand what is happening in the text, we can choose to carry out an analysis that shows the structure of both finite and non-finite clauses.

Activity 2.10

The next activity provides extra practice in analysing finite clauses, including the identification of adjuncts, using an extract from Text 2.9 (*Letter to the Editor*).

(a) First divide the text into finite clauses, using double lines || to separate one finite clause from another.

(b) Then identify the SVOCA structure of each clauses, using single lines | to separate one clause element from another. Write the appropriate symbol over each clause element (S = Subject, V = Verb, O = Object, C = Complement, A = Adjunct). You can ignore connectors such as *that* and *however* in your analysis.[3]

The first clause has already been analysed as an example.

     S   V   C

|| I | was | interested to read the article about proposed drug testing in our schools. ||

I generally support the idea of drug testing in schools. However it is important

that it is carried out the right way, not with 'sniffer dogs'. A more subtle

approach is necessary . . . Children should be informed that random tests are

regularly carried out, . . . I feel the testing should be done by an outside body

as expressed by J.G.

This chapter has focused on three areas of grammar: imperative clauses, passive voice, and adjuncts. These grammatical resources are used in many types of text, but they are particularly common in talking about procedure. The way they are used may vary depending on whether the function is instructing, describing, recommending, or reporting a procedure. The chapter began with a passage on kitemaking from a Chinese website, which illustrated problems in using these grammatical resources effectively. To finish, compare Text 2.1 with the following passage, also taken from a Chinese website, and evaluate its effectiveness.

Text 2.12 Kitemaking

Figure 2.3

The delicate procedure of making a kite can be divided into three parts. Firstly, pare and flex bamboo into thin strips for the frame of kites, making full use of the tenacity of the bamboo. According to taste, kites can have shapes as diverse as that of a dragonfly, swallow, centipede or butterfly. Secondly, paste paper onto the framework. The paper is required to be tough and thin with even and long fibers. Some high quality kites are even covered with thin silk. Finally, decorate the kites with colorful chiffon, ribbons and paintings.

> While the basic procedure remains the same, styles of kite-making vary in different regions. The kites in the 'World Kite Capital' of Weifang in Shandong Province are well known for their exquisite craftsmanship, materials, painting, sculpture and flexible flying movement [. . .]

(http://www.travelchinaguide.com/intro/arts/kites.htm)

Compared with Text 2.1, this is clearly a much more effective text. Imperatives, passives, and adjuncts are all used correctly, the clause structure is faultless, and there is no difficulty in understanding what each clause means. At the level of form, the text is unproblematic. However, the text still reads a little oddly, and the problem seems to be that the communicative function is not entirely clear. Some sentences provide instructions that a reader could follow in order to make a kite, as in *Firstly, pare and flex bamboo into thin strips*. But other sentences seem to be describing kitemaking in general, as in *styles of kite-making vary in different regions*. The mixture of description and instruction detracts a little from the overall effectiveness of the text.

Text 2.12 demonstrates that, even when a text is grammatically flawless, it may still not quite work as a piece of communication. Where a traditional formal grammar would stop short at analysing the grammatical structure, a more communicative approach to grammar involves considering form in relation to function – whether, for example, the writer or speaker wants to instruct, to recommend, to report, or (as the next chapter will explore) to describe.

2.5 Summary

Imperative clauses involve an imperative form of the verb, e.g. *Wait! Don't go! Let's talk!* Imperative verbs do not mark tense or number, and do not require a subject.

Verbal groups may be in either passive or active voice. A passive verb form involves the use of BE (or GET) together with a past participle, e.g. *was checked, will be appointed, has got damaged*.

The object of a transitive verb in the active voice becomes its subject in the passive voice; e.g.

S	V	O
They	*spray on*	<u>*a coat of Teflon primer*</u>.

S	V
<u>*A coat of Teflon primer*</u>	*is sprayed on.*

Use of the passive voice makes it possible to downplay agency. The agent of the action may be given in a by-phrase, or may simply be omitted; e.g.

Two men are being questioned <u>by the police</u> in connection with the robbery.

Two men are being questioned in connection with the robbery.

Adjuncts are clause elements that provide information about circumstances such as when, where, how, or why something happens; e.g.

V	O	A	A
hold	*rear paws*	*tightly*	*with left hand.*

V	O	A	A
push	*pill*	*to back of mouth*	*with right forefinger.*

Adjuncts are typically optional (the clause is grammatically correct without them) and can be moved to different positions in the clause; e.g.

Hold rear paws tightly.

Tightly hold rear paws.

Hold rear paws.

2.6 Answer key

Activity 2.3

Interrogative

Is the baby crying or breathing?

Have you got a boy or a girl?

Is it a boy or a girl?

Declarative

Yes, it's crying.

what I want you to do is gently wipe off the baby's mouth and nose.

I need a clean towel!

You need a couple.

I don't know yet.

Imperative

And dry the baby off with a clean towel.

Then wrap the baby in a clean, dry towel

Lift him up!

Just wipe the baby's mouth and nose first.

Minor (verbless) clauses

Quick!

One to dry the baby off with and one to wrap him up with.

A little boy.

Congratulations

Right

OK

Yeah?

Activity 2.5

Text 2.7: If Teflon is non-sticky . . .	Text 2.8: Coating and primer formulation . . .
Active	**Active**
is (a pain to work with)	*No examples*
is (nonsticky)	
do they get	**Passive**
sandblast	*are sandblasted*
spray on	*is (then) applied*
is (thin)	*are abandoned*
spray on	*is applied*
bake	*are (then) dried*
will stick	*<are> (finally) sintered*
Passive	
is (then) baked	

Activity 2.6

Active	Passive
was (interested)	*is carried out*
support	*should be informed*
is (important)	*are (regularly) carried out*
is (necessary)	*should be done*
(My concern) is	*are found*
is adding	*should be offered*
feel	*should be notified*
	should be kept

You may have identified *was interested* as a passive verb form, and this would be a possible analysis if you see it as related to a corresponding active version: *I was interested to read the article* ↔ *To read the article interested me.* However, it is more satisfactory to treat *interested* as an adjective, as will be discussed in Chapter 3.

You may also have identified *proposed* and *expressed* as passive (in *proposed drug testing* and *as expressed by J.G.*). However, the activity focuses on finite verbal groups, and these are non-finite.

Activity 2.7

have been fermented

is . . . sliced, <is> dipped . . . and <is> deep-fried

is . . . consumed

is made

can be preserved

are soaked . . ., <are> dehulled and <are> cooked

are spread out

is used

are . . . mixed . . ., <are> wrapped . . . and <are> left

is . . . covered and <is> bound together

Activity 2.8

The missing verbs were:

was performed

were conducted

were selected

was presented

were sliced

could see

was coded

were asked

were placed

marked

thought

fit

were determined

In American English, the past tense of *fit* is *fit*; in British English it would be *fitted*.

81

The adjuncts are indicated in the analysis below. We have also included other information to help you see how they fit within the clause structure. To simplify the analysis, some clause elements have been shortened. Connectors are shown in italics. The clause elements are separated by | and indicated using the abbreviations:

S	Subject
V	Verb
O	Object
C	Complement
A	Adjunct

S
The visual descriptive sensory analysis of the smoked cheese samples
  V
| was performed |

         A   A
by the University of Wisconsin . . . Laboratory | under conditions . . .

         S   V
Three separate sensory panels | were conducted

  A   S   V
For each panel, | 28 volunteers . . . | were selected

  S   V   O
Each panelist, | was presented with | four smoked cheese samples on a plastic plate

  S   V   A   A
The samples | were sliced | about 1 cm thick | perpendicularly to the smoked surface

   S   V   O
the panelists | could see | the smoked exterior and unsmoked interior of the samples

   S   V   A
Each sample | was coded | with a different three-digit numerical code

   S   V
The panelists | were asked . . .

   S   V   A
Descriptors | were placed | 1.0 cm from each end of the scale

   S   V   O
Panelists | marked | the line

    S V
where | they | thought

     S   V A
that | each sample | fit | best

 S   V   A
Scores | were determined | by measuring . . . with a template

Activity 2.10

Connectors are shown in italics. The clause elements are separated by | and indicated using the abbreviations:

S	Subject
V	Verb
O	Object
C	Complement
A	Adjunct

 S A   V   O
|| I | generally | support | the idea of drug testing in schools ||

	S	V	C
However	it	is	important

S	V	A	A
that it	is carried out	the right way	not with 'sniffer dogs'

S	V	C
A more subtle approach	is	necessary

S	V
Children	should be informed

	S	V	A	V[4]
that	random tests	are	regularly	carried out

S	V
I	feel

S	V	A	A
the testing	should be done	by an outside body	as expressed by J.G.

Notes

1 The name of a special type of paper.

2 The convention [. . .] indicates where part of a text has been removed.

3 Note that in this book we will use the term **connector** to refer to words which link together either clauses or sections of the text. Connectors thus include conjunctions such as *and, but.*

4 Notice that the verbal group *are carried out* is discontinuous; it is interrupted by the adjunct *regularly.*

three

Describing

3.1 Introduction

Scenario

A primary student who has to write a school science project on dogs has found the following two texts on the Internet. Would either text be useful for the project? Why/why not?

Text 3.1 Dog

Figure 3.1

Domestic dog

Domestic dog	
Fossil range: Late Pleistocene - Recent	
Conservation status	
Domesticated	
Scientific classification	
Domain:	Eukaryota
Kingdom:	Animalia
Phylum:	Chordata
Class:	Mammalia

The **dog** (*Canis lupus familiaris*) is a domesticated subspecies of the wolf, a mammal of the Canidae family of the order Carnivora. The term encompasses both feral and pet varieties and is also sometimes used to describe wild canids of other subspecies or species. The domestic dog has been (and continues to be) one of the most widely-kept working and companion animals in human history, as well as being a food source in some cultures. There are estimated to be 400,000,000 dogs in the world.

The dog has developed into hundreds of varied breeds. Height measured to the withers ranges from a few inches in the Chihuahua to a few feet in the Irish Wolfhound; color varies from white through grays (usually called *blue*) to black, and browns from light (tan) to dark ('red' or 'chocolate') in a wide variation of patterns; and, coats can be very short to many centimeters long, from coarse hair to something akin to wool, straight or curly, or smooth.

(http://en.wikipedia.org/wiki/Dog)

Text 3.2 Candy

Candy is a dear little Jack Russell terrier. She's quite young, less than a year old, and although lively she's very obedient, and is already house-trained. Candy was found abandoned and desperately needs someone to care for her. She will make a delightful companion as she is so affectionate.

  Candy is truly a darling! She's such fun to be with and loves going for walks or playing with a ball. She's so good around the house and never causes any trouble. Candy would be happiest in a home where she can be the centre of attention. She isn't at all aggressive, but she can get a little jealous if there are other dogs around. All she wants is to be with you!

(Author's personal data)

Text 3.1 is an encyclopaedia entry, designed to provide factual information about dogs in general. It comes from the online encyclopaedia Wikipedia, which can sometimes be an unreliable source, since the entries are compiled by the general public rather than a panel of experts. However, the information provided here about dogs is objective information that can easily be checked and verified. It is the right sort of information for a school science project. For a primary student, however, the language might be rather forbidding. The description is quite technical, with several specialist terms such as *domesticated subspecies* and *wild canids*. A primary student would probably need some help in making sense of the text, otherwise the temptation might be to copy and paste the information without really understanding it.

Text 3.2, on the other hand, uses language that would be more accessible to a youngster, with no specialist terminology. However, the text is not written to provide objective information about dogs in general, but to describe one particular dog, Candy. It appears on a website advertising dogs who need a home, and is designed to appeal to prospective owners, with the use of subjective terms such as *delightful* and *such fun to be with*. Unlike the encyclopaedia entry, it includes opinions as well as fact. Text 3.2 is not likely to be useful for a school science project, as it does not provide factual information about dogs in general, but a mixture of facts and opinions about one particular dog.

We can describe many different kinds of thing, whether systems, processes, entities, or concepts, and the information we give may be general or particular, more objective or more subjective. But whatever the topic, describing something involves presenting information about its qualities, features, and characteristics. This information is often provided in clauses with the structure subject–verb–complement, such as *The dog is a domesticated subspecies of the wolf*. Typically, descriptive details occur in nominal groups (NGs) or adjectival groups (AdjGs), and so Chapter 3 will focus on examining these areas of grammar. It will consider both the simplest kind of nominal group, consisting of a single pronoun or noun, and more complex nominal groups that include determiners and modifiers. We begin by looking at nominal groups consisting of just a pronoun, but by the end of the chapter you will be able to analyse the structure of more complex nominal and adjectival groups, and appreciate the way these grammatical resources contribute to different kinds of descriptive text.

3.2 Pronouns

The simplest nominal group consists of a single noun or pronoun identifying what you are talking about, e.g. *dogs*, or *Candy*, or *she*.

Have a look at the following clauses from Text 3.2 (*Candy*); they all have the same basic structure, with a complement describing the subject. Can you see a pattern in the choice of the subject in these clauses?

As Chapter 1 pointed out, a 'group' may consist of one or more words.

Complement was introduced in Chapter 1.

Subject	Verb	Adjunct	Complement
Candy	is		a dear little Jack Russell terrier
she	is		quite young
she	is		very obedient
She	will make		a delightful companion
Candy	is	truly	a darling
she	is		such fun to be with

In a description, it's quite common for the phenomenon that is being described to appear frequently in the subject position. Text 3.2 is about Candy, but although the dog's name appears at the beginning of each paragraph, it is replaced in subsequent clauses by the pronoun *she*. Pronouns are used to refer to something that doesn't need to be specified in full, either because the information has already been provided earlier in the text (**anaphoric** reference), or because it is clear from the context (**exophoric** reference). The item that a pronoun refers to is known as the **referent**. In the clause *She is such fun to be with*, the referent of the pronoun *she* is *Candy*.

In a conversation, the pronouns *I* and *you* refer exophorically to the speaker and listener(s), respectively, and the pronouns *it*, *he*, *she*, or *they* may refer either anaphorically to something/someone that has been mentioned, or exophorically to something/someone that can be identified in the context. The **demonstrative pronouns** *this*, *that*, *these*, and *those* work in a similar way. Notice how the pronouns are used in this brief classroom exchange:

T: *What's <u>this</u>?*	Exophoric: *this* refers to a picture the teacher is holding up
S: *<u>I</u> don't know.*	Exophoric: *I* refers to the student speaking
T: *What do <u>you</u> think?*	Exophoric: *You* refers to the student listening
S: *Is <u>it</u> a bulldog?*	Anaphoric: *It* refers back to the question *What's this?*
T: *<u>That's</u> right.*	Anaphoric: *That* refers back to the answer *It's a bulldog*

Activity 3.1

Text 3.3 is an extract from an ecosystems lecture at an American university. As an example of spoken data, it has been transcribed verbatim, including the false starts, repetition, and hesitation that are typical of speech. Written punctuation has not been added; instead, a full stop is used to indicate a brief pause with falling intonation, and a comma to indicate other brief pauses. (Throughout this book you will note that different conventions are used to transcribe spoken language, depending on the source.)

Some of the pronouns in this transcript have been underlined. Look at these pronouns and identify the referent of each one as precisely as possible. If there are any cases where you cannot identify the referent, think about why that might be.

Text 3.3 Rivers

okay, then, what i want to talk about is um, a little bit about the processes of rivers, and understanding and understanding more about what the purpose of a river is. and so, rivers are basically they're great, levellers that transport material from high in the landscape, and <u>they</u> wash it out to lower in the landscape. so they're moving this material from upward, down, to lower grounds and water basins and then <u>they</u> get deposited there. and <u>they</u> carry a large amount of material with them, this material is called alluvium, any material transported by a river is called alluvium. and this diagram here the one up, here shows, that there are different types of materials, that the river carries. one type is this bed load, which, is just, located in the bottom, <u>it</u> moves very, slowly it kind of rolls with the river but it s, it's along the bottom, and <u>those</u> are where the coarsest materials are found. so <u>they</u> kinda roll and tumble along, the, lower surface of, the river. and then <u>you</u> also have suspended load, which are the finer particles that get carried with the flow of water. and, uh <u>we</u> talked about this before that depending on how fast the water is moving would depend on, wh- what size of particles settle out. so those clays which are the finest materials, <u>they</u> will say s- stay suspended in that flow, until it, <u>it</u> almost comes to a complete stop. and then the clays with- would um settle out. but if the river's moving faster <u>it</u>'ll be able to carry larger particles. and over here this term saltation is what is referred to when, the river's moving much larger particles. and it's actually, just, <u>it</u>'s sort of a bouncing, leaps and tumbles of larger particles, that occur when <u>they</u> get picked up by either wind, or by water.

Michigan Corpus of Academic Spoken English, English Language Institute, University of Michigan (http://quod.lib.umich.edu/cgi/c/corpus/corpus?c=micase;cc=micase;q1=drainage;view=transcript;id= LES425SU093)

You have probably noticed that most of the pronouns in this extract are used anaphorically, to refer back to something the lecturer has already mentioned. The lecturer also uses occasional **personal** pronouns (*I*, *we*, *you*, *he*, *she*, *it*, *they*) to refer exophorically. In a face-to-face situation it's normal to use personal pronouns to identify the speaker and listener(s), and although a formal lecture might avoid this sort of interpersonal engagement, here the lecturer uses a fairly informal style. Another instance of exophoric reference is the demonstrative pronoun *those*, which refers to something in the lecture room; from the written transcript alone we cannot tell exactly what this is, though it is probably something in the diagram.

You may also have noticed another puzzling pronoun in the utterance *so they're moving this material from upward, down, to lower grounds and water basins and then <u>they</u> get deposited there*. At first glance the pronoun seems to refer to *rivers*, but from the meaning it becomes clear that the lecturer is explaining that *this material* gets deposited. In writing, if you used a plural pronoun such as *they* to refer to a singular nominal group such as *this material* you would probably spot the mistake and correct it. In spoken language, it is much harder to keep track of referents, so this sort of slip is not uncommon, and is often not even noticed by the listeners.

In analysing spoken texts, we need to recognise that the grammar of spoken English differs in some ways from the grammar of written English (Carter and McCarthy 1997). Chapter 1 pointed out, for example, that one difference is clause structure. Because speakers need to process what they say in real time, there may also be hesitations, repetitions, and false starts. For example, it seems that the lecturer started out to say something like *depending on how fast the water is moving, the particles settle out according to size*, but halfway through changed to a different structure, producing instead the utterance *depending on how fast the water is moving would depend on, wh-what size of particles settle out*. If you examine this carefully, neither the grammatical structure nor the literal meaning is exactly what the lecturer may have intended, but in spoken language this sort of blending rarely causes problems for the listeners.

3.3 Nominal group structure: determiners and heads

Pronouns are the simplest possible type of nominal group, consisting of only one word, but most nominal groups are more complex. To look at these in more detail, we'll focus on some of the clauses from Text 3.3 (*Rivers*) that have been set out below. (Some of the speech-like features of the clauses have been simplified in order to focus on the NG structure.) In these particular clauses, the subjects, objects, and complements are all nominal groups; from these examples, what can you say about the structure of nominal groups?

Subject	Verb	Object	Complement	Adjunct(s)
rivers	*are*		*great levellers*	
they	*are moving*	*this material*		*from upward, down to lower grounds and water basins*

Subject	Verb	Object	Complement	Adjunct(s)
they	carry	a large amount of material		with them
this material	is called		alluvium	
any material transported by a river	is called		alluvium	
one type	is		this bed load	
you	have	suspended load		also
the clays	would settle out			
the river	is moving			faster
the river	is moving	much larger particles		

The simplest nominal group consists of a single noun or pronoun identifying what you are talking about, e.g. *alluvium*, or *rivers*, or *they*. This is known as the **head** of the nominal group. Occasionally a head may consist of two or more nouns or pronouns that are joined by conjunctions, e.g. *you or me*, or *trains, boats, and planes*.

There may also be a determiner before the head, and **modifiers** before or after the head. Here are some examples from Text 3.3:

Determiners were introduced in Chapter 1.

Determiner	Premodifier	Head	Postmodifier
that		flow	
	much larger	particles	
the	lower	surface	of the river
		leaps and tumbles	of larger particles
this		term	saltation

Notice in the last example that it is possible to have two nominal groups alongside each other, both referring to the same thing (*this term* = *saltation*). The second nominal group (*saltation*) is a modifier, telling us more about *this term.* Compare *Dhaka, the capital of Bangladesh,* or *her father, a poor farmer.*

Modifiers will be covered in more detail later in the next section. First, though, we need to examine the role of determiners, which are typically the first element in a nominal group, as in <u>the</u> *clays,* or <u>this</u> *material,* or <u>one</u> *type.* Determiners comprise a number of different items, including:

Articles:	*the, a/an*
Quantifiers:	*some, any, all, many, much, both, half, few, several, etc.*
Demonstratives:	*this, that, these, those*
Possessives:	*his, my, Steven's, the owner's, the King of Spain's, etc.*
Numerals:	*one, two, a hundred, etc.*

Notice that some of these items may be used both as pronouns (on their own) and as determiners (at the beginning of a nominal group); for example:

Pronoun	*have a look at <u>this</u>*
Determiner	*they're moving <u>this material</u>*

The use of determiners is influenced by whether or not the head of the nominal group is **count** or **mass** (alternative terms are 'countable' and 'uncountable'). Broadly speaking, we use a mass noun when we regard something as an indistinguishable mass (such as *water*), and a count noun when we regard it as having its own distinct shape (such as *a river*). This is a matter of how things are viewed in English, rather than an inherent quality of the things themselves. For example, *work* is treated as mass (an unbounded activity), while *a job* is treated as count (something with a recognisable beginning and end). Many nouns can be used either way, with a change of meaning. In Text 3.3, for example, *clays* is used as a plural count noun, although it is more frequently used as a mass noun, and *material/materials* is used as both count and mass within the space of a few clauses. If you want to check on the way a particular noun is used, you can experiment by running an Internet search. For example, we found about 3.9 million results for *clays*, about 1.5 million for *a clay*, and about 96 million for *clay* – suggesting that the uncountable form is much more frequent.

The use of determiners is related to the choice of count or mass noun, singular or plural, and these choices work together to indicate whether the reference of the nominal group is generic, definite, or indefinite. The table below sums up the most common options:

	Mass	Singular count	Plural count
generic	*mud*	*a river*	*rivers*
definite	*the mud*	*the river*	*the rivers*
indefinite	*(some) mud*	*a river*	*(some) rivers*

A **generic** nominal group refers to things in general as a class; for example: *rivers are great levellers*. An **indefinite** nominal group is used to refer to items that are new to the listener or reader, and that they will not necessarily be able to identify. These may be specific items, e.g. *I've just had an idea* (a particular idea) or non-specific, e.g. *I'm looking for a pencil* (any pencil). A **definite** nominal group is used when the listener or reader can be expected to recognise which item(s) are referred to; this may be because:

- it has already been mentioned, e.g.
  Each cell contains a nucleus, and the nucleus . . .;

- enough information is provided in the nominal group itself, e.g.
  We stayed in the most expensive hotel in town;

- it is obvious from the context or from general knowledge, e.g.
  They live in San Diego, near the zoo.

The first of these possibilities involves anaphoric reference, which was discussed earlier in relation to pronouns. Compare:

Each cell contains a nucleus, and the nucleus . . .

Each cell contains a nucleus, and it . . .

Activity 3.2

The short text below is from a website designed for overseas Vietnamese, and describes a traditional musical instrument. Some of the nominal groups are underlined. Have a look at these and, in each case, try to account for the use of determiners by considering whether the reference of nominal groups is generic, indefinite, or definite.

Text 3.4 T'rung

This traditional folk-musical instrument is made of short bamboo tubes differing in size, with a notch at one end and a beveled edge at the other. The long big tubes give off low-pitched tones while the short small ones produce high-pitched tones. The tubes are arranged lengthwise horizontally and attached together by two strings.

In the majestic Central Highlands, T'rung is often played after back-breaking farm work and during evening get-togethers in the communal house around a bonfire with young boys and girls singing and dancing merrily. The sounds of the gong and T'rung also mingle together at wedding parties and village festivals.

(http://www.vnstyle.vdc.com.vn/myhomeland/arts_style/traditionalinstruments/T_rung.html)

Like the encyclopaedia entry in Text 3.1, this extract aims to provide general information about the topic, t'rung. As a result, most of the nominal groups involve generic reference (e.g. *young boys and girls*) or indefinite reference (e.g. *a notch, a beveled edge*). In some contexts, when an indefinite nominal group refers to something non-specific, the distinction between generic and indefinite can become fuzzy. Consider for example *evening get-togethers . . . around a bonfire*. Clearly *get-togethers* involves generic reference, but *a bonfire* could be interpreted as either one indefinite bonfire, or bonfires in general. In this context, the distinction is not important. In a similar way, we can say either *She enjoys a brisk walk* (indefinite) or *She enjoys brisk walks* (generic), without much difference in meaning.

Some of the definite nominal groups in Text 3.4 involve anaphoric reference; *This traditional folk-musical instrument,* for example, refers back to the heading *T'rung.* Several definite nominal groups, however, depend on the reader's ability to infer what is referred to from the context (exophoric reference). *The majestic Central Highlands* can be identified quite easily – even if you've never heard of them before you can work out what they are. *The communal house,* however, is perhaps less obvious, and seems to assume that the reader knows the features of a typical Vietnamese village. Without this background knowledge, the reader has to do more work to understand the text. For writers, the ability to judge what readers will and will not be able to identify is an important skill, which may affect grammatical choices right down to the level of determiners.

3.4 Nominal group structure: modifiers

Activity 3.3

The extracts below are from a homework assignment in geography by two secondary students. Each student has written a paragraph on deforestation in the Amazon.

(a) Read quickly through the texts. Which assignment do you think got a higher grade, and why?
(b) Now underline any nominal groups which include a modifier before the head (known as a **premodifier**). Do you notice any difference between the way they are used in the two assignments?

Text 3.5 Deforestation (by Kelly)

Since 1970, over 600,000 square kilometers of Amazonian rainforest have been destroyed. Small-scale subsistence agriculture practices contribute to about a third of this, but the main cause is cattle ranching, which requires widespread land clearance for pastures. Usually the land is planted with African savannah grasses but

> *sometimes it is just cleared for investment purposes. The problems are inappropriate government tax policies and land tenure regulations, as well as commercial exploitation. For example, pasture is more profitable than forest land because of the low tax on agricultural income. In addition, anyone who clears forest land to keep cattle can claim the land, and this encourages the destruction of the forest.*

(Author's personal data)

Text 3.6 Deforestation (by Jake)

> The Amazon has lost a vast extent of its rain-forest in the last forty years! What has caused this great destruction? Many people blame subsistence farmers, but actually they only cause 30% of the deforestation. Most of it is down to the ranchers who clear huge acres of forest to keep their cattle, and plant Savannah grasses to make their pastures. But it is not only the ranchers who are responsible, as the government's policies can encourage people to clear the forest for investment. This is because you can claim forest land by clearing it and keeping some cattle on it, and then you pay lower taxes because you are in the agriculture sector.

(Author's personal data)

As you probably realised, Kelly received a higher grade for this project than Jake. Although the work would have been assessed for its subject matter, the way in which the information is presented has contributed to its effectiveness as a piece of writing. Compared with Jake, Kelly makes more use of premodifiers, and these enable her to build up a more detailed and precise description of the causes of deforestation. The difference is not only in the frequency of premodifiers, but also the type. Look again at each premodifier and try this simple test: is it possible to combine the premodifier with a **degree** adverb such as *very*, *rather*, or *quite*? As you apply the test, consider what factors influence your results.

Adverbs were introduced in Chapter 1.

The first and fairly obvious point to notice is that, if a premodifier is a noun, it cannot take a degree adverb. We cannot talk, for example, of **quite cattle ranching*, **slightly savannah grasses*, or **very tax policies*. But not all adjectives can take a degree adverb either. Those that do are known as **gradable** adjectives; examples from the text include *small-scale*, *low*, and *inappropriate*. Several adjectives, however, are not gradable; we cannot normally say, for example, **very agricultural income*. Some adjectives may be either gradable or ungradable, depending on their meaning, and this change of meaning gives a clue to what is going on. Compare, for example:

*rather Amazonian rainforest	*a rather Amazonian woman*
*very commercial income	*a very commercial proposition*

The gradable adjectives on the right describe some quality that applies to the NG head; a *rather Amazonian* woman is a strong, assertive woman, and a *commercial* proposition is one that seems to be profitable. Ungradable adjectives, however, are not descriptive; instead, they delimit a particular subcategory of the NG head. *Amazonian rainforest*, for example, is a particular type of rainforest located in the Amazon region, and *commercial income* is a particular type of income derived from commerce.

This distinction allows us to identify two types of premodifier:

Epithets   premodifiers that describe a quality of the head, typically gradable adjectives

Classifiers   premodifiers that delimit a subcategory of the NG head, typically ungradable adjectives or nouns

---

This distinction is based on semantic criteria, but it has grammatical reality as well, since in the ordering of elements in a nominal group, epithets always come before classifiers; e.g.

Det	E	C	Head
the	*most widely-kept*	*working and companion*	*animals*

E	C	C	Head
inappropriate	*government*	*tax*	*policies*

Although we have talked about adjectives and nouns as premodifiers, it would be more accurate to say adjectival groups and nominal groups (bearing in mind that a group may contain one or more words). Notice, for example, the structure of the example above:

	Nominal group 1	
Premodifier	Premodifier	Head of NG 1
(Adjectival group)	(Nominal group 2)	
small-scale	*subsistence agriculture*	*practices*

The heavy use of nominal groups as premodifiers is particularly common in scientific and technical writing, but also occurs in other contexts such as estate agents' listings (e.g. *City centre two bedroom ground floor flat*), advertising notices (e.g. *Summer half price kitchen sale)* and newspaper headlines (e.g. *BANK HOLIDAY TRAFFIC CHAOS WARNING*). You might like to look for examples of headlines or slogans with heavy premodification – or try constructing your own!

Modifiers may be embedded inside each other like Russian dolls. The process of nesting similar components inside one another is known as **recursion**, and is an important property of all human languages. It is particularly common in English with postmodifiers, where it allows the speaker or writer to build up an increasingly specific description of an object or phenomenon, e.g. *a solo from the lady in the front row of the central section of the choir*. In this case, the postmodifier involves several prepositional phrases, one inside another. (A prepositional phrase (PP) is a phrase with a preposition at its head, such as *by the window* or *after the war.*)

One way to show the structure is with a tree diagram:

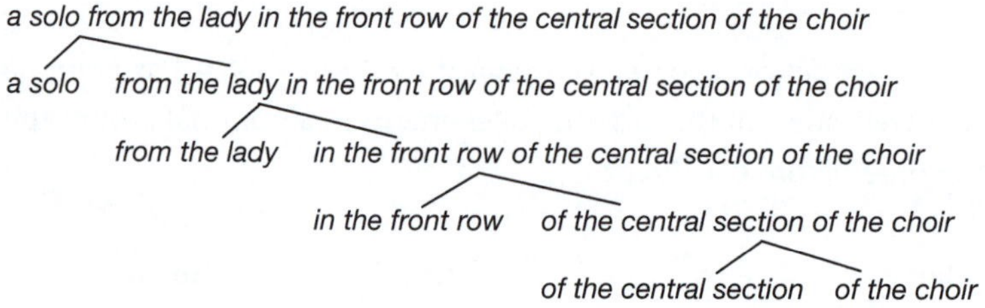

Figure 3.3
Tree diagram

a solo from the lady in the front row of the central section of the choir
a solo   *from the lady in the front row of the central section of the choir*
    from the lady   *in the front row of the central section of the choir*
      in the front row   *of the central section of the choir*
        of the central section   *of the choir*

Other ways to show structure are bracketing:

a solo [by the lady [in the front row [of the central section [of the choir]]]]

and table form:

Nominal group

Det	Head	Postmodifier			
		Prepositional phrase 1			
			Prepositional phrase 2		
				Prepositional phrase 3	
					Prepositional phrase 4
a	*solo*	*from the lady*	*in the front row*	*of the central section*	*of the choir*

Analysing the structure of complex nominal groups involves under-standing the way that words are grouped together. It is often helpful to rephrase the nominal group, to see which words tend to stay together, e.g.

city centre two bedroom ground floor flat

a flat in the city centre with two bedrooms on the ground floor

a ground floor flat in the city centre with two bedrooms

a two bedroom flat in the city centre on the ground floor

The rephrasing suggests that we can analyse the nominal group as:

[city centre] [two bedroom] [ground floor] [flat]

Although nominal groups are often ambiguous, we use our knowledge of the world to work out the meaning, usually without even noticing the ambiguity. If you pass a sign advertising *cheap ladies' shoes*, for example, you would assume they were:

cheap [ladies' shoes]

not

[cheap ladies'] shoes.

Similarly, if someone tells you they have a holiday photo of *a tribesman hunting a wild pig with a bow and arrow*, you would expect to see the bow and arrow with the tribesman, not the pig:

> *a tribesman [hunting a wild pig] [with a bow and arrow]*

not

> *a tribesman [hunting a wild pig [with a bow and arrow]]*

Occasionally, though, this sort of ambiguity can cause misunderstanding or absurdity, and careful writers need to check that what they have written will be interpreted in the way they intended. The next activity features cases where this has not happened; although these particular examples are constructed, they are based on real newspaper advertisements.

Activity 3.4

The classified advertisements placed in newspapers by private individuals are not always carefully edited. The examples below all involve an unfortunate ambiguity in the nominal group structure. Use bracketing to show the two different interpretations, and suggest a way of rewriting the advertisement to remove the ambiguity.

Text 3.7 Classified ads

FOR SALE
Renault Clio with one lady owner, serviced regularly.

LOST
English bulldog, neutered, like one of the family.

WANTED
Young lady to baby-sit for toddler who does not smoke.

FOR SALE
Baby cot that converts into bed, wardrobe, gas cooker and lawn mower.

FOR SALE
Antique chair suitable for gentleman with three legs.

WANTED
Thick sheet metal welder

As you have probably noticed, different grammatical structures may be used as postmodifiers in a nominal group. The most common possibilities are shown below with examples, and will be discussed in the following sections.

- Prepositional phrase
  the low tax <u>on agricultural income</u>
- Adjectival group
  antique chair <u>suitable for gentleman</u>
- Non-finite clause (with **participle**)
  any material <u>transported by a river</u>
  short bamboo tubes <u>differing in size</u>
- Non-finite clause (with infinitive)
  someone <u>to care for her</u>
- Relative clause
  anyone <u>who clears forest land to keep cattle</u>

3.5 Adjectival groups

Compare the following two utterances; what do you think is the effect of the different grammatical choices?

The driver was angry; he blasted the horn.
The angry driver blasted the horn.

In the first case, the adjective *angry* is used as a complement of the subject, *the driver*. In the second case, it is used as a modifier within the nominal group, *the angry driver*. The first utterance claims that the driver was angry, while the second presupposes it. Adjectives used as modifiers make it possible to express ideas more concisely, as part of a nominal group, but they can sometimes give the impression of pushing a reader or listener into accepting a particular viewpoint.

This section explores adjectival groups (AdjGs) used within nominal groups or as complements. An adjectival group may consist of a single adjective, such as *angry*, or a group of words with an adjective as its head, such as *not very angry,* or two or more adjectives joined together by a conjunction, such as *hot, tired, and angry.*

103

Activity 3.5

The following extract is a piece of travel writing from a website where freelance writers can post their articles.

(a)   Identify any adjectival groups and identify whether they are used as modifiers in a nominal group, or as complements.

(b)   Why do you think the frequency of adjectival groups varies in the different parts of this article?

Text 3.8 Peaceful environs of Bentota hotels

Bentota Beach in Sri Lanka is a small but very attractive southern village located about 62 kilometers from the capital city of Colombo. The resort village attracts a huge number of international tourists, especially the Germans and Italians. The superb beach island has a distinctive culture all of its own. A stay in Bentota hotels surrounded by serene and peaceful environs of Bentota Beach provide a fabulously and enriching experience where the mind experiences absolute calmness! The friendly waters of the beach are simply too alluring to resist. On your visit to this tourist friendly destination one can take time out to have a first hand glimpse into one of the main traditional occupations 'tapping the toddy'. Toddy, a fermented sap used as alcoholic drink is transferred by the tappers from palm tree to palm tree on a network of tightropes to tap and collect the 'jungle juice'.

Bentota offerings

There's this little place at Bentota Beach called 'the Turtle Hatchery Project' where turtle eggs are gathered and placed in the premises for them to hatch. This place has been given the thumbs up by many tourists and finds itself on the visitors' itinerary. Once the turtles have hatched, they are safely released to the ocean. A visit to the hatchery costs a nominal fee while for the children entry is free. At the hatchery one will find on display several species of turtles and the visitors are allowed, rather encouraged to pet and hold the turtles. However, be prepared to be asked for voluntary donations at the end of the guided tour.

(http://www.articledashboard.com/Article/Peaceful-Environs-of-Bentota-Hotels/341100)

There are twenty-one adjectival groups in this text, but only two of them are used as complements: *simply too alluring to resist* and *free*. You may perhaps feel that the writer is pushing his views rather strongly, although this effusive style is not unusual in travel writing. Notice, though, that adjectival groups are more frequent in the first half of the extract. This may be partly because the writer wants to 'hook' the reader in, but it's also probably related to the nature of the topic, with the first part describing the place itself, while the second part focuses more on what happens, dealing with events rather than things.

One problem for analysis is the nominal group *a fabulously and enriching experience*, where the writer appears to have made a mistake. This could be corrected either by using two adjectives joined together by a conjunction (*a fabulous and enriching experience*), or by using *fabulously* as a degree adverb (*a fabulously enriching experience*). Degree adverbs (e.g. *very*, *really*, *quite*, *slightly*) are used with adjectives to strengthen or weaken their meaning. Here are some other examples:

<u>simply too</u> alluring to resist
<u>so</u> good around the house
<u>much</u> larger
<u>not very</u> common

When an adjectival group is used as the complement, it functions as a clause element on its own, for example:

Subject	Verb	Complement
Nominal group		**Adjectival group**
the friendly waters of the beach	*are*	*simply too alluring to resist*
entry	*is*	*free*
pasture	*is*	*more profitable than forest land*

When an adjectival group is used as a premodifier, however, it functions as part of a nominal group. In the first example in the table, *friendly* does not function as a clause element in its own right; it is part of the nominal group *the friendly waters of the beach*.

Activity 3.6

In the clauses below, which are taken from Text 3.2 (*Candy*), some of the verbs are underlined. These are all **copular** verbs, which relate a subject to a complement. But what kind of complement is it – an adjectival group or a nominal group?

Candy <u>is</u> a dear little Jack Russell terrier

although lively she<u>'s</u> very obedient

and <u>is</u> already house-trained

She <u>will make</u> a delightful companion

as she <u>is</u> so affectionate

Candy <u>is</u> truly a darling

She<u>'s</u> such fun to be with

Candy <u>would be</u> happiest in a home

[[where she <u>can be</u> the centre of attention]]

3.6 Clauses as modifiers

Look at the following nominal groups taken from Text 3.8 (*Peaceful environs of Bentota hotels*). Can you find the NG head in each case, and identify any postmodifiers?

a distinctive culture all of its own

a first hand glimpse into one of the main traditional occupations

a visit to the hatchery

this little place at Bentota Beach called 'the Turtle Hatchery Project' where turtle eggs are gathered and placed in the premises for them to hatch

The NG heads *culture*, *glimpse*, and *visit* are each followed by a prepositional phrase postmodifier. (Notice that the preposition in a prepositional phrase does not necessarily come first; occasionally there is a degree adverb at the beginning, as in *all of its own*. Other examples are *totally out of reach* and *right by my side*.)

The last example is rather more complicated, as the NG head is followed by three postmodifiers:

this little place [at Bentota Beach] [called 'the Turtle Hatchery Project'] [where turtle eggs are gathered and placed in the premises for them to hatch]

The first postmodifier is a prepositional phrase, but the other two contain verbs: the non-finite verb *called*, and the finite verbal group *are gathered and placed*. As they contain verbs, they are both clauses; the first one is a non-finite clause, and the second one is a finite clause. However, they are still acting as postmodifiers inside the nominal group.

This section will focus on the use of finite and non-finite clauses as modifiers in nominal groups, beginning with relative clauses. A **relative clause** is a clause that adds further information about the head of a nominal group. It is usually introduced by a **relativiser** (*which, who, whom, whose, that, where, when, why* – also known as 'relative pronouns'). Some examples of relative clauses from previous texts are:

a home <u>where she can be the centre of attention</u>

great levellers <u>that transport material from high in the landscape</u>

the ranchers <u>who clear huge acres of forest to keep their cattle</u>

Activity 3.7

This activity also focuses on a description of a place – this time a hotel review written by a disgruntled guest and posted on Tripadvisor.com. For obvious reasons, we've deleted the name of the hotel. Identify any relative clauses in the text, and indicate the NG head which the relative clause relates to.

Text 3.9 Abandon all hope, you who enter here!

Looking at the other reviews, this must be a place one either loves or hates. Positive reviews seem to come from college students who know it is an 'anything goes' hotel. Our room was far nastier than one I visited in an outer province in China, (which at least had courteous and attentive service). Most of the staff at the XXX Resort was sullen and almost determinedly unhelpful. Our room was never cleaned during a 3 day stay and smelled so badly we had to keep the balcony door open at night for air – not a problem since the door wouldn't latch. The pool looked like a toxic waste dump, and the loud, drunken, openly sexual behavior of young adults went on at poolside until 3am each night. My only amusement was listening to comments of other guests who could not believe they were stuck in this pit. The place allows dogs; you'd do better to leave yours in a kennel, which is guaranteed to be cleaner.

(http://www.tripadvisor.com)

Although relative clauses are usually introduced by a relativiser, it is often possible to omit this. Have a look at the clauses below and identify which of them have no relativiser present. Would it be possible to omit the relativiser in any of the other clauses? Can you make a general rule about when this is/is not possible?

1   *you (who enter here)*

2   *a place (one either loves or hates)*

3   *college students (who know it is an 'anything goes' hotel)*

4   *one (I visited in an outer province in China)*

5   *one . . . (which at least had courteous and attentive service)*

6   *other guests (who could not believe they were stuck in this pit)*

7   *a kennel (which is guaranteed to be cleaner)*

The two clauses where the relativiser is optional are (2) and (4). In the other cases it is not possible to omit the relativiser as the resulting clause could be difficult for a reader or listener to understand. Consider the following sentence, for example:

*Positive reviews seem to come from college students know it is an 'anything goes' hotel.

Why is this sentence confusing when omitting the relativiser causes no problems in a sentence such as the one below?

This must be a place one either loves or hates.

The problem stems from the grammatical role that the relativiser has to play in the two different sentences. If the relativiser is the subject of the relative clause, then it cannot be omitted. If it is the object, it can be omitted. Compare:

S	V
College students	*know . . .*

S	V	A	S	V
Positive reviews	*seem to come*	*from college students*	*[[who*	*know . . .]]*

S	A	V	O
One	*either*	*loves or hates*	*the place*

S	V	C	O	S	A	V
This	*must be*	*a place*	*[[<which>*	*one*	*either*	*loves or hates]]*

In these cases, the relative clause acts as a postmodifier, embedded within the structure of the nominal group:

Subject	Verb	Complement			
		Nominal group			
		Head	Postmodifier		
			Subject	Adjunct	Verb
This	*must be*	*a place*	*one*	*either*	*loves or hates*

Embedding occurs whenever one structure is contained within another structure, so that it functions at a lower level; in this case, the clause *one either loves or hates* is contained within a nominal group. In an analysis, embedded elements are indicated by square brackets: *This must be a place [[one either loves or hates]]*.

Not all relative clauses, however, are embedded. Compare, for example, the two relative clauses in the sentence below. Try reading the sentence aloud; where do you pause, and why? Now read the sentence twice, but each time omit one of the relative clauses; what does this tell you about their role in the sentence?

Our room was far nastier than one I visited in an outer province in China, (which at least had courteous and attentive service).

The first relative clause (*I visited in an outer province in China*) provides information that is necessary in order to identify which '*one*' the writer is talking about. If you leave it out, the sentence becomes unintelligible. This is known as a **restrictive** (or 'defining') relative clause. The second relative clause, however, does not identify which hotel is involved; it simply provides extra descriptive information about it. This is known as a **non-restrictive** (or 'non-defining') relative clause. In speech, non-restrictive relative clauses are often marked by a slight pause and a separate intonation pattern. In writing, they are often separated from the rest of the sentence by commas, brackets, or dashes.

To check whether a relative clause is restrictive or not, you can try reading the sentence aloud without the relative clause or writing it with brackets around it. Another test is to try replacing the relativiser with *and* + pronoun. If these tests result in an acceptable sentence, then the relative clause is non-restrictive. For example:

you'd do better to leave your dog in a kennel, which is guaranteed to be cleaner.

you'd do better to leave your dog in a kennel

you'd do better to leave your dog in a kennel (which is guaranteed to be cleaner).

you'd do better to leave your dog in a kennel, and this is guaranteed to be cleaner.

In this case the clause is non-restrictive, and is therefore not an integral part of the nominal group. A non-restrictive relative clause is not embedded in the nominal group, but functions as a separate clause.

you'd do better to leave your dog in a kennel || which is guaranteed to be cleaner.

Occasionally it can be difficult to know what the writer or speaker intended. For example, in the sentence *Positive reviews seem to come from college students who know it is an 'anything goes' hotel*, is the writer identifying the particular sort of students who write positive reviews (restrictive), or suggesting that all college students write positive reviews (non-restrictive)? Both interpretations seem possible in this case.

110

Activity 3.8

Like Text 3.9, the following text might also be read by someone planning a trip. However, this extract is taken from a website for Thomson holidays, so it aims to attract prospective customers, not to put them off! The text illustrates a variety of different clause types, but this activity focuses just on the nominal groups shown in italics. Identify the head of each of these nominal groups, and mark any determiners, premodifiers, or postmodifiers that you find. If there are any embedded clauses, put square brackets around the embedded material.

Text 3.10 Odjo D'Agua Hotel

If you're seeking *a boutique-style hotel that captures the relaxed Cape Verdian spirit perfectly*, the Odjo d'Agua does it to a T. Curving around *its own secluded cove* – it's a real romantic retreat. Step out from the cool reception area and *a tangled riot of cascading bougainvillea* greets you, along with *the swaying palms and lush fruit trees that flank the Roman-style pool*. It's *the picture postcard views over the twinkling seas* that really wow the flip-flops off you, though. Stone steps lead down to the bone-white beach, where you'll also find the serene 'Alma Spa', hidden behind fluttering canvas sails. Hear the clinking of ice cubes as *a zesty 'caiparinha' cocktail* is poured for you at *the brightly painted beach bar*. Then simply sit back on a sunbed and soak up the magical setting. Once discovered, this place brings people back time and time again. But apart from *its obvious charms*, what is it that makes this hideaway oh-so special? Well, there are the bedrooms for a start. Flooded with light, they look out over the shimmering shores and are tastefully decorated with *large black and white tiled bathrooms*. Then there's *the restaurant with to-die-for panoramic vistas*, jutting out over the ocean. And perching below here, *a rustic-style terrace with seating made for sipping fruity cocktails as you gaze out to sea*. Oh, and after dark, don't forget to pop in to *the circular underground bar that bursts into life with live music and scintillating island rhythms*. If you like *laid-back chic with a colourful twist*, then this is your dream destination.

(http://www.thomson.co.uk/destinations/africa/cape-verde/cape-verde-islands/santa-maria-cape-verde-isl/hotels/odjo-dagua-hotel.html)

You have probably identified the three relative clauses as embedded; in each case the writer uses the information to identify the hotel, the trees, and the bar. These restrictive relative clauses help to contribute to the impact of the advertisement, suggesting that it's not just any hotel, but *a hotel* [[*that captures the relaxed Cape Verdian spirit*]], not just any trees, but *trees* [[*that flank the Roman-style pool*]], not just any bar, but a *bar* [[*that bursts into life with live music and scintillating island rhythms*]]. In the last case, you may feel that the information is not really identifying at all, but just descriptive. However, the way it is presented without any punctuation does suggest that the writer wants us to regard it as a defining characteristic, contributing to the exclusivity of the hotel.

One nominal group that may have puzzled you is this: *a rustic-style terrace with seating made for sipping fruity cocktails as you gaze out to sea*. The head is *terrace*, and this is modified by a prepositional phrase (*with . . .*). But what did you make of the clause *as you gaze out to sea*? Its function appears to be describing the circumstances as you sip fruity cocktails, so if this was a complete sentence we could analyse it as:

S	V	O	A
You	*sip*	*fruity cocktails* ‖	*as you gaze out to sea* ‖

But *sipping fruity cocktails* isn't functioning as a complete sentence; it's embedded within the phrase *made for sipping cocktails*. And even now we don't have a complete sentence, as *made for sipping cocktails* is itself embedded within the prepositional phrase *with seating* (or perhaps it's modifying *the terrace* rather than *the seating* – this is not entirely clear). We could show this either by bracketing:

a rustic-style terrace [[made for [[sipping fruity cocktails [[as you gaze out to sea]]]]]]

or in a table:

Det	Premodifier	Head	Postmodifier		
			Non-finite clause		
				Non-finite clause	
					Finite clause
a	*rustic-style*	*terrace*	*made for*	*sipping fruity cocktails*	*as you gaze out to sea*

Notice that the embedded items here include not only the finite clause *as you gaze out to sea* but also non-finite clauses. A non-finite clause is a clause built up around a non-finite verb form. This may be the infinitive form, either with or without *to*, or a participle (e.g. *sipping, made*).

Activity 3.9

What would Text 3.10 look like if it was written, not as a piece of publicity, but as a traveller review, like Text 3.9 (*Abandon all hope*)?

(a) To find out, experiment on the extract below by changing it to the past.
(b) When you've done this, highlight the finite verbs (the ones that are marked for tense) and underline the non-finite verbs (the ones that are not marked for tense).
(c) What do you think is the function of the non-finite verbs in this extract?

But apart from its obvious charms, what is it that makes this hideaway oh-so special? Well, there are the bedrooms for a start. Flooded with light, they look out over the shimmering shores and are tastefully decorated with large black and white tiled bathrooms. Then there's the restaurant with to-die-for panoramic vistas, jutting out over the ocean. And perching below here, a rustic-style terrace with seating made for sipping fruity cocktails as you gaze out to sea.

In considering the function of the non-finite verbs in this text, we need to consider what other options the writer had. Each non-finite verb can be seen as the nucleus of a potential finite clause. It could have been written as a finite verb, accompanied by a Subject, Object, Complement, and/or Adjunct. For example, the writer could have produced clauses such as:

> *The bedrooms are flooded with light.*
>
> *The shores shimmer.*
>
> *The restaurant juts over the ocean.*

But this is not what the writer chose to do. Instead, the non-finite verbs have been backgrounded, and made dependent on another clause. In this extract, most non-finite verbs are used to provide further description of a nominal group; for example:

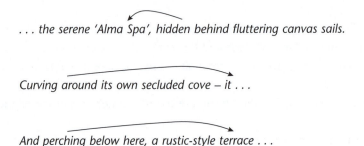

Flooded with light, they looked out . . .

Then there was the restaurant . . . jutting out over the ocean.

Notice that, in these examples, the non-finite clause is separate from the nominal group, not embedded inside it. These are non-restrictive clauses, providing additional descriptive information about the nominal group. Some more examples from Text 3.10 are:

. . . the serene 'Alma Spa', hidden behind fluttering canvas sails.

Curving around its own secluded cove – it . . .

And perching below here, a rustic-style terrace . . .

Just as with relative clauses, non-finite clauses can be either restrictive or non-restrictive. In contrast to the previous examples, the non-finite clauses below are restrictive. These clauses are embedded as postmodifiers in the nominal group, and provide information that identifies the NG head:

seating <u>*made for sipping fruity cocktails*</u>

any material <u>*transported by a river*</u>

short bamboo tubes <u>*differing in size*</u>

a fermented sap <u>*used as alcoholic drink*</u>

Participles may also be used as premodifiers within the nominal group, as in:

the <u>*relaxed*</u> Cape Verdian spirit

its own <u>*secluded*</u> cove

<u>*cascading*</u> bougainvillea

the <u>*swaying*</u> palms

When a participle is used in this way, you may wonder whether it should still be regarded as a verb form. Wouldn't it be easier just to call it an adjective? The question is whether the participle describes an action (e.g. *the gates were <u>locked</u> every night*) or a state (e.g *I couldn't get in because the gates were <u>locked</u>*). Some cases can be decided by checking whether you could use a degree adverb such as *very* or *rather* in front of the participle. If you can, this indicates that it is functioning as an adjective, as in the first two examples below:

> the <u>rather</u> relaxed Cape Verdian spirit
>
> its own <u>very</u> secluded cove
>
> *<u>quite</u> cascading bougainvillea
>
> *the <u>very</u> swaying palms

Unfortunately, this rule of thumb doesn't always apply, and in some cases it may be impossible to decide whether you are dealing with a participle functioning as a verb or an adjective.

Participles raise particular problems for the traditional approach to word-classes (parts of speech). We've already seen that they can be used as verbs and adjectives, and, to complicate matters further, the *-ing* participle can also be used as a noun (as in *I wish I'd done <u>cooking</u> at school*). Traditional grammar exercises sometimes involve classifying the *–ing* form according to 'part of speech', verb, adjective, or noun, and these forms even have different names (participle, gerund, and gerundive).

The traditional treatment of parts of speech is outlined in Chapter 1.

We would argue that it is more important to focus on function rather than form, and taking this approach has the added advantage of simplifying the analysis. Talking about premodifiers in a nominal group (rather than adjectives, nouns, and participles) focuses on the fact that, regardless of word-class, they fulfil the same function of providing information describing the NG head.

3.7 Summary

Nominal groups consist of a head noun or pronoun, which may be accompanied by a determiner, premodifiers, and postmodifiers. These possibilities are listed below, with examples.

Determiner	Premodifiers	Head	Postmodifiers
Article	Adjectival group	Pronoun	Prepositional phrase
the	*rather pretty*	*one*	*over the fireplace*
Quantifier	Nominal group	Noun	Adjectival group
several	*herbicide*	*programs*	*suitable for small farms*
Possessive	Participle		Non-finite clause (with infinitive)
her	*growing*	*desire*	*to compete*
Demonstrative			Non-finite clause (with participle)
these		*materials*	*transported by rivers*
Numeral			Relative clause
two		*strings*	*that hold the tubes together*

Relative clauses may be classified as restrictive or non-restrictive. Restrictive clauses are embedded within the structure of a nominal group, whereas non-restrictive clauses stand as separate clauses. The same distinction applies to non-finite clauses.

Apart from occurring as modifiers within a nominal group, adjectival groups may also stand alone as the complement in an SVC clause, e.g. *She is <u>so good around the house</u>*.

3.8 Answer key

Activity 3.1

In cases of anaphoric reference, the referent is indicated in the text by a box. In cases of exophoric reference, a note at the side suggests something in the context that is the most likely referent (to be certain, you would need to be present at the lecture).

okay, then, what **i** want to talk about is um, a little bit about the processes of rivers, and understanding and understanding more about what the purpose of a river is. and so, rivers are basically they're great, levellers that transport material from high in the landscape, and **they** wash it out to lower in the landscape. so they're moving this material from upward, down, to lower grounds and water basins and then **they** get deposited there. and **they** carry a large amount of material with them, this material is called alluvium, any material transported by a river is called alluvium. and this diagram here the one up, here shows, that there are different types of materials, that the river carries. one type is this bed load, which, is just, located in the bottom, **it** moves very, slowly it kind of rolls with the river but it's, it's along the bottom, and **those** are where the coarsest materials are found. so **they** kinda roll and tumble along, the, lower surface of, the river. and then **you** also have suspended load, which are the finer particles that get carried with the flow of water. and, uh **we** talked about this before that depending on how fast the water is moving would depend on, wh- what size of particles settle out. so those clays which are the finest materials, **they** will say s- stay suspended in that flow, until it, **it** almost comes to a complete stop. and then the clays with- would um settle out. but if the river 's moving faster **it**'ll be able to carry larger particles. and over here this term saltation is what is referred to when, the river's moving much larger particles . and it's actually, just, **it**'s sort of a bouncing, leaps and tumbles of larger particles, that occur when **they** get picked up by either wind, or by water.

→ the lecturer

→ Presumably 'they' refers to 'this material', and the lecturer has made a slip in using a plural form.

→ There is no obvious referent. Perhaps the lecturer is pointing to something in the diagram?

→ This probably refers to people in general, rather than to the students.

→ the lecturer and students

→ 'it' probably refers to 'that flow', which has just been mentioned, but it could also be understood to refer to the water or the river.

Activity 3.2

Generic reference

low-pitched tones	Generic, plural count noun with no determiner
back-breaking farm work	Generic, mass noun with no determiner
young boys and girls	Generic, plural count noun with no determiner
wedding parties and village festivals	Generic, plural count noun with no determiner

Indefinite reference

short bamboo tubes differing in size	Some unidentified tubes, plural count noun with no determiner

a notch	One unidentified notch, singular count noun with indefinite article
two strings	Plural count noun with numeral. Notice that the number simply tells you how many, without specifying which ones.
a bonfire	One unidentified bonfire, singular count noun with indefinite article

Definite reference

This traditional folk-musical instrument	*This* refers back to the heading *T'rung* (anaphoric).
the other (end)	If one end has already been mentioned, then you know which end is the other end.
The long big tubes	The writer has already said there are tubes of differing sizes, so the reader should be able to recognise what this refers to.
the majestic Central Highlands	This is obvious from the context – they must be the Central Highlands of Vietnam.
the communal house	This is also clear from the context, though it requires a little more inference. Presumably the writer expects readers to know that a Vietnamese village would normally have a communal house.
The sounds of the gong and T'rung	Sounds haven't been explicitly mentioned before, but the reference is obvious from context.

Activity 3.3

The nominal groups with premodifiers are listed below:

Det	Premodifier	Head	Postmodifier
over 600,000 sq. kms. of	*Amazonian*	*rainforest*	
	small-scale subsistence agriculture	*practices*	

Det	Premodifier	Head	Postmodifier
	cattle	ranching	
	widespread land	clearance	
	African savannah	grasses	
	investment	purposes	
	inappropriate government tax	policies	
	land tenure	regulations	
	commercial	exploitation	
	forest	land	
the	low	tax	on agricultural income
a	vast	extent	
this	great	destruction	
	subsistence	farmers	
	huge	acres	of forest
	savannah	grasses	
	forest	land	
	lower	taxes	
the	agriculture	sector	

Activity 3.4

Analysis

Renault Clio [with one lady owner] [serviced regularly]
Renault Clio [with one lady owner [serviced regularly]]

English bulldog, [neutered] [like one of the family]
English bulldog, [neutered [like one of the family]]

Young lady [to babysit for toddler] [who does not smoke]
Young lady [to babysit for toddler [who does not smoke]]

Baby cot [that converts into bed], wardrobe, gas cooker and lawn mower
Baby cot [that converts into bed, wardrobe, gas cooker and lawn mower]

Antique chair [suitable for gentleman] [with three legs]
Antique chair [suitable for gentleman [with three legs]]

[Thick [sheet metal]] welder
[Thick] [sheet metal] welder

Suggested rewriting

For sale: Renault Clio, serviced regularly, one lady owner.

Lost: Neutered English bulldog, like one of the family.

Wanted: Young lady, non-smoker, to babysit for toddler.

For sale: Wardrobe, gas cooker, lawn mower, and baby cot that converts into bed.

For sale: Antique chair with three legs, suitable for gentleman.

Wanted: Welder to work with thick sheet metal.

Activity 3.5

The adjectival groups are underlined below:

peaceful environs

a small but very attractive southern village

a huge number

international tourists

the superb beach island

a distinctive culture

serene and peaceful environs

a fabulously and enriching experience

absolute calmness

the friendly waters of the beach

are simply too alluring to resist

this tourist friendly destination

a first hand glimpse

the main traditional occupations

a fermented sap

alcoholic drink

this _little_ place

a _nominal_ fee

is _free_

voluntary donations

the _guided_ tour

Activity 3.6

Candy is _a dear little Jack Russell terrier_	nominal group
although lively she's _very obedient_	adjectival group
and is already _house-trained_	adjectival group
She will make _a delightful companion_	nominal group
as she is _so affectionate_	adjectival group
Candy is truly _a darling_	nominal group
She's _such fun to be with_	nominal group
Candy would be _happiest_ in a home	adjectival group
[[where she can be the centre of attention]]	nominal group

Activity 3.8

Det	Premodifiers	Head	Postmodifiers
a	boutique-style	hotel	_[[that captures the relaxed Cape Verdian spirit perfectly]]_
its own	secluded	cove	
a	tangled	riot	of cascading bougainvillea
the	swaying	palms	
	lush fruit	trees	_[[that flank the Roman-style pool]]_
the	picture postcard	views	over the twinkling seas

a	*zesty 'caiparinha'*	*cocktail*	
the	*brightly painted beach*	*bar*	
its	*obvious*	*charms*	
	large black and white tiled	*bathrooms*	
the		*restaurant*	*with to-die-for panoramic vistas*
a	*rustic-style*	*terrace*	*with seating [[made for sipping fruity cocktails as you gaze out to sea]]*
the	*circular underground*	*bar*	*[[that bursts into life with live music and scintillating island rhythms]]*
	laid-back	*chic*	*with a colourful twist*

Activity 3.9

But apart from its obvious charms, what **was** it that **made** this hideaway oh-so special? Well, there **were** the bedrooms for a start. <u>Flooded</u> with light, they **looked** out over the <u>shimmering</u> shores and **were** tastefully decorated with large black and white <u>tiled</u> bathrooms. Then there **was** the restaurant with <u>to-die-for</u> panoramic vistas, <u>jutting</u> out over the ocean. And <u>perching</u> below here, a rustic-style terrace with seating <u>made</u> for <u>sipping</u> fruity cocktails as you **gazed** out to sea.

four

Talking about
the past

4.1 Introduction

When we think objectively about the past, we often have a tendency towards creating chronologies, making sense of events by locating them in relation to each other, in the order they happened. However, this does not always match the way we experience or remember things – when you recall your childhood or adolescence, for example, you may find that certain events stand out with greater clarity, while your memories of other events are more diffuse and elusive. In the visual medium, film-makers often exploit techniques such as slow motion or flashbacks to manipulate the audience's perception of time. Similarly, the narrator of a piece of fiction may wish to create a sense of the passing of time that does not necessarily coincide with calendar time, and even in non-fiction a writer may have particular reasons to present events non-chronologically. Each medium has its own resources for representing time – compare, for example, how it is treated in cartoons, in TV serials, or in novels – and each language too has its own grammatical resources for this purpose. Translating a story from one medium to another, or from one language to another, may involve difficult decisions on how to represent time while retaining the dramatic impact of the original.

Scenario

The extract below comes from the novel *Vanity Fair*, written by William Thackeray between 1847 and 1848. The scene occurs as two friends, Becky and Amelia, are left behind in Brussels while their husbands, Rawdon and George, are sent off to fight at the battle of Waterloo. How could this part of the book be portrayed in a film? What features of the written text affect the way you visualise the story?

Text 4.1 Waterloo

All that day from morning until past sunset, the cannon never ceased to roar. It was dark when the cannonading stopped all of a sudden.

All of us have read of what occurred during that interval. The tale is in every Englishman's mouth; and you and I, who were children when the great battle was won and lost, are never tired of hearing and recounting the history of that famous action. [. . .]

All day long, whilst the women were praying ten miles away, the lines of the dauntless English infantry were receiving and repelling the furious charges of the French horsemen. Guns which were heard at Brussels were ploughing up their ranks, and comrades falling, and the resolute survivors closing in. Towards evening, the attack of the French, repeated and resisted so bravely, slackened in its fury. They had other foes besides the British to engage, or were preparing for a final onset. It came at last: the columns of the Imperial Guard marched up the hill of Saint Jean, at length and at once to sweep the English from the height which they had maintained all day, and spite of all: unscared by the thunder of the artillery, which hurled death from the English line – the dark rolling column pressed on and up the hill. It seemed almost to crest the eminence, when it began to wave and falter. Then it stopped, still facing the shot. Then at last the English troops rushed from the post from which no enemy had been able to dislodge them, and the Guard turned and fled.

No more firing was heard at Brussels – the pursuit rolled miles away. Darkness came down on the field and city: and Amelia was praying for George, who was lying on his face, dead, with a bullet through his heart.

(William Thackeray (1847/48) *Vanity Fair*, chapter 32)

One striking feature of this extract is the way it moves through time and space. It opens in Brussels as the women listen to the cannon, and returns again to Brussels at the end of the battle. The story does not unfold chronologically, though. After summing up the whole day in the opening sentence (*from morning until past sunset*), Thackeray takes a paragraph (abridged in this extract) to reflect how famous these events have become. The reader may well know what happened at Waterloo, but is left in suspense as to what has happened to Rawdon and George. In paragraph three Thackeray moves back in time and place to the battlefield, but maintains the suspense as he describes the battle swinging to and fro till victory is finally secured. The fate of the two protagonists is swallowed up in the battlefield mêlée, until we are returned in paragraph four to the women in Brussels, as the cannon fall silent. We are back where we started – except that George is now dead. We have been told nothing of his death, and for readers who have followed his exploits through several chapters of the book, it comes as a shock to have a protagonist so suddenly dispatched.

The scene is powerfully written, and it's easy to imagine how a film-maker might try to recreate its impact. But how does Thackeray achieve this verbally? The lexical choices are clearly important, particularly the repetition, such as *all that day, all of us, all day long* at the beginning of each paragraph, or *the women were praying* (paragraph two) and *Amelia was praying* (paragraph three). Thackeray also makes use of poetic devices of alliteration and rhythm (e.g. *receiving and repelling*). But notice the part played by the verbs – the present tense forms in the second paragraph interrupting the forward movement of the story, the *-ing* forms as the battle swings in the balance (*were ploughing . . . falling . . . closing in*), and the switch to simple past for the final push, culminating in the decisive moment when *the Guard turned and fled*. Notice too how George's death takes place unseen, revealed only indirectly through the adjective *dead*, and how the final moments of the day seem to be frozen in time with the use of the verbs *was lying* and *was praying*.

Telling stories is an important part not only of literature, but of our everyday lives, and this chapter explores the grammar resources that we use for this purpose. As the commentary above suggests, verb forms play a key role in narrative, and most of the chapter will focus on the two systems of **tense** (present and past) and **aspect** (perfect and progressive) that allow us to build narratives which are more than just a chronology of events. The final section on **temporal expressions** will examine the role of adjuncts and dependent clauses in expressing temporal relationships.

4.2 Time and tense

It is important not to confuse tense – a grammatical system involving different forms of the verbal group – with the phenomenon of time itself. We all experience time as part of our everyday reality, but different languages have different grammatical resources for indicating when things happen. Some languages (such as Chinese or Malay) have no tenses as such, although they have alternative ways of representing time, while other languages may categorise tenses in very different ways.

In English, every finite verbal group is necessarily marked as either present or past (with the exception of imperatives, as explained in Chapter 2). It is the first word of the verbal group that indicates tense, e.g:

Present tense verbal groups	Past tense verbal groups
swims	*swam*
are pretending	*were* pretending
has fallen over	*had* fallen over
can be collected	*could* be collected
will have been waiting	*would* have been waiting

These tenses do not map exactly onto time – present tense can sometimes be used to talk about the past, and past tense to talk about the present. However, broadly speaking, present and past tense bear some relationship to present and past time.

If we imagine a timeline that emerges from the past and points towards the future, then tense establishes two points along the timeline: the **utterance time** (the time at which the speaker is speaking or the writer is writing), and the **reference time** (the time which they are talking about).

When we use past tense, we are usually talking about a previous time, so the reference time is somewhere before the utterance time. For example, if someone tells you *I went to the cinema yesterday*, they are referring to yesterday, but speaking now. In Figure 4.1, X represents the event of going to the cinema, RT represents the reference time, and UT represents the utterance time:

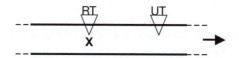

Figure 4.1

When we use present tense, we are talking about things that are true now, as we speak, so the reference time and utterance time coincide (though not necessarily exactly). For example, if you say *I'm just having a cup of tea*, you are speaking now, and you are also talking about now. In Figure 4.2, X represents the action of having a cup of tea.

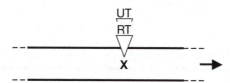

Figure 4.2

The reference time itself is elastic; *in 1815*, for example, sets up a reference time (then) that itself is a year long, while *as I speak* sets up a reference time (now) that is measured in minutes rather than hours.

Thackeray's account of the battle of Waterloo is set in the past, and the overwhelming majority of verbal groups are past tense, e.g.

stopped

were praying

were heard

slackened

marched

had maintained

began to wave and falter

was heard at Brussels

was lying

Present tense forms occur only in paragraph two, where Thackeray describes the situation in his own day.

Activity 4.1

Consider the following clauses from paragraph three. If you had to show the information diagrammatically, how would you mark the events on the timeline in Figure 4.3 below? Show the time of each event (a–f) within the dotted lines, using any techniques you like to make the chronology clear.

(a)   the women were praying ten miles away
(b)   the lines of the dauntless English infantry were receiving and repelling the furious charges of the French horsemen
(c)   the attack of the French slackened in its fury
(d)   the columns of the Imperial Guard marched up the hill of Saint Jean
(e)   the English troops rushed from the post
(f)   the Guard turned and fled.

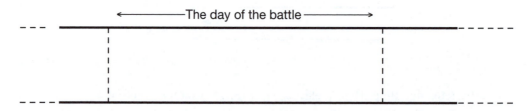

Figure 4.3

Trying to diagram this information draws attention to a difference between events that happened one after another within a relatively short period of time – (c) *slackened*, (d) *marched*, (e) *rushed*, (f) *turned and fled* – and situations that carried on over a longer period of time – (a) *were praying* and (b) *were receiving and repelling*. For instance, you might mark a cross on the diagram to show an event, and a wavy line to show an ongoing situation. Alternatively, you could use a single letter for an event, and a row of repeated letters for a situation (as in the Answer key).

A narrative typically moves forward through a series of events, in which each clause answers the question, 'What happened next?'. It is often accompanied by background information that doesn't advance the narrative, but answers the question, 'What was it like?' or 'What was going on?'. Section 4.3 focuses on the way a narrative presents the chronology of <u>events</u>, while Section 4.4 focuses on the way background <u>situations</u> are represented.

4.3 The structure of verbal groups

The text below is taken from a website that investigates urban legends. It's written not simply to relate a series of events, but also to make this interesting for the readers. What finite verbal forms does the writer use? How do these contribute to the effectiveness of the text?

Text 4.2 WGASA

Some years ago, the San Diego Zoo opened a second, larger branch called the San Diego Wild Animal Park. The Park is built around an enormous open-field enclosure where the animals roam free. To see the animals, visitors ride on a monorail called the Wgasa Bush Line which circles the enclosure. Here's the true story of how the Wgasa Bush Line got its name.

They wanted to give the monorail a jazzy, African sounding name. So they sent out a memo to all their staff, saying: 'What shall we call the new monorail in the Wild Animal Park?' One of the memos came back with 'WGASA' written on the bottom. The planners loved it and the rest is history. What the planners didn't know was that the staff member hadn't intended to suggest a name. He was using an acronym which was popular at the time. It stood for 'Who gives a shit anyhow?'

(http://www.snopes.com/business/names/wgasa.asp)

The text begins with a past tense verbal group (*opened*), which sets up the reference time for the story – *some years ago, when the San Diego Zoo opened a second branch*. The next four finite verbal groups use present tense (*is built, roam, ride, circles*), as they describe the current layout of the San Diego Zoo, at the time of writing. These clauses provide background information (orientation) that the reader needs to understand the story that follows.

The tense switches at the point when the story is introduced: *Here's the true story of how the Wgasa Bush Line got its name*. The story itself is told using past tense forms (except for the quotation, which uses the original verb form). However, the narrator brings it back to the present with the clause *the rest is history*, providing a comment on the significance of the story. But notice what comes next. While the story moved, like most stories, through a chronological sequence of events – *they wanted, they sent, it came back, they loved it* – the last few clauses take a retrospective focus and comment with hindsight on what was really going on with the choice of name. Rather in the way that Thackeray held back the news of George's death, the writer here has held back the 'punchline' of the story. The punchline is emphasised, too, with the construction *What the planners didn't know was that* . . . rather than the more normal *The planners didn't know that* . . .

Narratives involve a sequence of events, but very often the narrator manipulates this sequence, changing the order of events or slowing down the pace. The choice of verb forms is an important part of these narrative techniques.

A verbal group always includes a lexical verb, which identifies a process, e.g. *open, build, get, say, have*. The lexical verb may also be accompanied by one or more auxiliaries, which provide more information about how the process is to be interpreted, e.g.

> Auxiliaries and lexical verbs were introduced in Chapter 1.

was opening

has been opened

could be opening

may have been opened

Each auxiliary determines the form of the verb that follows:

- **Modal** auxiliaries are followed by the base form of a verb, without any inflectional ending, e.g. *may need, should arrive, can play, must be*.

- The **perfect** auxiliary *HAVE* is followed by the past participle of a verb, e.g. *have found, has decided, have spoken*. This usually ends in *–ed*, but because there are many irregular forms such as *gone, taken*, or *driven*, it is sometimes called the *–en* form.

- The **progressive** auxiliary *BE* is followed by the present participle (the *–ing* form of the verb), e.g. *am thinking, was laughing*. The progressive is also called the 'continuous'.

- The **passive** auxiliary *BE* is followed by the past participle, e.g. *is reported, were given*.

Auxiliaries appear in the following sequence:

Modal	Perfect	Progressive	Passive	Lexical verb
	HAVE	BE	BE	
(followed by base form)	(followed by –en form)	(followed by –en form)	(followed by –ing form)	
shall				call
	hadn't			intended
		isn't		using
			was	broken
could	have			said
	has		been	changed
must		be	being	cleaned

Remember that it is always the <u>first</u> word in a finite verbal group that is marked for present or past tense. Using this information, it is possible to read off the name of the verb form from the headings of the columns. So, for example, *has been changed* is a present perfect passive form, *could have said* is a past modal perfect form, and *must be being washed* is a present modal progressive passive form. (Some linguists do not regard modal verbs as having tense, so they would label the last two examples 'modal perfect' and 'modal progressive passive'. This issue will be discussed in Chapter 5.) Finite verb forms that do not involve any auxiliaries are called **simple present** or **simple past** forms (unless of course they are imperative, e.g. *Fire! Stop!*).

Passive forms were introduced in Chapter 2.

Activity 4.3

Text 4.3 is a paragraph from a university student's essay on the topic: *To what extent did the Inquisition affect the pursuit of scientific knowledge in sixteenth century Spain?*

(a) Underline the finite verbal groups and try to identify their form using the information set out above. You will encounter some problems with this exercise – in each case, see if you can work out what causes the problem.

(b) What do you think is the function of this paragraph? Would you call it a narrative? Why/Why not?

Text 4.3 The Inquisition

In 1559 the Inquisition issued its first index of prohibited books. The aim of the index was to counter the new Protestant literature, which was seen as a threat to the Catholic faith. Once a book was considered to be heretical it would be put on trial. In the Inquisition's view the aura created by a book being on trial would be enough to separate the book from the popular masses and restrict it to academic circles, which were dominated by Catholics. The outcome of the trial was that the book would either be altered to remove its heretical contents; or it could be banned outright. Once a book was found to be guilty of heresy it had to be controlled. This involved surveillance operations in bookshops, libraries, printing houses, and at ports and borders. All of these measures were riddled with inefficiency and loopholes. The Spanish Inquisition was not at the command of the pope, but was a council of the crown of Spain. This meant that although the king could control things in Castile, he did not have complete authority over the other regions. Therefore if somebody wished to have a book published but could not get a licence to do so in Castile, they would simply travel to another region and get their book published there. The control on the imports of banned books was also only effective in Castile. Spain was also reliant on the import of books for its access to literature. The biggest problem with trying to control books in Spain though was that the majority of people in the book trade simply ignored the legislation. Spanish printers were allowed to reprint books without having to apply for a new licence to do so, even if the book had been substantially changed since its first edition. The majority of Spanish authors would go and get their books printed outside Spain, mostly in France or Italy. All of this meant that the Inquisition had minimal control over the content of the scientific literature that existed in Spain.

(Author's personal data)

Not surprisingly, all the finite verbal groups in this paragraph are in past tense, since the reference time is the sixteenth century. Half are simple forms, but there are also several instances of modal and passive forms. The text contains several **verbal group (VG) complexes**, which may have caused you problems in your analysis. A VG complex involves more than one lexical verb. This may occur when two verbal groups have been linked by coordination, as in *The majority of Spanish authors <u>would go and get</u> their books printed outside Spain*. The two lexical verbs *go* and *get* are coordinated by *and*, and the modal element *would* applies to both of them.

Like Texts 4.1 and 4.2, Text 4.3 also uses past tense forms, but its function is quite different, as it does not set out to tell a story. The high frequency of modal and passive verb forms may have alerted you to the fact that something different is going on in this passage. In particular, consider the use of modal *would* in the following examples:

> *Once a book was considered to be heretical it <u>would</u> be put on trial.*
>
> *The outcome of the trial was that the book <u>would</u> either be altered to remove its heretical contents; or it could be banned outright.*
>
> *if somebody wished to have a book published . . . they <u>would</u> simply travel to another region.*
>
> *The majority of Spanish authors <u>would</u> go and get their books printed outside Spain.*

The actions represented here are not part of a sequence of events that make up a narrative; they are actions that were repeated many times over a period. Like *used to*, the modal *would* is used here to indicate habitual events in the past. A diagrammatic representation might look something like Figure 4.4 below, with a single cross for a single event, a row of crosses for repeated events, and a wavy line for an ongoing situation:

Figure 4.4

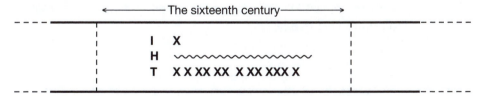

Key   I   the Inquisition issued its first index of prohibited books
      H   the king did not have complete authority over the other regions
      T   [publishers] would simply travel to another region

Single events in the past may form part of a narrative sequence. Repeated events, however, can be seen as describing the customs and routines of the past, and Text 4.3 involves this kind of description. Specifically, it describes the procedures involved in the banning of books, and explains their consequences.

Notice the passive verb forms associated with procedures, as discussed in Chapter 2.

Although Text 4.3 is not itself a narrative, there are narratives that do include descriptive material, as in Text 4.1 (*Waterloo*). This may be about states (e.g. *George . . . was lying on his face*) or about repeated actions (e.g. *the artillery . . . hurled death from the English line*). This aspect of narrative technique will be re-examined in Section 4.5, after a further look at the language used to narrate a sequence of events.

4.4 Perfect aspect

The choice of tense is important in establishing a chronology of events, but it is not the only factor involved, as the next activity demonstrates.

Activity 4.4

Text 4.4 also deals with a historical topic, but is taken from a history learning website rather than from an undergraduate essay. This extract comes from a page about Louis Pasteur, the French scientist who developed the rabies vaccine.

(a) First identify the finite verbal groups and list them in a table as we did on page 131.

(b) Then focus on the chronology of the events. From the list at the end of the text, work out what happened when, and plot each event on the timeline (Figure 4.5) below. One event is already shown in the diagram to help you get started.

Figure 4.5

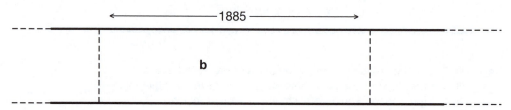

Text 4.4 Louis Pasteur

In 1885, a young boy, Joseph Meister, had been bitten by a rabid dog, and was brought to Pasteur. The boy almost certainly would have died an agonising death if nothing was done so Pasteur took the risk of using his untested vaccine.

> The death of this child appearing to be inevitable, I decided, not without lively and sore anxiety, as may well be believed, to try upon Joseph Meister, the method which I had found constantly successful with dogs. Consequently, sixty hours after the bites, and in the presence of Drs Vulpian and Grancher, young Meister was inoculated under a fold of skin with half a syringeful of the spinal cord of a rabbit, which had died of rabies. It had been preserved (for) fifteen days in a flask of dry air. In the following days, fresh inoculations were made. I thus made thirteen inoculations. On the last days, I inoculated Joseph Meister with the most virulent virus of rabies.
>
> Pasteur

The boy survived, and Pasteur knew that he had found a vaccine for rabies. Three months later, when he examined Meister again, Pasteur reported that the boy was in good health.

(http://www.historylearningsite.co.uk/louis_pasteur.htm)

(a)   Joseph Meister had been bitten by a rabid dog.

(b)   He was brought to Pasteur.

(c)   Pasteur took the risk of using his vaccine.

(d)   He had found the method successful with dogs.

(e)   Meister was inoculated with the spinal cord of a rabbit.

(f)   The rabbit had died of rabies.

(g)   The spinal cord had been preserved (for) fifteen days.

(h)   Thirteen inoculations were made.

(i)   The boy survived.

As you might expect, the verbs in this text are almost all past tense; the one exception occurs when Pasteur steps outside the narrative to comment on the reader's probable reaction (*as may well be believed*). A diagram of these events is shown in the Answer key. Your own version may not look exactly like this, but if you read the passage carefully you should have been able to order the events in the same chronological sequence.

In a narrative, the default assumption is that events will be mentioned in sequence. For example, if you hear *I went into town and bought some shoes* you are likely to assume that the shoes were bought after going into town, and vice versa for *I bought some shoes and went into town*. Like many narratives, though, the text above mentions some events that are out of sequence, and these events are indicated by the use of a perfect form, e.g. *had been bitten*, *had found*. The perfect performs a function similar to the use of flashbacks in films; like blurring the image or switching to black and white, a perfect form signals a movement back in time. In a film it is not always necessary to signal a flashback explicitly, and in speaking or writing too, perfect forms are often optional. This is because verb forms interact with other features of the text, particularly expressions of time, and these features may be enough to make the chronology clear to the listener or reader.

Many grammar books explain the **past perfect** as indicating that one event happened before another. This is often true, particularly in embedded clauses; e.g.

Young Meister was inoculated under a fold of skin with half a syringeful of the spinal cord of a rabbit <u>which had died of rabies</u>.

Often, though, the effect is not simply to order one event relative to another event, but to shift to a different time frame. Consider, for example, the very first paragraph of the novel *Captain Corelli's Mandolin*, by Louis de Bernières (1994). As you read, ask yourself where and when we are as the novel opens.

Text 4.5 Dr Iannis

Dr Iannis had enjoyed a satisfactory day in which none of his patients had died or got any worse. He had attended a surprisingly easy calving, lanced one abscess, extracted a molar, dosed one lady of easy virtue with Salvarsan, performed an unpleasant but spectacularly fruitful enema, and had produced a miracle by a feat of medical prestidigitation.

(Louis de Bernières (1994) *Captain Corelli's Mandolin*, chapter 1)

Did you envisage the doctor at home at the end of a busy day, looking back over what had happened? This effect is produced by the use of perfect forms (which continue for several more paragraphs). Their function is not to locate these events before some other events – no other events have been mentioned. Rather, they produce a retrospective effect, locating the narrator in a period of time from which he can look back on events. Perfect forms indicate **aspect** – a way of viewing the temporal location of events – rather than tense, which is more to do with the distinction between present and past.

There was no grammatical reason why de Bernières had to start his novel this way; he could have used simple past forms. Here, and in many other cases, use of the perfect is optional. A writer or speaker may choose to use a perfect rather than a simple form, perhaps to make the chronology comprehensible to the reader or listener, or perhaps to produce a 'retrospective' effect.

Present perfect verb forms function in much the same way as past perfect verb forms. Notice for example how they are used in the following text:

Text 4.6 Dear Agony Aunt

I have recently had an operation. There is still some sensitivity and soreness in my arm, and I can't seem to get away from well-meaning but thoughtless people who pull on my arm trying to get my attention, hit it while laughing about something, or pat it when offering comfort. Please tell these well-wishers to avoid hitting or touching someone who has undergone any type of surgery or who has suffered an injury or illness.

– Mrs N in Baltimore

The present perfect can be used to order one event relative to another, as in: *avoid hitting or touching someone who has* (previously) *undergone any type of surgery*. More frequent, though, is the 'retrospective' use, when the present perfect is used to shift the time frame, as in I <u>have</u> recently had an operation, which looks back retrospectively on the operation from the perspective of the present time.

Many grammar books explain perfect forms in terms of completed or finished actions. This can be a little misleading, however, as perfect verb

137

forms do not always show completed actions. This depends on the type of process that is being described or narrated. Some processes have a natural endpoint, and you can't look back retrospectively on them until they have finished. For example, you can't truthfully say *I've sent off my tax form* until you actually have done so. Other processes, however, have no endpoint built in, and in these cases you can talk about them retrospectively without implying that the action is finished. For instance, *I've lived in Bristol for three years* doesn't imply that you no longer live there – quite the opposite, in fact.

Aspect is also signalled by the use of progressive verb forms, and these can cancel out any suggestion of completed action with processes that have a natural endpoint. So, while *I've written a letter* suggests it's finished, *I've been writing a letter* suggests the opposite. With both perfect and progressive aspect, the precise meaning of a particular verb form depends very much on the context in which it is used. The selection of aspect is often a stylistic choice made by the writer or speaker, rather than a grammatically obligatory feature. The next section will explore in more detail the way in which progressive aspect is used.

Activity 4.5

The text below comes from the diary kept by a hospital patient, but each finite verbal group has been removed. Using the lexical verb shown in brackets, decide what form you would use. The first one has been written in as an example. Often there are alternative possibilities; what factors do you think affect your choice?

Text 4.7 Last day in hospital

Feb 23rd

Time (PASS) **has passed** *quickly, and Mr Gomez* (AGREE) _____ *that I* (GO) _____ *home today.*
Sadly he (DO) _____ *his ward round whilst I* (HAVE) _____ *a bath, but he* (LOOK) _____

---

at the charts and (GIVE) _____ *permission for my escape. Alf* (COME) _____ *and we* (WAIT) _____ *in the day room for the medicines to come from the pharmacy. In for a check* (BE) _____ *a young Chinese mother who* (SPEAK) _____ *little English. She* (SHARE) _____ *my ward earlier and we* (HAVE) _____ *some fun teaching each other English and Chinese, all of which I* (FORGET) _____ *now, except 'ho-foo' meaning good luck. That* (BE) _____ *probably wrong too!*

(Author's personal data)

Most of this extract presents a narrative of the events of the day, so verb forms are mainly past tense. However, diaries are frequently written on the same day as the events they relate, and from the first sentence of the extract we can see that the diarist was still in the hospital when she wrote this entry. The reference time for the beginning of the entry is 'now', and from this point she sums up the highlight of the day – that she *can go home*. It would be possible to say either that the surgeon *has agreed* (present perfect because he has given his agreement earlier) or that *he agrees* (simple present because he is still in agreement).

After this brief introduction, the diary entry moves back to the reference time of the ward round, and narrates what happened through the rest of the day. Notice the use of a past progressive form in the clause *whilst I was having my bath*, indicating that this is not part of the narrative sequence of events, but background information about the timing of the surgeon's ward round. Progressive aspect is very common in contexts like this, where there is an element of the unexpected or accidental – use of a simple past form here might suggest that the two events had been deliberately coordinated!

The events are mainly narrated in sequence, except for the information about the diarist's previous meeting with the Chinese woman: *She shared my ward earlier and we had had some fun teaching each other English and Chinese*. Both these events happened earlier, and both could be related using a past perfect form. However, perfect aspect is not obligatory here, because the sequence of events is clear without it. In the first clause, the adjunct *earlier* signals anteriority, and the second clause obviously relates to the same time period. The diarist actually used simple past in the first clause and past perfect in the second clause, but any combination of the two verb forms would be possible here. As is often the case, perfect aspect is optional.

The clause *all of which I have forgotten now* returns us to the reference time of 'now', with a present perfect form indicating a process that happens earlier. Here again the perfect is optional; the diarist could have said *I forget now*, with a focus more on her present knowledge of Chinese rather than on the process of forgetting over time.

The diary entry uses present and past tense in a way that is also quite common in conversational anecdotes, with the main sequence of events in past tense, sandwiched between a brief introduction and a brief conclusion, both in present tense, that serve to anchor the story to 'now'.

Activity 4.6

Before moving on to the next section, you may want to use Text 4.7 to practise clause structure analysis. Divide the extract into finite clauses by adding double lines || to separate one finite clause from another. Identify the SVOCA structure of each clause and write the appropriate symbol over each clause element (S = Subject, V = Verb, O = Object, C = Complement, A = Adjunct). You can ignore connectors such as *that* and *however* in your analysis. The first clause has already been analysed as an example.

```
        S        V        A
|| Time | has passed | quickly, || and Mr Gomez agrees I can go home today.
```

Sadly he did his ward rounds whilst I was having a bath, but he looked at the

charts and gave permission for my escape. Alf came and we waited in the day

room for the medicines to come from the pharmacy. In for a check was a young

Chinese mother who spoke little English. She shared my ward earlier and we

had had some fun teaching each other English and Chinese, all of which I have

now forgotten, except 'ho-foo' meaning good luck. That's probably wrong too!

Perfect aspect views events or situations 'retrospectively' from a reference time, with present perfect forms locating them in a period earlier than 'now', and past perfect locating them in a period earlier than 'then'.

4.5 Progressive aspect

Activity 4.7

The text below is an oral narrative, in which an American relates an embarrassing incident during a visit to Japan. Identify the past tense verbs that relate the sequence of events in this narrative. Then consider the other verb forms, and work out what you think their function is.

Text 4.8 The Japanese bath

Anyway, what was I say- Oh we were at the Japanese bath and um they didn't tell us, first of all, that we were going into the bath, so we were standing in the room, and they said 'Okay, take your clothes off.' We're like 'What?!' and um and they gave us these kimono and we put the kimono on. They brought us to this other room, and they said, 'Okay take the kimono off.' And we're like 'What are you talking about?' So then the teacher left. We were kind of wandering around, we saw the bath, so we figure out the deal, so we went down, got in the bath, and sitting there, this 74 year old man who was in our group from Austria

> jumped over our heads into a three foot bath, splashed all over the place and started doing the back- backstroke in the tub So the teacher's back at this time and he's going 'Oyogenai de kudasai.' 'Don't swim!'

(Deborah Tannen (2007) *Talking Voices: Repetition, dialogue and imagery in conversational discourse*, second edn, Cambridge: Cambridge University Press)

As in previous examples, the narrative is moved forward mainly by finite verbal groups in past simple form: *said, gave, put, brought, said, left, saw, went, got, jumped, splashed, started*. Unlike previous examples, though, there are also several present tense forms; this use of present tense to relate events in the past is known as the **historic present**, and is a typical feature of oral narratives. It tends to occur in particular at key points of the narrative, where the switch to present tense creates a dramatic effect by making the events seem more immediate: *We're like 'What?!' . . . And we're like 'What are you talking about?' . . . so we figure out the deal . . . So the teacher's back at this time and he's going 'Oyogenai de kudasai.' 'Don't swim!'*

The use of *we're like* is a relatively recent feature of spoken English that has spread in particular among younger people. It can be used to report what someone says, but more often seems to occur as a way of representing someone's emotional response. In this narrative there is an ambiguity between the two possibilities. It seems unlikely that the group as a whole (*we*) chorused the words *What are you talking about?* – but did anyone say them, or were they just thought? A slightly different example occurs at the end, where *he's going* is also used to introduce reported speech. It seems likely that in this case the words *Oyogenai de kudasai* were actually spoken, but why use a progressive rather than a simple form? The narrator may perhaps want to imply that the words were repeated several times, but it seems more likely that the progressive is used here simply to 'slow down' the action – to freeze it at the point where the Japanese teacher's horror becomes apparent.

The previous section mentioned the way that progressive aspect can cancel the suggestion of completed action. While perfect aspect takes a retrospective view of events, progressive aspect views them as it were from inside ⌄, as they are in progress.

Progressive verb forms in narrative are therefore often found in a scene-setting role, indicating what was happening in the background as the sequence of events unfolded. In Text 4.8, this kind of scene-setting occurs in the clauses *so we were standing in the room*, and *We were kind of wandering around*. The other past progressive form is used slightly differently, as it reports what was (or in this case was not) said: *they didn't tell us, first of all, that we <u>were going</u> into the bath*, where the actual words would have been '*You are going into the bath*'. Here the progressive form *are going* has future reference, though it can be argued that it refers to future events that are already 'in progress' in some way. (Chapter 5 will look in more detail at ways of talking about the future.)

While perfect aspect indicates that an event or situation precedes the reference time, progressive aspect indicates that an event or situation is ongoing at the reference time. Compare:

	Perfect	Progressive
RT = 1980	*By 1980 he'd worked in India.*	*In 1980 he was working in India.*
RT = 'now'	*They've done their homework.*	*They're doing their homework.*

Diagrammatically, the two types of aspect can be shown as follows, with a cross representing an event, and a wavy line representing an ongoing situation:

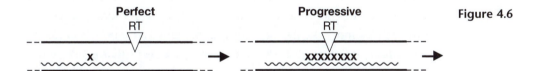

Figure 4.6

The meaning of the progressive depends upon the context in which it is used, and, in particular, the type of event that it relates to. If an event has no natural endpoint, then a progressive form suggests that the event is temporary, while a simple form suggests habitual action. Compare:

The children <u>sleep</u> in the attic. (habitual)

The children <u>are sleeping</u> in the attic. (temporary)

If the event does have a natural endpoint, then a progressive form may represent the event as in progress rather than completed, e.g.

> They _marched_ up the hill. (completed)
>
> They _were marching_ up the hill. (in progress)

Some events are of such short duration that the only way to envisage them as being in progress is as repeated occurrences, rather than a single event, e.g.

> He _sneezed_. (single occurrence)
>
> He _was sneezing_. (repeated occurrences)

The nature of progressive aspect means that it is unlikely to occur with some types of verb. Think, for example, of a subject complement that you could use to complete each of the following clauses:

> You're . . .
>
> You're being . . .

With the simple present, you could choose from a wide range of possible complements to complete the clause, such as _You're gorgeous_, _You're too thin_, _You're prone to exaggeration_, _You're very hard-working_, _You're a pain in the neck_, _You're sunburnt_, _You're an angel_, etc. But with the progressive, you are forced to choose a complement that represents some temporary feature seen as under the person's control, perhaps _You're being a nuisance_, or _You're being ridiculous_. If the verb represents an event that is inherently static, then it is incompatible with the progressive. So while _You're too thin_ is a normal utterance, *_You're being too thin_ would be a strange thing to say.

There are several factors that affect a writer's or speaker's choice of progressive aspect. First of all are their overall purpose and the meaning they want to convey, but another important factor is the nature of the event they are talking about (whether single or repeated, with or without a natural endpoint, permanent or temporary).

For both perfect and progressive aspect, it is also important to bear in mind the reference time – that is, the time that the writer or speaker is talking about. In any given utterance, the reference time may be understood from:

another event:

> *I was cooking dinner <u>when the phone rang</u>.*
>
> *A vacuum is created in the jar <u>because the contents have contracted</u>.*

an expression of time:

> <u>*In 1972*</u> *they were living in Paris.*
>
> <u>*By the end of 2004*</u> *blogs had established themselves as a key part of online culture.*

the context:

> *Look! I'm balancing on one leg!*
>
> *Oh no, the milk's boiled over.*

The final section of this chapter will examine the language used to establish the reference time of an event.

4.6 Expressions of time

Activity 4.8

Read the newspaper story below and identify any parts of the text that provide information about <u>when</u> things happened. What grammatical resources are used to do this?

Text 4.9 Stricken ship poses threat

By KATHERINE DANKS in Sydney

OIL SPILL FEAR ON POPULAR BEACH

A MASSIVE coal ship is threatening to leak tonnes of oil off Newcastle's most popular beach after it ran aground during wild weather on the Hunter coast yesterday.

There are fears another two ships could also become stranded after they all apparently ignored warnings from the Newcastle Port Corporation about weather forecasts of heavy seas and strong winds.

The Panama-registered, 225m-long Pasha Bulker was waiting to load 58,000 tonnes of coal from Newcastle Port when it ran aground off Nobbys Beach about 9.15am yesterday.

It was pounded by 18m waves and vicious winds during the wild weather, which has blacked out many Newcastle homes in a storm that was predicted to worsen last night.

NSW Ports Minister Joe Tripodi said there were signs of damage on the starboard side of the ship, which is carrying 700 tonnes of fuel oil, 38 tonnes of diesel and 40 tonnes of lube oil.

As emergency crews scrambled to prepare for a possible oil leak, the ship's 21 foreign crew were airlifted from the stricken vessel in a dramatic rescue.

One of the Westpac rescue helicopter crewmen Glen Ramplin said the weather was unlike anything he had ever experienced.

"They're the worst conditions I've ever been in ... even though we're so close to shore. I've never experienced anything like that," he told reporters.

(*Northern Territory News* (Australia), 9 June 2007 Saturday)

As explained in Chapter 2, a clause often includes adjuncts that indicate the circumstances surrounding an event, and answer questions such as when? where? how? and why? In Text 4.9, there are several adjuncts that indicate time; these are known as **temporal** adjuncts:

S	V	A	A	A
|| it	ran aground	during wild weather	on the Hunter coast	yesterday ||

S	V	A	A	A
|| it	ran aground	off Nobbys Beach	about 9.15am	yesterday ||

S	V	A
|| that	was predicted to worsen	last night ||

S V   A   V   O

|| *I* | *'ve* | <u>*never*</u> | *experienced* | *anything like that* ||

Some of these expressions of time are prepositional phrases (*during wild weather, about 9.15am*) while others are adverbial groups (*yesterday, never*). There are also some nominal groups that can be used as temporal adjuncts, such as *last night, tomorrow morning*, or *next year*. Finally, an important grammatical resource for expressing time is the use of dependent clauses. A dependent clause is a clause that does not function independently; instead, it is linked to another clause and provides information about that clause. Consider this example from Text 4.9:

Dependent clauses were introduced in Chapter 1.

> *A massive coal ship is threatening to leak tonnes of oil off Newcastle's most popular beach after it ran aground during wild weather on the Hunter coast yesterday.*

This consists of two finite clauses, centred around the finite verbal groups *is threatening to leak* and *ran aground*. The first clause could stand on its own: *A massive coal ship is threatening to leak tonnes of oil off Newcastle's most popular beach*. The second clause, however, would be incomplete on its own: *after it ran aground during wild weather on the Hunter coast yesterday*. Its function is to tell us more about the circumstances of the threat reported in the first clause.

As you saw in Chapter 1, a dependent clause is usually introduced by a subordinating conjunction such as *when, while, until, because, if*, and *so that*. An independent clause may stand alone, or may be linked to another independent clause by a coordinating conjunction such as *and, or, nor, but*, and *yet*.

Dependent clauses may occur before or after the clause to which they are linked. For example, both of the sentences below are grammatically well formed:

> *As emergency crews scrambled to prepare for a possible oil leak, the ship's 21 foreign crew were airlifted from the stricken vessel in a dramatic rescue.*

> *The ship's 21 foreign crew were airlifted from the stricken vessel in a dramatic rescue, as emergency crews scrambled to prepare for a possible oil leak.*

147

It is also possible for a dependent clause to interrupt another clause, for example:

All day long, whilst the women were praying ten miles away, the lines of the dauntless English infantry were receiving and repelling the furious charges of the French horsemen.

For clarity we can separate the interrupting clause:

A   **S**
|| All day long . . . | the lines of the dauntless English infantry | were

V   **O**
receiving and repelling | the furious charges of the French horsemen ||

S   **V**   **A**
<< whilst | the women | were praying | ten miles away >>

The angle brackets << >> are used to show that this is an interrupting clause.

Although dependent clauses provide additional information about another clause, they are not embedded in it. They still function as clauses, not as an element inside another clause. Compare the following sentences, which include dependent clauses shown between double lines and embedded clauses shown in square brackets. Try reading the sentences without including the embedded/dependent clause. As you do this, notice the difference between the two types of clauses:

Dependent clauses

The aim of the index was to counter the new Protestant literature, || which was seen as a threat to the Catholic faith. ||

The boy almost certainly would have died an agonising death || if nothing was done. ||

Three months later, << when he examined Meister again, >> Pasteur reported that the boy was in good health.

It was pounded by 18m waves and vicious winds during the wild weather, || which has blacked out many Newcastle homes. ||

|| As emergency crews scrambled to prepare for a possible oil leak, || the ship's 21 foreign crew were airlifted from the stricken vessel in a dramatic rescue.

Embedded clauses

Here's the true story of [[how the Wgasa Bush Line got its name.]]

[[What the planners didn't know]] was that the staff member hadn't intended to suggest a name.

The Inquisition had minimal control over the content of the scientific literature [[that existed in Spain.]]

Please tell these well-wishers to avoid hitting or touching someone [[who has undergone any type of surgery.]]

One of the Westpac rescue helicopter crewmen Glen Ramplin said the weather was unlike anything [[he had ever experienced.]]

It is usually possible to omit a dependent clause and still have a sentence that is grammatically correct and meaningful. Omitting an embedded clause, however, leaves a sentence that is incomplete, whether grammatically, such as **Here's the true story of*, or semantically, such as *The weather was unlike anything*.

As explained in Chapter 3, a restrictive relative clause provides information that is needed to identify what is being talked about. In the example above, the relative clause *he had ever experienced* identifies *anything*; without it, the sentence no longer makes much sense. A non-restrictive relative clause, however, gives additional information that is not essential for identification, as in the following sentence: *The aim of the index was to counter the new Protestant literature, which was seen as a threat to the Catholic faith.* If you omit the relative clause here, the sentence still makes sense, as the reader can identify *the new Protestant literature*. Restrictive relative clauses are embedded, whereas non-restrictive relative clauses are dependent.

Activity 4.9

The sentences below are taken from Text 4.10, which is printed in full in the next activity. Identify the finite clauses and put double lines || around each one. Highlight any dependent clauses. Then identify any embedded clauses and put square brackets [[ ]] around them.

(a) When they left for Morningside, the roads were even busier than on the way out.

(b)   But theirs seemed to be the only vehicle going north: everyone else was heading in the opposite direction.

(c)   They were flagged down several times by helpful people who wanted to make sure they knew where they were going.

(d)   It was late afternoon when they came into Sungei Pattani.

(e)   Now Sungei Pattani was empty no longer: everywhere they looked there where soldiers.

(f)   In the town's parks and roundabouts – where children usually played – they saw groups of exhausted men.

This chapter has focused on the grammatical resources that enable us to talk about the past, for example in telling stories or relating historical events. It has discussed the use of tense (present and past), aspect (perfect and progressive), and time expressions (adjuncts and dependent clauses), not only to establish a chronology of events, but also to provide a particular perspective on them. The choices we make in deploying these resources are not determined by rigid grammatical rules, but reflect a speaker's or writer's own decisions about how best to tell their story. We began by considering the stylistic choices made in a nineteenth-century novel, and in the final activity we turn again to literature, this time to a modern novel: *The Glass Palace* (2000), by Amitav Ghosh. This presents a family saga against the changing political background of India, Burma, and Malaya in the twentieth century.

Activity 4.10

In the following scene from *The Glass Palace*, as the Japanese invasion moves south into Malaya, the protagonists are heading north, trying to reach the car they have left at the Morningside tea estate.

How does the writer build up the tension in this part of the story? How do the verb forms and temporal expressions contribute to his narrative technique?

Text 4.10 Sungei Pattani

When they left for Morningside, the next day, the roads were even busier than on the way out. But theirs seemed to be the only vehicle going north: everyone else was heading in the opposite direction – towards Kuala Lumpur and Singapore. Heads turned to stare as they drove by; they were flagged down several times by helpful people who wanted to make sure they knew where they were going.

They passed dozens of army trucks, many of them travelling two abreast, with their klaxons blaring, crowding them off the road. Over long stretches they were forced to drive on the grassy verge, crawling along at speeds of fifteen to twenty miles an hour.

It was late afternoon when they came into Sungei Pattani: it was just a day since they'd last driven through, but the town already seemed a changed place. In the morning, they'd found it empty and ghostlike: most of its inhabitants had scattered into the countryside; its shops had been boarded and locked. Now Sungei Pattani was empty no longer: everywhere they looked there were soldiers – Australians, Canadians, Indians, British. But these were not the orderly detachments they had grown accustomed to seeing; these were listless, weary-looking men, bunched together in small groups and ragged little clusters. Some were ambling through the streets with their guns slung over their shoulders, like fishing rods; some were lounging in the shade of the shophouse arcades, eating out of cans and packets, scooping out the food with their fingers. Their uniforms were sweat-stained and dirty, their faces streaked with mud. In the town's parks and round-abouts – where children usually played – they saw groups of exhausted men, lying asleep, with their weapons cradled in their arms.

They began to notice signs of looting: broken windows, gates that had been wrenched open, shops with battered shutters. They saw looters stepping in and out of the breaches – soldiers and locals were milling about together, tearing shops apart. There were no policemen in sight. It was clear that the civil administration had departed.

'Faster, Ilongo.' Dinu rapped on the truck's window. 'Let's get through . . .'

(Amitav Ghosh (2000) *The Glass Palace*, Harper Collins, chapter 37)

Perhaps the most striking feature of this extract is the way it sets up a number of contrasts. Apart from the contrast in space, as Dinu and Ilongo move north while everyone else moves south, there is also a contrast in time: the situation now compared with the situation the day before – empty/crowded, civilian/military, orderly/chaotic. This contrast is marked by the choice of perfect aspect, with past perfect finite verbs providing a retrospective view of the earlier situation: *had driven through, had found, had scattered, had been boarded and locked*. With the words <u>Now</u> *Sungei Pattani was empty no longer*, the reader is brought back to the current point in the story, as Dinu and Ilongo drive through town. The scene is described using past progressive verb forms – *were ambling, were lounging, were milling about* – which have the effect of slowing down the forward movement of the narrative. This impression is also reinforced by the frequent use of non-finite verb forms such as *eating, scooping out, lying, stepping in and out*. The verb forms contribute to the rising sense of urgency as the narrative, like the truck, seems to slow down in the chaos of the town. The scenes that Dinu and Ilongo are seeing also make them realise the most alarming change: that *the civil administration* <u>*had departed*</u>. Once again, a past perfect verb form emphasises the contrast with the earlier situation. The reader is likely to share the sense of rising panic that leads to Dinu's plea *'Faster . . . Let's get through'*.

Did you notice the way that temporal expressions were distributed in the extract? In the first part, there are several adjuncts and dependent clauses that help establish the contrast in time, such as *in the morning, now, as they drove by*, and *since they'd last driven through*. But temporal expressions vanish after the sentence <u>Now</u> *Sungei Pattani was empty no longer*, and their absence contributes to the loss of forward movement in the narrative. Verb forms and temporal expressions are not of course the only resources the writer uses to tell his story, but they are an important part of the narrative technique.

4.7 Summary

A verb group consists of a lexical verb that may be preceded by one or more auxiliaries. Auxiliaries occur in the order: modal, *HAVE* (perfect), *BE* (progressive), and *BE* (passive).

The first word of a finite verb group is marked for present or past tense. Typically, past tense locates events in a period before the time of utterance, while present tense locates them at the time of utterance.

Events presented in simple past tense are generally assumed to occur in chronological sequence, unless there are indications otherwise.

The perfect or progressive aspect varies the way we view the temporal location of events. Perfect verb forms typically present events seen retrospectively, while progressive verb forms typically present events as ongoing, rather than completed actions.

Temporal expressions include adjuncts and dependent clauses. Dependent clauses are introduced by subordinating conjunctions such as *while*, *after*, and *as soon as*.

4.8 Answer key

Activity 4.1

There are many ways that you could complete the diagram, and the answer below is just one suggestion.

Figure 4.7

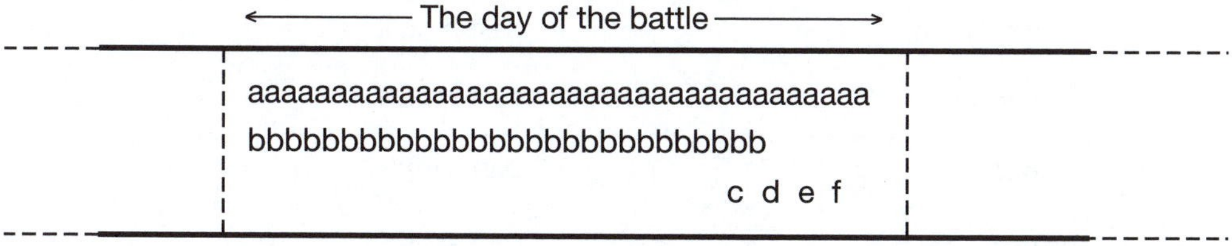

```
                   ←————— The day of the battle —————→
- - - - ┬─────────────────────────────────────────────────────┬ - - - -
        ¦   aaaaaaaaaaaaaaaaaaaaaaaaaaaaaaaaaaaaaaaaa           ¦
        ¦   bbbbbbbbbbbbbbbbbbbbbbbbbbbbbb                      ¦
        ¦                                       c d e f        ¦
- - - - ┴─────────────────────────────────────────────────────┴ - - - -
```

Activity 4.3

issued	past simple
was	past simple
was seen	past passive
was considered to be	past passive (VG complex)
would be put	past modal passive
would be	past modal
were dominated	past passive
was	past simple
would be altered	past modal passive

could be banned	past modal passive
was found to be	past passive (VG complex)
had to be controlled	past modal passive[1]
involved	past simple
were	past simple
was	past simple
was	past simple
meant	past simple
could control	past modal
did not have	past simple
wished to have	past simple (VG complex)
could not get	past modal
would travel	past modal
<would> get	past modal
was	past simple
was	past simple
was	past simple
ignored	past simple
were allowed to reprint	past passive (VG complex)
had been changed	past perfect passive
would go and get	past modal (VG complex)
meant	past simple
had	past simple
existed	past simple

Activity 4.4

Modal	Perfect	Progressive	Passive	Lexical verb
	HAVE	BE	BE	
(followed by base form)	(followed by –en form)	(followed by –en form)	(followed by –ing form)	
	had		been	bitten
			was	brought
would	have			died
			was	done
				took
				decided
may			be	believed
	had			found
			was	inoculated
	had			died
	had		been	preserved
			were	made
				made
				inoculated
				survived
				knew
	had			found
				examined
				reported
				was

Figure 4.8

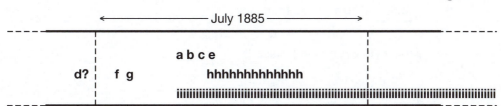

July 1885

d?   f g   a b c e
hhhhhhhhhhhhh
iiiiiiiiiiiiiiiiiiiiiiiiiiiiiiiiiiiiiiiiiiiiiiiiiiiiiiiiiiiiiiiiiiiiiiiiiiiiiiiiii

Activity 4.5

The original diary entry reads as follows, though these are not the only possible verb forms. If you have made different choices, think about your reasons.

Feb 23rd

Time __has passed__ quickly, and Mr Gomez __agrees__ that I __can go__ home today. Sadly he __did__ his ward round whilst I __was having__ a bath, but he __looked__ at the charts and __gave__ permission for my escape. Alf __came__ and we __waited__ in the day room for the medicines to come from the pharmacy. In for a check __was__ a young Chinese mother who __spoke__ little English. She __shared__ my ward earlier and we __had had__ some fun teaching each other English and Chinese, all of which I __have forgotten__ now, except ' ho-foo' meaning good luck. That__'s__ probably wrong too!

Activity 4.6

S	V	A	
|| Time	has passed	quickly ||	

	S	V	
|| and	Mr Gomez	agrees ||	

S	V	A	A
|| I	can go	home	today ||

A	S	V	O
|| Sadly	he	did	his ward rounds ||

	S	V	O
|| whilst	I	was having	a bath ||

	S	V	O
|| but	he	looked at	the charts ||

156

	V	O	
	and	gave	permission for my escape	

S	V
	Alf	came	

	S	V	A	A
	and	we	waited	in the day room	for the medicines to come from the pharmacy	

	C	V	S*
	In for a check	was	a young Chinese mother	

S	V	O
	who	spoke	little English	

S	V	O	A
	She	shared	my ward	earlier	

	S	V	O	A
	and	we	had had	some fun	teaching each other English and Chinese	

O	S	V	A	V	A
	all of which	I	have	now	forgotten,	except 'ho-foo' meaning good luck	

S	V	A	C	A
	That	's	probably	wrong	too!	

*Notice the inversion here: the normal order would be *A young Chinese mother was in for a check*.

Activity 4.9

Finite clauses are shown between double lines, dependent clauses are highlighted, and embedded clauses are shown in square brackets.

(a) || When they left for Morningside || the roads were even busier than on the way out ||

(b) || But theirs seemed to be the only vehicle going north: || everyone else was heading in the opposite direction ||

(c) || They were flagged down several times by helpful people [[who wanted to make sure they knew where they were going]] ||

(d) || It was late afternoon || when they came into Sungei Pattani ||

(e) || Now Sungei Pattani was empty no longer || everywhere [[they looked]] there were soldiers ||

(f) || In the town's parks and roundabouts . . . they saw groups of exhausted men || << – where children usually played – >>*

* Notice that this is an interrupting clause; it's shown separately here so that you can see the two clauses more easily.

Notes

1   *Have to* behaves in some ways like a modal verb (cf. *must be controlled*), and this is how it has been analysed here.

five

Predicting and hypothesising

5.1 Introduction

Scenario

Read the following extract from a service contract with a phone provider (referred to here as COMPANY). Given these conditions, would you be happy to sign the contract?

Text 5.1 Dispute resolution

8.1. This section applies to any dispute between you and COMPANY arising out of or relating to this agreement, including any dispute you may have regarding the services, charges for services, advertising, or any other dispute that either you or COMPANY has that is related to this agreement, even if the dispute arises after your service has terminated. All disputes must be resolved as described in this section. You agree that any dispute will not be resolved by a judge or jury in court (except for small claims court, if applicable). You further agree that any dispute you may have against COMPANY cannot be joined with the dispute of any other person or entity in a lawsuit, arbitration or any other proceeding, or resolved on a class-wide basis.

(http://www.gripe2ed.com/scoop/story/2004/11/8/112534/236)

This extract is quoted in an article entitled 'What you can do to preserve your constitutional right to go to court against businesses that rip you off', written by a professor of law. It draws attention to the increasing use of contracts that trick consumers into signing away their rights – in this case, the rights to trial by jury and to bringing a class action. These contracts have been the subject of a series of court cases brought by an American public interest law firm (see http://www.tlpj.org/).

There are a number of reasons why the language of contracts can often bamboozle members of the public. One factor is the use of complex grammatical structures, such as nominal group postmodifiers (e.g. *any dispute between you and COMPANY arising out of or relating to this agreement, including any dispute you may have regarding the services, charges for services, advertising*) and dependent clauses (e.g. *even if the dispute arises after your service has terminated*). Another factor arises when the contract refers to conditions that may conceivably occur in the future. The future cannot be known – it can only be conceived of in some non-factual way, for example as imagined, or planned, or predicted. As a result, a contract that refers to future possibilities may be more open to question. In this case, the contract applies to *any dispute you may have* (in future), and talks about what *must*, *will* and *cannot* be done in these circumstances.

This chapter explores the language used to talk about non-factual information relating to the future. The main focus is on the verbal group, and the way it is used to indicate future, modal, and hypothetical meanings. The chapter will also consider aspects of clause structure characteristic of texts dealing with the future, particularly dependent clauses that indicate time or condition.

5.2 Verbal groups referring to future events

Activity 5.1

Text 5.2 is the transcript of a BBC weather forecast, which has been broken into clauses to make analysis easier. Identify the finite verbal groups. Which of them refer to the future?

Text 5.2 Weather forecast

hello there

for many of us it's been a grey and a gloomy start to Friday

and we're going to keep a lot of cloud as well especially for England and Wales

as we go through the rest of the afternoon with some drizzle

more substantial rain though for Scotland and for Northern Ireland will continue to work its way south and eastwards

as we head through the rest of the day

so some fairly blue skies eventually working in across the far north and west of Scotland

but for central and southern areas more rain's to come

although the rain perhaps not quite as heavy

as it was this morning

for England as a whole it's going to be quite cloudy through the rest of the day

could be some drizzle around here and there

but some brighter spells perhaps working into the London area

as we head through the afternoon

any brightness tending to be fairly unreliable

there will be a lot of cloud out there

as we head through the rest of the afternoon

and with light winds for southwest England and Wales we should see temperatures climbing to around 14 degrees

now the cloud will thicken up across the far north and west of Wales and for the Isle of Man

so some rain pushing in here

as we head through Friday afternoon

but eventually some brighter skies just working in across the far north and west of Northern Ireland

(Chris Fawkes, *BBC online weather forecast*, 14.00 Friday 26 October 2007)

One thing that may have struck you in this text is the variety of verb forms used to talk about the future. The future differs from present or past time in that we have no experience of it, so while we can talk about the events in the past or the present in factual terms, we can only talk about the future in terms of plans, predictions, possibilities, and so on. This aspect of our experience is reflected in the English verb system. Unlike present and past, the future is not associated with any morphological marking of the verb – there are no 'future tense endings'. Instead, we tend to talk about the future using present tense and modal verbs.

Events in the future are often represented using present tense forms (either simple or progressive), and this is the standard way to refer to the future in clauses of time or condition:

Progressive forms are discussed in more detail in Chapter 4.

as we <u>head</u> through the afternoon

when we<u>'re not expecting</u> it.

if it <u>rains</u>

Present tense is also used when talking of future events that are seen as predetermined or already planned:

The sun <u>sets</u> at 6.35 tomorrow.

My flight <u>gets in</u> early in the morning.

They can't come next weekend; they<u>'re moving</u> house.

Another way of referring to the future is to use the **semi-modal** *be going to*. (Semi-modals are verbs, such as *going to*, *have to*, *need to*, and *ought to*, that function like modals but do not share all the same grammatical features.) *Going to* is used to indicate things that have been decided:

It's no good, he <u>isn't going to change</u> his mind

or things that the speaker thinks are certain, based on current evidence:

it<u>'s going to be</u> quite cloudy through the rest of the day.

The use of *going to* doesn't mean that something necessarily <u>is</u> certain, just that the speaker is expressing it that way. If someone says, for example,

I'm going to be famous one day, the verb form tells us more about their attitude than about the reality of their future life.

Another common way of referring to future events is by using a modal verb, and the choice of modal also indicates the speaker's judgement about the likelihood of their prediction; compare, for example:

> the cloud <u>will thicken up</u> across the far north and west of Wales
>
> <u>could be</u> some drizzle around here and there
>
> we <u>should see</u> temperatures climbing to around 14 degrees.

The finite clauses in Text 5.2 are each built up around a finite verb group, but you may have noticed some minor clauses that do not have a finite verb at all. Sometimes part of the clause has been ellipted, and the missing information can be easily supplied by the hearer (or reader). For example, in the line *could be some drizzle around here and there*, it is possible to fill in the missing subject, *there*. In an analysis, you can show the ellipted elements within angle brackets: *<There> could be some drizzle around here and there*.

One particularly striking feature of Text 5.2 (*Weather forecast*) is the number of nominal groups that stand on their own as minor clauses, rather than functioning as the subject or object of a finite clause. They follow a rather similar pattern, as the table shows, with a head noun followed by a postmodifier:

Minor clauses were introduced in Chapter 2.

Notice the use of participles as postmodifiers, which we also examined in Chapter 3.

Determiner	Premodifier	Head	Postmodifier
some	*fairly blue*	*skies*	*eventually working in across the far north and west of Scotland*
the		*rain*	*perhaps not quite as heavy*
some	*brighter*	*spells*	*perhaps working into the London area*
any		*brightness*	*tending to be fairly unreliable*
some	*brighter*	*skies*	*just working in across the far north and west of Northern Ireland*

Consider what might have been ellipted in, for example, *some brighter spells perhaps working into the London area*. You might reconstruct this minor clause in several different ways: *<There are> some brighter spells perhaps working into the London area*, or *Some brighter spells perhaps <will be> working into the London area* or *<We may see> some brighter spells perhaps working into the London area*, or something else – it is impossible to be sure. If analysts start filling in texts with what they <u>imagine</u> might be missing, there are clearly potential problems about distortion of the data. Generally, ellipsis is only recognised when the missing elements can be reconstructed with confidence. If not, then it may be necessary simply to label the unit as a minor clause, without trying to identify the subject, verb, object, and so on.

The pattern of a head noun followed by a participial postmodifier is particularly common in weather forecasts. Presumably, one of the reasons is that much of the information in a weather forecast is very predictable and doesn't need to be made explicit. Another reason may be stylistic, related to the trend for announcements to be made in a casual, conversational style. The informal style of Text 5.2 stands in contrast to the formal, legal language of Text 5.1.

5.3 Modal verbs

Activity 5.2

Text 5.3 (Figure 5.1) was written by an eight-year-old boy after a discussion with his mother, who encouraged him to write down his ideas. What grammatical resources does he use to refer to the future? Does anything strike you as unusual about his use of verbs?

Text 5.3 When I take over the world

Figure 5.1

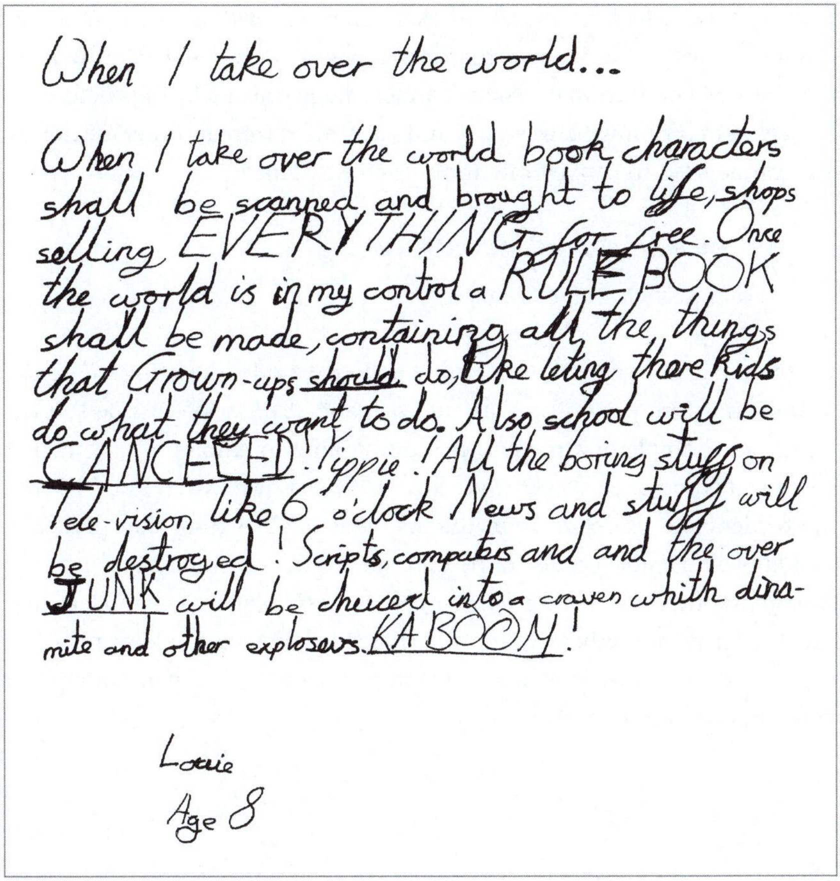

> When I take over the world...
>
> When I take over the world book characters shall be scanned and brought to life, shops selling EVERYTHING for free. Once the world is in my control a RULE BOOK shall be made, containing all the things that Grown-ups should do, like leting there kids do what they want to do. Also school will be CANCELED! Yippie! All the boring stuff on Tele-vision like 6 o'clock News and stuff will be destroyed! Scripts, computers and and the over JUNK will be chucced into a craven whith dina-mite and other explosevs. KABOOM!
>
> Louie
> Age 8

(Author's personal data)

Text 5.3 uses the same grammatical resources to talk about the future as Texts 5.1 and 5.2. Finite verbal groups in present tense are used in time clauses referring to the future: *when I take over the world, once the world is in my control*. Modal verbs are frequent, as in *all the things that grown-ups should do*. In most cases, though, they are used in the passive, e.g. *school will be cancelled*. Louie seems already to understand that the passive can be used as the voice of authority – compare the similar use of the passive in Text 5.1, e.g. *All disputes must be resolved* ... The use of capitals to highlight key words is also typical of this type of text.

Perhaps the most striking feature of Louie's writing is the use of *shall*, which is a relatively low-frequency modal verb. When his mother asked why he'd used *shall*, he explained that if he used *will*, it would sound as though things would happen that way anyway, so he used *shall* to stress that he was going to make them happen. Louie has picked up here on a difference in meaning between *will* and *shall*. Apart from its other meanings, *will* can be used to convey intention, even insistence:

> *We will meet you at the station at 9.00.*
>
> *I will not be spoken to like that!*

Traditional grammar books sometimes included a rule restricting *will* to the second and third person (*you*, *he*, and *she*) and *shall* to the first person (*I*). This is an example of a prescriptive rule seeking to enforce a pattern that never seems to have existed in practice. However, it may have arisen from the tendency to use *shall* when the insistence derives from the speaker. A well-known example occurs in the traditional story of Cinderella, when the fairy godmother says, *Cinderella, you <u>shall</u> go to the ball!* making it clear that she, the fairy godmother, will ensure that this happens. Louie seems to be using *shall* in the same way in his writing, stressing his own anticipated powers as world dictator!

Activity 5.3

Look at the following extract from a newspaper horoscope.

(a) Find the finite verbal groups in the text and use them to help you divide it into finite clauses. (Embedded finite clauses are already shown in square brackets and don't need to be analysed separately.)

(b) How would you account for the form of the verbal groups in this text?

Text 5.4 Your daily horoscope

TAURUS (April 21–May 21)
An emotional-looking full moon in your sign warns you could lose your temper for no reason. Something [[that nine times out of ten would not bother you in the slightest]] will get you all worked up and you will say things [[you do not really mean]]. You may have to make a few apologies tomorrow.

[...]

LEO (July 24–Aug. 23)
You may be inclined to make a snap decision about your work or career but the full moon warns that is probably not a good idea. You are more likely to make the right decision if you wait until your anger with certain people subsides, which it will do once today's full moon starts to wane.

VIRGO (Aug. 24–Sept. 23)
Be aware that if you start something new today you will most likely lose interest in it after a few weeks. It's good that you want to do something creative but timing is all-important and you are more likely to make the right choice if you wait until Mercury, your ruler, turns direct on November 1st.

LIBRA (Sept. 24–Oct. 23)
A friend or colleague may have a change of heart today about a project [[you have been working on together]] but there is no need to worry because by this time tomorrow they will have changed back again. Today's full moon will be a disruptive influence but no real harm will come of it.

(Sally Brompton, 'Your Daily Horoscope', *Globe Life*, Friday 26 October 2007)

Although Text 5.4 deals mainly with the future, it includes a few verbal groups referring to present time (e.g. *the full moon warns, there is no need to worry*) and one example of a present perfect form (*a project you have been working on together*).

Text 5.4 also contains several dependent clauses of time (e.g. *once today's full moon starts to wane*) and of condition (*if you wait*). These refer to future time, but the verb forms are present, as required in such clauses.

The use of present tense forms in dependent clauses that refer to the future can be explained in terms of their communicative function. Look at the dependent clauses numbered 1–4 in the example below. Which of them make a prediction?

> *You are more likely to make the right decision:*
>
> 1   *if you wait*
>
> 2   *until your anger with certain people subsides,*
>
> 3   *which it will do*
>
> 4   *once today's full moon starts to wane.*

Clauses 1, 2, and 4 do not make any prediction about the future; they simply describe possible situations. It is only in clause 3 that the astrologer predicts what will happen. Notice the contrast between clause 2 and clause 3, which talk about the same event, first as a description, then as a prediction: *until your anger <u>subsides</u> . . . which it <u>will do</u>*.

The same point applies to the relative clause in *you will say things you do not really mean*. Here *will say* makes a prediction, but *do not really mean* simply describes what kind of *things*, without making any prediction. The distinction may be easier to see if you contrast two similar clauses:

> *you will say things you do not really mean*
>
> *you will say things you will regret*

Both clauses make a prediction about *saying*, but the second clause also makes a prediction about *regretting*.

The modal verb *will* is used, not so much to refer to future time, as to convey modal meanings such as prediction and intention. If no such modal meanings are involved, then the writer or speaker is more likely to use a present simple or progressive verb form to refer to the future.

As an astrologer, the writer of Text 5.4 is professionally required to claim knowledge of the future. It's not surprising then to find frequent use of *will* to make predictions, as in *today's full moon will be a disruptive influence*. Notice also the modal perfect verb form in *by this time tomorrow they <u>will have changed back</u> again*, where the perfect creates a retrospective effect, looking back from the reference time of *this time tomorrow*. Apart from *will*, other modal verbs are occasionally used to express less certainty, as in *you could lose your temper for no reason*, or *you may have to make a few apologies*. Modal meanings are also conveyed using adverbs (*probably*) and adjectives (*likely*). Although there are no examples in this text, modal nouns, such as *possibility*, can also be used.

Modal verbs differ grammatically from lexical verbs in a number of ways. For example, they:

1 are always finite;

2 are always used as auxiliaries;

3 do not take an –s suffix (*he musts, *she mays);

4 cannot combine with each other (*I will can do it later).

Semi-modal verbs do not share all these grammatical restrictions; for example, they may be combined with modals, as in *you may have to make a few apologies*. But, like modal verbs, they also refer, not to facts, but to the speaker's attitude or stance towards what he or she says. Modal and semi-modal verbs have a range of meanings, which can be broadly grouped under two main headings:

Epistemic modality concerns the speaker's assessment of the validity of what they are saying. It involves logical meanings such as certainty, logical necessity, probability, and possibility:

Looking at the other reviews, this must be a place one either loves or hates.

You can't be serious!

We should see temperatures climbing to around 14 degrees.

There could be some drizzle around here and there.

Deontic modality concerns the speaker's assessment of the desirability of an event or situation. It involves meanings such as obligation, desirability, inclination, and permission.

You must never tell anyone about this.

Testing should be done by an outside body.

Can I park here?

Activity 5.4

The year 2006 saw the publication of the *Stern Report*, which examined the impact of climate change. It considers the possible effects of climate change (a natural context for epistemic modal meanings) and recommends possible responses (a natural context for deontic modal meanings). In the extract below, identify any modal or semi-modal verbs and classify them as either deontic or epistemic.

Text 5.5 Climate change

Climate change will affect the basic elements of life for people around the world – access to water, food production, health, and the environment. Hundreds of millions of people could suffer hunger, water shortages and coastal flooding as the world warms.

[. . .]

Because climate change is a global problem, the response to it must be international. It must be based on a shared vision of long-term goals and agreement on frameworks that will accelerate action over the next decade, and it must build on mutually reinforcing approaches at national, regional and international level.

Climate change could have very serious impacts on growth and development. If no action is taken to reduce emissions, the concentration of greenhouse gases in the atmosphere could reach double its pre-industrial level as early as 2035, virtually committing us to a global average temperature rise of over 2°C. In the longer term, there would be more than a 50% chance that the temperature rise would exceed 5°C. This rise would be very dangerous indeed; it is equivalent to the change in average temperatures from the last ice age to today. Such a radical change in the physical geography of the world must lead to major changes in the human geography – where people live and how they live their lives.

[. . .]

Adaptation to climate change – that is, taking steps to build resilience and minimise costs – is essential. It is no longer possible to prevent the climate change that will take place over the next two to three decades, but it is still possible to protect our societies and economies from its impacts to some extent – for example, by providing better information, improved planning and more climate-resilient crops and infrastructure. Adaptation will cost tens of billions of dollars a year in developing countries alone, and will put still further pressure on already scarce resources. Adaptation efforts, particularly in developing countries, should be accelerated. The costs of stabilising the climate are significant but manageable; delay would be dangerous and much more costly.

The risks of the worst impacts of climate change can be substantially reduced if greenhouse gas levels in the atmosphere can be stabilised between 450 and 550ppm CO^2 equivalent (CO^2e). The current level is 430ppm CO^2e today, and it is rising at more than 2ppm each year. Stabilisation in this range would require emissions to be at least 25% below current levels by 2050, and perhaps much more. Ultimately, stabilisation – at whatever level – requires that annual emissions be brought down to more than 80% below current levels.

[...]

It would already be very difficult and costly to aim to stabilise at 450ppm CO_2e. If we delay, the opportunity to stabilise at 500–550ppm CO_2e may slip away. Action on climate change is required across all countries, and it need not cap the aspirations for growth of rich or poor countries.

The costs of taking action are not evenly distributed across sectors or around the world. Even if the rich world takes on responsibility for absolute cuts in emissions of 60–80% by 2050, developing countries must take significant action too. But developing countries should not be required to bear the full costs of this action alone, and they will not have to. Carbon markets in rich countries are already beginning to deliver flows of finance to support low-carbon development, including through the Clean Development Mechanism. A transformation of these flows is now required to support action on the scale required.

(*Stern Review: The Economics of Climate Change.* Executive Summary. HM Treasury (http://www.hm-treasury.gov.uk/media/9/9/CLOSED_SHORT_executive_summary.pdf))

The epistemic and deontic modal verbs are shown in the Answer key. These are not, however, the only resources for making modal meanings, and you may have noticed the use of *is essential*, *is possible*, and *is required* in this text. The table below indicates how some modal verbs correspond to some modal adjectives:

Modal verb	Epistemic meanings	Deontic meanings
must	*is obvious*	*is obligatory*
will	*is certain/predictable*	*is obligatory*
can	*is possible*	*is able/permitted*
may	*is possible*	*is permitted*
should	*is likely*	*is desirable/advisable*

5.4 Real and unreal conditions

As noted earlier, modal verbs behave rather differently from other verbs, and the relationship between their present and past tense forms is one of those differences. Sometimes the past tense form of a modal is used to talk about the past, just as with other verbs. This is the case in the following example, where there is a straightforward relationship between the present and past tense versions:

Our hotel's disappointing. You   *Our hotel was disappointing.*
can only see the sea from the   *You could only see the sea*
bathroom window and you   *from the bathroom window*
have to walk across a main   *and you had to walk across a*
road to get to the beach.   *main road to get to the beach.*
We won't stay here again.   *We wouldn't stay there again.*

In many cases, though, this pattern breaks down. Text 5.5 contains several examples of past tense modal verbs relating to present or future time, such as:

Hundreds of millions of people could suffer hunger, water shortages and coastal flooding

This rise would be very dangerous indeed

Adaptation efforts, particularly in developing countries, should be accelerated.

With modal verbs, past tense has more to do with unlikely or tentative modality than with past time. Some linguists argue that tense simply does not apply to modal verbs. For example, Steven Pinker (1999: 89) recognises *could* as the past tense of *can*, but comments that:

Other pairs of modal auxiliaries – *may-might, will-would* and *shall-should* – began life as different tenses of the same verb, but the couples divorced long ago and *might, would* and *should* are no longer past tense forms.

An alternative position, though, is to focus on the similarities between past tense meanings for both modal and lexical verbs, recognising that in

English, past tense is not simply about past time. Have a look at the examples below and think about why past tense is used in these cases:

(a)   *We stayed in a lovely hotel. It <u>was</u> right on the beach.*

(b)   *We <u>were going</u> to my mother's this weekend, but the car's broken down.*

(c)   *It's time you <u>were</u> in bed.*

(d)   *I wish they <u>didn't live</u> so far away.*

(e)   *If I <u>had</u> enough money, I'd buy a new one.*

(f)   *If you <u>could just move</u> back a little, please . . .*

(g)   *I <u>was wondering</u> if I could speak to you later this morning.*

The first example looks like a straightforward reference to past time, except that the hotel is presumably still on the beach right now. The past tense doesn't necessarily mean that an event or situation is over; it may simply be that the speaker is presenting it as background to a narrative, not of relevance to the current time. In (b), the past tense refers to an intended action in the future, but one that is no longer expected to take place. Again, the past tense signals a lack of current relevance. Example (c) also seems to refer to a future event, but in this case the past tense signals something counter to reality: you should be in bed, but actually you are not. Similarly, in (d), the past tense is used to express a wish, and in (e) to express a condition, both of them counter to reality. Example (f) looks similar to (e), except that the if-clause expresses a request rather than a condition. In (g), however, the past tense is used even though the process is actually happening – the speaker <u>is</u> wondering as they say the words *I <u>was</u> wondering*.

Examples such as these have led some linguists to move away from a view of tense as simply reflecting distinctions of time. George Yule (1998: 58), for example, explains:

> Conceptually, the present tense form ties the situation described closely to the situation of utterance. The past tense form makes the distinction more remote from the situation of utterance. There is a very regular distinction in English which is marked by *then* versus *now*, *there* versus *here*, *that* versus *this*, and past tense versus present tense. In each of these examples, one is distant or remote from the speaker's situation and the other

is not. In this analysis, past tense means 'remote' and present tense means 'non-remote'.

Past tense forms are used when an event or situation is seen as remote from the current situation, and this may be for one of three reasons:

- **past time**: an event or situation is located in a time in the past, either real or imaginary (as in a novel);

- **hypothetical**: an event or situation is presented as being unreal or unlikely;

- **tentative**: a past tense form is used to suggest that the speaker is tentative or doubtful; the indirectness of this normally conveys politeness.

This analysis of the past tense makes it possible to analyse both modal and lexical verbs in the same way. Like lexical verbs, modal verbs may express past time, e.g. *I could play the piano when I was young*, or hypothetical situations, e.g. *I wish you wouldn't shout*, or tentativeness, e.g. *Could you possibly give me a hand?*. However, because modals express modality rather than fact, they are particularly associated with hypothetical and tentative meanings, whereas lexical verbs in the past tense are more often associated with past time meanings. The less common meanings are shaded in the table below:

Past tense meanings:	with lexical verbs	with modal verbs
past time	*We stayed in a lovely hotel.*	*I could play the piano when I was young.*
hypothetical	*If I had enough money, I'd buy a new one.*	*I wish you wouldn't shout.*
tentative	*I was wondering if I could speak to you later.*	*Could you possibly give me a hand?*

Activity 5.5

The transcript below comes from a public hearing in the USA on testing in maths. In this extract, the chair, Gary Phillips, is questioning one of the experts, Fran Berry.

(a)   Identify any past tense modal verbs in this extract.

(b)   How would you account for their use?

Text 5.6 Committee meeting

PHILLIPS:	You mentioned that you would like to see the test divided into two 45-minute sessions.
	Do you have a view about whether or not it should be the same day or on separate days?
	Would it be acceptable to have like one in the morning and one in the afternoon?
	There is a test security issue that has to be dealt with.
BERRY:	There is a test security issue. There is also the issue of impacting student's schedule within the middle school.
	And that's, the balance between that. I mean, the middle school in which I taught, I was given a 45-minute class period to work with students.
	And granted, I had all those. I had 150 students over the course of the day.
	But to think about trying to assess all 150 students in two 45-minute blocks on the same day, I'm just trying to think how I could have gotten my teammates to help me do that because, you know, it would have impacted what we had done that day.
	And I think there would have been the reasonability of doing that.
	If you were going to think along those lines, I would suggest that you do, you know, a sample.

First sample the section A in the morning and section B in the afternoon and a second sample of kids hopefully that have the same demographics or the same ability level.

And then, switch it around so that they have sample B in the morning and sample A in the afternoon.

PHILLIPS: But would it be an examination nightmare if we had the test 45 minutes in the morning and 45 minutes in the afternoon?

Or would it – we have to think about thousands of schools taking this test.

BERRY: Exactly.

PHILLIPS: Would it be – I know that when the committee was thinking about this, they were recommending or considering having 45 minutes on two separate days, if I remember correctly.

DOSSEY: Right.

BERRY: Well, when you talk about test security, are you thinking you would give them the entire test and let them work as far as they could in 45 minutes?

PHILLIPS: Well –

BERRY: Or are you going to have two separate packages?

PHILLIPS: No, if we had two separate days, we have to have the test divided into two parts.

BERRY: Right.

PHILLIPS: And part one would be administered on one day. And part two would be kept secure probably in a bundle, shrink-wrapped, things like that.

BERRY: Yes.

PHILLIPS: Which would be opened the second day.

BERRY: Right.

(http://www.athel.com/sample.html)

A large part of this dialogue is concerned with Berry's suggestion to divide the test into two 45-minute parts. The suggestion may not be adopted, and Berry acknowledges this by using past tense in the clause *If you were going to think along those lines*. The hypothetical past tense is also used by Phillips in the clause *if we had the test 45 minutes in the morning and*

45 minutes in the afternoon. Both these are **conditional** clauses introduced by *if*, and the consequences are expressed using a past modal verb:

> *If you were going to think along those lines, I <u>would suggest</u> that you do . . . a sample.*

> *But <u>would it be</u> an examination nightmare if we had the test 45 minutes in the morning and 45 minutes in the afternoon?*

This construction is typical of the conditional sentences presented in grammar books. What is not always made clear is that the past modal form may occur even when there is no *if*-clause, and the condition is understood rather than expressed. Throughout Text 5.6, the discussion proceeds on the understanding that it concerns what <u>would</u> happen if this suggestion was implemented. Past modal forms are therefore used even in clauses when the condition is not made explicit. At the end, for example, there are three past modal passive verbal groups outlining the (hypothetical) procedure: *would be administered*, *would be kept*, and *would be opened*.

You may also have noticed that at one point Berry discusses, not the possible future implementation of the proposal, but the counterfactual idea of how she might have implemented it in the past: *I'm just trying to think how I <u>could have gotten</u> my teammates to help me do that*. A past tense form (*could*) is required here, as in the other examples, to indicate that the idea is purely hypothetical. However, the clause also relates to a past time, and English does not have a means of marking past tense twice on the same verb to show both past time and hypothetical meaning. Instead, perfect aspect is brought in to provide a retrospective angle. The past modal perfect forms (*could have gotten*, *would have impacted*, and *would have been*) thus involve both past time and counterfactual situations.

The modal verbs in this extract are used in a fairly typical way, to discuss events and situations, not factually, but hypothetically. The situation is also fairly formal, and it is possible that some of the modal verbs reflect the speaker's concern to appear polite. For example, when Berry says *If you were going to think along those lines, I would suggest that you do, you know, a sample*, she treats her own proposal as a hypothesis, and uses past tense forms. She could, however, have chosen to be more assertive, by saying *If you <u>are</u> going to think along those lines, I <u>suggest</u> . . .* The past tense forms may therefore signal both hypothetical and tentative meanings; it is not always possible to distinguish between the two.

177

Activity 5.6

Text 5.7 is taken from a magazine article that discusses turning points in history – and how things might have turned out differently. Which parts of the extract does the writer present as factual or possible, and which parts as counterfactual?

Text 5.7 What if . . .?

... there are some events – usually overlooked or undervalued, like the flap of the butterfly's wings – that really did set off convulsive effects and rejigged the history of the past 1,000 years. The big issues in the world history of our millennium have concerned the clash of civilisations, in which China, Islam and 'the west' have contended for supremacy. The big issue of the future is how the cultural diversity of our 'multi-civilisational world' will be perpetuated or resolved. The balance that has emerged has been delicate, shifting and prone to sudden lurches. The outcome we have experienced has happened by accident and is unlikely to last. Any of the following eventualities might have forestalled it – and others like them are likely to upset it.

If Seljuk, the 11th-century Turkish war-chief, had remained a pagan ... if he had remained uninspired by a dream, in which he imagined himself ejaculating fire over the world, he might never have pursued all-conquering ambitions in alliance with Islam. The nomad manpower of central Asia would never have been recruited to refresh Muslim strength. The crusader kingdoms would have survived. Islam would have withered or become a marginal force in the world. Eventually, the nomads would have succumbed to those emasculating religions, Christianity and Buddhism.

If the great grassland belt of Africa had been united in the Middle Ages by an imperial people ... an avenue of cultural exchange would have spanned the continent. The civilisations of the Niger would have been linked with Christian Ethiopia. Cultural cross-fertilisation tends to nourish technological innovations. If the grassland had developed as a corridor of east-west communications, Africa might never have ceded to Europe the vast technical advantage that crushed resistance to western imperialism in modern times.

We should live in a world of equipollent continents. African civilisation would have contended on equal terms with those of Eurasia and the Americas. White abuse of black slavery would have been impossible, modern racism unthinkable.

(Felipe Fernandez-Armesto (1999) 'What if the Armada had landed . . .?', *The New Statesman,* 20 December 1999 (http://www.newstatesman.com/199912200027))

The first paragraph of Text 5.7 deals mainly with information that is presented as factual or possible. The writer refers to some things that really have happened, e.g. *China, Islam and 'the west' have contended for supremacy*. He also uses modal verbs and adjectives to speculate about what may happen in future (*. . . will be perpetuated or resolved, is unlikely to last, are likely to upset it*). But at the end of this paragraph we encounter the first clause involving counterfactuality: *Any of the following eventualities might have forestalled it*. This introduces the remainder of the text, which explores events that did not really happen, and are therefore purely hypothetical.

The following paragraphs deal mainly with counterfactual conditions expressed in *if*-clauses (e.g. *If Seljuk . . . had remained a pagan*), and the consequences of those conditions (e.g. *The crusader kingdoms would have survived*). These clauses involve past tense (to indicate hypothetical situations), modal verbs (to indicate epistemic modality), and perfect forms (to provide a retrospective view). There is one exception to this pattern, where a consequence is expressed, not retrospectively, but in terms of what would be the case now (*We should live in a world of equipollent continents*). In this case, a perfect form is not needed.

A few clauses, however, are not presented as counterfactual. The clause *Cultural cross-fertilisation tends to nourish technological innovations* makes a general statement, which the writer presents as evidence to support his reasoning. There are also two relative clauses that, although part of the hypothetical scenario, are themselves factual, and therefore involve past tense used in its more common function, signalling past time. These clauses are: *in which he imagined himself ejaculating fire over the world*, and *that crushed resistance to western imperialism in modern times*.

Traditional grammars often presented just three types of conditional sentences, as though these were the only possible verb forms:

First conditional: *If you come by train I will meet you at the station.*

Second conditional: *If you came by train I would meet you at the station.*

Third conditional: *If you had come by train I would have met you at the station.*

Within a communicative framework, when we look at the way conditions are expressed in real-life situations, we find that there is a wide range of possible verb forms, depending on the combination of meanings. The table below shows some of these possibilities; notice in particular the use of past tense verbs to show hypothetical (unreal or unlikely) meanings.

	Condition	Consequence in the past	Consequence now	Consequence in the future
Unreal past	*If Krakatoa had not blown apart in 1833 . . .*	*it would not have thrown up so much ash*	*the island would still be there now*	*it would probably explode soon*
Unlikely present/ future	*If there were intelligent aliens on Mars . . .*	*scientists would already have discovered them*	*they might be watching us now*	*we could try to communicate with them*
Possible present/ future	*If you pass the exam . . .*	*you must have cheated*	*you deserve a prize*	*you may get a promotion*

Activity 5.7

Text 5.8 is from a book that discusses the evolution of the human brain. Here, the writer speculates on the development of stone tools among early hominids *Australopithecus robustus* and *Homo erectus*. What do you think accounts for the use of both present and past tense forms in this extract?

Text 5.8 Stone tools

The development of stone tools is [. . .] probably characteristic only of the line that led to *Homo*. Stone tools seem to have been primarily associated with the cutting and scraping of carcasses, and thus with the eating of meat. Whereas *robustus* adapted to life on the dry grassland and woodland environment by seeking plant foods, *Homo* probably scavenged for animal meat, and by 1.6 million years ago, *H. erectus* is thought to have consumed animal meat at a higher level than any living nonhuman primate. Since sources of meat would have been widely dispersed, this would have encouraged cooperation among males in the search for meat. We begin to see, then, the emergence of a social order in which specialized tools and perhaps ways of communicating became important.

There has been some debate as to whether the manufacture of stone tools represents a conceptual advance, or whether it was essentially at the level of, say, the shaping of twigs for termiting, as practiced by chimpanzees. The actual manufacturing process was scarcely more complex; the tools were made by simply striking the core stone with a hammerstone, and it has been suggested that no more than three or four blows were required, a technique that could probably be learned by simple observation. Indeed, it has been successfully taught to an orangutan and even to graduate students in California.

(Michael C. Corballis (1991) *The Lopsided Ape: Evolution of the generative mind*, Oxford University Press, chapter 3)

One of the features of academic writing is a focus not only on what is or was actually the case, but also on the evidence involved. In this passage, present tense forms are mainly used when the writer is dealing with epistemic modality – that is, the degree of certainty. Alongside the present tense verb forms we also see other expressions that reflect certainty/uncertainty, such as*: is probably, seem to have been, is thought to have consumed, There has been some debate, it was essentially, it has been suggested that.*

The past tense forms generally occur in statements about past time, as in *the line that led to Homo* and *the tools were made*. However, at several points the writer represents both the current state of knowledge and the evolutionary events in the same clause. This is achieved by using a verb in the present tense, followed by a non-finite perfect form:

> Stone tools *seem to have been* primarily associated
>
> H. erectus *is thought to have consumed* animal meat

Compare this with the use of the perfect after a modal verb in hypothetical conditions:

> Since sources of meat *would have been widely dispersed*
>
> this *would have encouraged* cooperation among males

In both cases, the perfect provides a retrospective focus. By contrast, the modal in *could probably be learned by simple observation* is not followed by a perfect form, since it involves a statement that is not limited to the past, but also applies now.

If we look again at the way the writers speculate in Text 5.7 (*What if ...?*) and Text 5.8 (*Stone tools*), one point of difference emerges. Whereas Text 5.7 speculates about things that we know to be counterfactual, Text 5.8 speculates about what really did happen. A modal verb followed by a perfect form is often counterfactual. For example, if someone says *I could have been a contender*, the implication is that, in reality, they were not a contender. This is the way such verbal groups are used in Text 5.7. In Text 5.8, however, there is no such suggestion of counterfactuality in the sentence: *Since sources of meat would have been widely dispersed, this would have encouraged cooperation among males in the search for meat.* The implication is 'if we are right, then we could predict that . . .' We understand statements as counterfactual, not simply because of the grammatical form of the clauses, but also through the way they function in context.

Activity 5.8

The following letter of complaint was written to a dentist (all the names have been changed). We have altered all the modal verbal groups by removing the auxiliaries and leaving only the lexical verb. What do you think the missing auxiliaries were? As you complete the text, think about the reasons for your choice of auxiliaries.

Text 5.9 Letter of complaint

Dear Mr Atkinson

You treat both my son, Peter, and my daughter, Claire. I am writing this letter of complaint following an appointment for Peter at your practice yesterday.

I _____ begin by saying that I have no complaints about the treatment that either Peter or Claire are receiving. I am very happy with this. Rather, I wish to complain about two matters: the new appointments system and the way it was introduced; and the manner in which I was treated at the reception desk yesterday.

Following Peter's appointment, I asked for a follow-up appointment in October. I was told that a new system had been instituted, and that for the type of work being carried out on Peter's teeth, the only appointment time available was on Thursday afternoon or early evening. While there _____ be good reasons for arranging your time in this way, it seems to me that it fails to take into account the fact that in our case – and I'm sure we are in no way exceptions – working parents have to take time off work to bring their children to appointments. Being limited to appointments on only one afternoon is an impossible restriction. Surely some flexibility _____ built into this. My further objection is that the first I heard of this new arrangement was when your receptionist told me as I made the appointment. Surely as a matter of courtesy to your patients and their parents, if new appointment arrangements are brought in, some written notification of this _____ made. When I suggested this to your receptionist, I was told that there had been papers to this effect at some time on the reception counter. I have never seen or been offered one and, when I asked for a copy, was given a copy of your 'Practice Policies'. As I'm sure you know, this makes no mention of details of appointment times or of any changes to the system.

My second complaint concerns the way I was treated by your receptionist. When offered a Thursday appointment time, I asked if another day _____ be possible as this was inconvenient. She explained that there was a new system and that was the only time available. I asked what I _____ do if I _____ not make this time. She simply shrugged her shoulders. When I asked why patients hadn't been notified about the changes, she said that papers had been available (but see above). When I asked if she _____ convey my view to you that I thought a more formal notification of this change _____ been helpful and polite, she said 'don't get moody with me', that 'I only work for the dentist', and that if I wanted to take up the matter I _____ raised it when I went into the surgery with Peter for his consultation. (I didn't *come into the treatment room – I have in front of me a piece of paper from the practice discouraging parents from coming into consultations with their children.) With a waiting room full of patients and parents, it _____ been inappropriate for me to ask to see you to take up the matter at the time.*

I hope I was polite to her throughout, but I don't consider the way she behaved and the way she spoke to me, lacking any concern or courtesy, was appropriate for someone who acts as a go-between between a patient and parents, and someone providing a medical service.

I look forward to your response in due course.

Yours sincerely,

(Author's personal data)

Although the Answer key indicates the verbal groups that were actually used in this letter, these may not match exactly with your own choices, which depend on the particular modal meanings you have tried to convey. For example, in the first case you might choose *will begin* to signal your intention, or *would begin* to make this more tentative, or *should begin* to indicate obligation, or *must begin* for a stronger obligation.

While the choice of modal verb is up to you, the decision of whether or not to use a perfect form depends on the context. Compare, for example, the two examples below.

(a) *if new appointment arrangements are brought in, some written notification of this could be made*

(b) *if I wanted to take up the matter I should have raised it when I went into the surgery*

Both deal with a counterfactual situation and therefore use past tense to show counterfactuality. However, (a) is framed in terms of what doesn't happen in the current system, while (b) is framed as what didn't happen at a particular time in the past. So, in (b) it is necessary to use perfect aspect to refer retrospectively to the past.

5.5 Summary

When we talk about the future, we are dealing not with facts, but with predictions, hypotheses, plans, and so on. English uses a variety of ways to talk about the future, reflecting these possibilities. Present tense is used to represent events as planned or predetermined, and is the normal choice in dependent clauses. Modal or semi-modal verbs are used to convey modal (non-factual) meanings.

Modal verbs are grammatically restricted (for example, they are always finite). Semi-modal verbs (such as *have to*, *ought to*) also convey modal meanings, but do not share all these grammatical restrictions.

Modal meanings may be epistemic or deontic. Epistemic meanings concern validity, e.g. *You must be wrong/It's obvious you're wrong.* Deontic meanings concern desirability, e.g. *You should complain/It's advisable to complain.*

Past tense can be used not only to refer to past time, but also to suggest a hypothetical or tentative meaning. Lexical verbs in the past tense are more frequently associated with past time. Modal verbs in the past tense are more frequently associated with hypothetical or tentative meanings.

Past tense only applies to finite verbs. With non-finite verbs, the perfect can be used to refer retrospectively to the past. This may happen in counterfactual statements that need to be marked as both hypothetical and past, e.g. *I could have been a contender.* It may also happen in complex verbal groups with the initial verb in the present, e.g. *He seems to have got lost.*

*　　*　　*

The first five chapters of this book have taken a broadly communicative approach to grammar, looking at grammatical forms but also investigating what these forms are used for. These chapters have provided an overview of the major areas of English grammar, and introduced you to much of the terminology you are likely to encounter in discussions of grammar. You have practised analysing the structure of sentences, clauses, and phrases, and have investigated the meanings conveyed by various grammatical choices. The focus has been, not simply on grammatical rules as illustrated in single sentences, but on the way they are used in authentic texts, both written and spoken.

This analysis, however, is based on traditional grammar, using grammatical categories and terminology, most of which have long been established and are widely used. The advantage of this approach is that it provides access to the way that grammar is discussed in the public domain, for example in official syllabuses, examination specifications, and assessment criteria. A communicative perspective on traditional grammar, however, makes it possible to take the rather sterile lists of grammatical points that often occur in such documents, and breathe life into them. Grammar, we believe, only comes alive when we look at it in real-life contexts, and only makes sense when we consider how people use it to make meaning.

But if we take this as the basis for understanding grammar, there is no reason to remain tied down to traditional grammatical concepts. Instead of focusing on grammatical forms and asking what functions they are used for, we could start from functions, and look at the way people make meaning in different contexts and for different purposes. This is the direction that will be taken in the remaining chapters.

5.6 Answer key

Activity 5.1

The finite verbal groups are listed below; those referring to the future are asterisked.

's been
're going to keep*
go through*
will continue to work*
head*
's to come*
was
's going to be*
could be*
head*
will be*
head*
should see*
will thicken up*
head*

There were also several non-finite verbal groups that you should <u>not</u> have included! Notice how these differ from the finite verbal groups above:

working in (twice)
working
tending to be
pushing in

Activity 5.3

|| An emotional-looking full moon in your sign **<u>warns</u>** ||

|| you **<u>could lose</u>** your temper for no reason ||

|| Something [[that nine times out of ten **<u>would not bother</u>** you in the slightest]] **<u>will get</u>** you all worked up ||

|| and you **<u>will say</u>** things [[you **<u>do not really mean</u>**]] ||

|| You **<u>may have to make</u>** a few apologies tomorrow ||

|| You **<u>may be</u>** inclined to make a snap decision about your work or career ||

|| but the full moon **<u>warns</u>** ||

|| that **<u>is</u>** probably not a good idea ||

|| You **<u>are</u>** more likely to make the right decision ||

|| if you **<u>wait</u>** ||

|| until your anger with certain people **<u>subsides</u>** ||

|| which it **<u>will do</u>** ||

|| once today's full moon **<u>starts to wane</u>**. ||

|| **<u>Be</u>** aware ||

|| that if you **<u>start</u>** something new today ||

|| you **<u>will most likely lose</u>** interest in it after a few weeks ||

|| It**<u>'s</u>** good ||

|| that you **<u>want to do</u>** something creative ||

|| but timing **<u>is</u>** all-important ||

|| and you **<u>are</u>** more likely to make the right choice ||

|| if you **<u>wait</u>** ||

|| until Mercury, your ruler, <u>turns</u> direct on November 1st ||

|| A friend or colleague <u>**may have**</u> a change of heart today about a project [[you <u>**have been working on**</u> together]] ||

|| but there <u>**is**</u> no need to worry ||

|| because by this time tomorrow they <u>**will have changed back**</u> again ||

|| Today's full moon <u>**will be**</u> a disruptive influence ||

|| but no real harm <u>**will come**</u> of it. ||

Activity 5.4

will affect	epistemic
could suffer	epistemic
must be	deontic
must be based on	deontic
will accelerate	epistemic
must build	deontic
could have	epistemic
could reach	epistemic
would be	epistemic
would exceed	epistemic
would be	epistemic
must lead	epistemic
will take place	epistemic
will cost	epistemic
will put	epistemic
should be accelerated.	deontic
would be dangerous	epistemic
can be substantially reduced	epistemic
can be stabilised	epistemic
would require	epistemic
would already be	epistemic

may slip	epistemic
need not cap	epistemic
must take	deontic
should not be required to bear	deontic
will not have to <bear>.	epistemic (will) + deontic (have to)

Activity 5.5

would like to see
should be
Would it be
could have gotten
would have impacted
would have been
were going to
would suggest
would it be
would it –
Would it be –
would give
could
would be administered
would be kept
would be opened

Activity 5.8

I **should** begin by saying that I have no complaints about the treatment that either Peter or Claire are receiving.

While there **may** be good reasons for arranging your time in this way,

Surely some flexibility **could be** built into this.

some written notification of this **could be** made.

189

*I asked if another day **would** be possible*

*I asked what I **should** do*

*if I **could** not make this time.*

*When I asked if she **would** convey my view to you*

*a more formal notification of this change **would have** been helpful and polite*

*I **should have** raised it when I went into the surgery*

*it **would have** been inappropriate*

six

From communicative to systemic functional grammar

6.1 Introduction

The first half of this book took what we have broadly described as a 'communicative' approach to English grammar. Communicative approaches to grammar use terminology from traditional formal grammar in order to explore what people **do** with language, not only in written language but also in spoken encounters.

In the second half of the book you will see how systemic functional grammar (SFG) builds on ideas from formal and communicative approaches to grammar, but radically rethinks them so as to systematically (and comprehensively!) relate grammar to meaning, function, and context. SFG forms part of a rich theory of language that has been developed within a branch of linguistics referred to as systemic functional linguistics (SFL). Three key features of this theory are:

1   it places great importance on how grammar varies in relation to context;

2   it views grammar as a meaning-making tool;

3   it is designed to be useful to professionals who engage with language-related real-world issues and problems (for example, educators, translators, and speech therapists).

Chapters 6–10 will guide you through key concepts in SFG and provide activities designed to develop practical skills in analysing grammar in action. The emphasis will be on meaning and function, but form will still play an important role. Grammatical structure is an important dimension in any exploration of language use, and as you will see, many of the grammatical terms and concepts explored in Chapters 1–5 are also used in SFG. However, there will be a certain amount of refocusing as we increasingly shift our attention to which language forms are used *in which contexts*, *for which purposes*, and *to what effect*. Most importantly, by focusing on how meaning is created and communicated more – or less – effectively across different contexts, we will illustrate how the tools of SFG make it possible to identify and engage with real-world issues and problems. These range from communication disorders, such as those suffered by stroke patients, to the difficulties experienced by school children and university students when trying to produce successful written assignments. The following scenario and activity are designed to give you insight into how problems in writing can be identified with reference, not only to grammatical structure, but also to key aspects of the social context in which the writing takes place.

Scenario

The letter below was produced by Raeesha, a Grade 4 primary school student (aged about ten). The class had participated in a unit of work on 'Local Government' and their task was to write to the local MP (member of parliament) protesting about the removal of a sports ground in a park near their school. Read the letter and consider how effective it is, taking into account its context.

Text 6.1 Dear Mr Gallone

Dear Mr Gallone

Hi my name is Raeesha. My principal told me about the sports ground near my school that there is going to be a big housing development there and I want to complain about that. If you put lots of houses there we won't have anywhere to play sport and when it is hot and sunny there will be nowhere to run around and there will be too much people and cars, noise and no place for us to get fit.

    from

    Raeesha

(Author's personal data)

Raeesha's letter to the MP is not altogether unsuccessful. She manages to present an argument as to why the local council should not demolish their sports ground. However, the letter would be regarded as displaying a limited level of competence – first, from the perspective of grammatical structure and, second, from the perspective of Raeesha's use of language in relation to the context.

Activity 6.1

Read Raeesha's letter again, and, this time, drawing on your grammatical knowledge from Chapters 1–5:

(a)   highlight the finite verbal groups
(b)   use double lines to divide the sentences into clauses
(c)   underline the nominal groups.

You came across verbal groups in Chapters 1 and 4 and nominal groups including embedded elements in Chapter 3. Use the convention || for breaking up clauses. See Chapter 1.

193

From the perspective of formal grammar we can see that there are two main problems with Raeesha's letter. First, the clause structure is clumsy. The second sentence, for example, would be clearer if rewritten as two clauses rather than three:

My principal told me about the big housing development that will be built on the sports ground near my school || I want to complain about that.

Second, there is a lack of agreement between the quantifier *much* and the (count) nouns *people* and *cars:*

The distinction between count and mass nouns was discussed in Chapter 3.

too much people and cars

Although these formal grammatical problems provide part of the explanation for why the text is not particularly successful, they do not tell the whole story. There are other problems with the text, problems that can only really be identified and explained if we take into account the communicative purpose and context of the text.

First, the way Raeesha addresses her audience (*Hi . . . from*) is inappropriately casual. Second, although she takes a clear position on the issue (the loss of the sports ground), the reasons for her position are not well explained. Third, her arguments are not effectively grouped together in well-organised paragraphs. In the last sentence, a series of reasons (for why the development should not go ahead) are strung together to form a long chain of five clauses (including an interrupting clause) more reminiscent of spoken language than carefully planned and edited written text.

In sum, there are three aspects of context that Raeesha fails to take into account:

1   The social activity and purpose: this is a letter to a local MP in which a careful argument needs to be made as to why the housing development should not go ahead.

2   The relationship between writer and reader: this is a letter from a school child to someone in a position of authority, and this needs to be reflected in a more formal style. In addition, because the writer is making an argument, she needs to engage and persuade the MP that the points she is making are important and valid.

3   The text is a formal written letter and therefore should be carefully planned and redrafted. It should be better organised and focused.

By neglecting to take the context of the letter into account, Raeesha produces an ineffective text. Not only was her writing marked down for poor sentence structure, but in addition for 'inappropriate use of informal language' and 'some confusion'. If you work within an educational context such descriptors may be familiar. You may even have received similar comments at some point in your own educational or professional career.

In essence, such comments point to a mismatch between context and language style. That is, in any culture, and in all social institutions (such as schools, universities, the media, or law), there are certain expectations about the way language will be used. These expectations derive from predictable language patterns becoming established over time. Problems with texts are often connected to expectations not being fulfilled, because of a mismatch between context and form. SFG offers a framework for investigating these relations and identifying mismatches. In the rest of this chapter we will

- explore further the relationship between grammar and context;
- introduce the SFG framework, which provides a systematic account of the relationship between key aspects of social context and language use.

6.2 Context and language patterns

Activity 6.2

Look at the following language fragments taken from newspapers around the world in the run-up to the 2008 Olympics in China. Using the grammatical categories and terms introduced in Chapters 1–5:

(a)   Underline the nominal groups. Note any articles that are included in these groups.

Articles were explained in Chapter 3.

(b)   Highlight the verbs. Make a note of the tense and whether any auxiliaries are used.

Tense and auxiliaries were explained in Chapter 4.

(c)   Now consider what the fragments have in common. What recurring features of language use can you detect?

(d)   What is the connection between these language features and the context in which they are used?

DEMONSTRATORS DISRUPT OLYMPIC TORCH LIGHTING

(The Daily Telegraph, UK)

Protesters disrupt Olympic ceremony

(The Boston Globe)

OLYMPICS TORCH WORRIES

(Bangkok Post)

OLYMPIC TORCH RELAY PROTESTS 'SHAMEFUL': CHINA

(The Times of India)

China vows tight security for Games torch

(New Zealand Herald)

The features that are repeated across the fragments above reflect the predictable and distinctive telegraphic style of newspaper headlines. They comprise:

•   the use of dense nominal groups with no definite or indefinite articles;

•   the use of the present tense of verbs;

•   the omission of verbs in the third and fourth headlines above (these are therefore minor clauses);

•   the use of simple rather than complex sentences.

In certain types of text, syndromes of recurring grammatical features such as those above become well established. This is because, given their context of use, they are functional and effective. News headlines, for example, need to be short and punchy in order to economise on space and to attract attention. In the rest of the book we will refer to the language features that occur across texts and that make a significant contribution to a text's meaning as language **patterns**.

The more people reach consensus on how to use language (for example, when conducting an interview panel, interacting in a law court, or writing an academic argument), the more established the style becomes. A useful analogy might be the development of a rural footpath – the more people tread their way through the countryside following a particular route, the more it becomes visible and establishes itself as the conventional path: it becomes the convenient way of going about things. It is, of course, always possible to step off the path, trample through bushes, etc., but often there is an element of risk or inconvenience attached. Once established, language conventions or norms remain reasonably stable for a period of time. As such, members of the community are able to make judgements regarding their appropriateness and effectiveness. When it comes to language, this applies as much to the structure of a text (as we shall see in Chapter 7) as it does to the overall language style.

It is of course the case that, while these conventions and norms usually come into existence for functional reasons, they may not always remain functional or effective. Just as paths can change direction over time, so too can language style. These shifts are usually indicative of social changes and transitions, which make them fascinating sites of study. Just to get you thinking, consider the differences in traditional and contemporary greetings and salutations:

Traditional
Dear Sir/Madam
Dear Mr/Mrs West
Good morning, Good afternoon (Edith/Mrs West)

Contemporary
Dear Kelly
K, Kelly (e.g. in emails)
Hello, Hi, Hiya, Hey, Hi there (Kelly)

Although, in contemporary society, language users may sometimes choose traditional ways of greeting, more personal and informal expressions such as those in the second box are more and more common, reflecting overall trends towards an increasingly informal society. What is significant is that language users have an element of choice as to how they word their greeting or salutation. This does not mean it is a completely open choice. It would be odd, for example, to start a formal letter to an unknown bank manager with the words *Hey, how's it going?*, but in other contexts English speakers have considerable freedom. We can, for example, choose to begin an email to a work colleague by putting

> *Dear Kieran*

or

> *Hi Kieran*

or simply

> *Kieran*

All these different salutations are acceptable and appropriate, although, interestingly, each one may convey a slightly different tone and meaning. *Dear Kieran*, for example, seems rather old fashioned and somewhat formal for a contemporary medium, whereas *Kieran* may come across as somewhat abrupt and direct (with efficiency rather than friendliness taking priority). In other words the choices we make in language are often influenced by the context. Conversely, our choices may themselves influence the context.

The fact that language users are constantly making selections from a set of possible choices is an area that we explore in the next section.

6.3 Context and language choice

Activity 6.3

If a six-year-old child wanted to find out about spiders, which of the following texts would you direct him/her to?

Text 6.2 Spiders

Spiders look very distinctive. They have two body parts, the head and the abdomen. They have eight legs. Spiders can be colourful but most are dark. They have spinnerets that make silk.

Spiders live everywhere. They can live in hot desert areas or cool mountain areas. Some spiders live in people's homes or gardens.

All spiders spin silk. They use the silk for egg sacs, to line their burrows and to make webs.

(http://www.questacon.com/html/assets/pdf/previsit_activities.pdf)

Text 6.3 Spiders

Spiders are predatory invertebrate animals that have two body segments, eight legs, no chewing mouth parts and no wings. They are classified in the order Araneae, one of several orders within the larger class of arachnids, a group that also contains scorpions, whip scorpions, mites, ticks, and opiliones (harvestmen). The study of spiders is called arachnology.

All spiders produce silk, a thin, strong protein strand extruded by the spider from spinnerets most commonly found on the end of the abdomen. Many species use it to trap insects in webs, although there are also many species that hunt freely.

Spiders are found all over the world, from the tropics to the Arctic, living underwater in silken domes they supply with air, and on the tops of mountains.

(http://en.wikipedia.org/wiki/Spider (accessed 11 August 2008))

It is likely that you selected Text 6.2 as the best source of information for a six year old. One reason would be the more familiar **lexis** (the technical term for vocabulary), compared with the greater use of **specialised lexis** in Text 6.3. That is, in order to understand lexical items such as *invertebrate*, *protein strand*, *abdomen*, *tropics*, some familiarity with specialised domains of knowledge (i.e. zoology and geography) is required, and a six year old is not yet likely to have such specialised knowledge.

The differences in grammatical form across the two texts also help to explain why Text 6.2 might be more accessible to a six year old than Text 6.3.

Activity 6.4

Use your knowledge of grammar that was built up over Chapters 1–5 to compare the texts from the perspective of grammatical form:

You came across verbal groups in Chapters 1 and 4 and nominal groups, including embedded clauses, in Chapter 3.

(a)   Highlight the verbal groups.

(b)   Break the texts into independent clauses and (if there are any) dependent clauses.

(c)   Underline the nominal groups, and use square brackets [[ ]] to indicate any embedded clauses within a nominal group.

Your analysis will reveal that, even though Text 6.3 is almost twice as long as Text 6.2, it contains fewer clauses that are not embedded. (A clause that is not embedded is known as a **ranking** clause.) This is because, in Text 6.3, many of the nominal groups are packed with information: the head nouns are built up through the use of both pre- and postmodifiers. As a result, Text 6.3 is denser and therefore more difficult to process than Text 6.2.

As explained in Chapter 3, premodifiers come before the head of a nominal group, and postmodifiers follow it.

Text 6.3 is fairly typical of written academic texts that are designed to be read by those with some understanding (though not necessarily expert knowledge) of the field. When texts are written for more expert members of a field, they tend to use more specialised lexis and are often 'lexically dense', with information packed into nominal groups. We can calculate the lexical density of a text by dividing the number of lexical items by the number of ranking (i.e. non-embedded) clauses. This is referred to as **lexical density**.

Activity 6.5

Calculate the lexical density of Texts 6.2 and 6.3 by following steps (a)–(c).

(a)   Count the number of ranking clauses for each text.

200

(b)   Count the number of **lexical items** for each text, that is, all the content-carrying words such as nouns, lexical verbs, adverbs, and adjectives. (Non-content-carrying words include prepositions, articles, conjunctions, auxiliary verbs, and pronouns.)

(c)   Divide the number of lexical items by the number of ranking clauses for each text.

The calculation of lexical density for each text (3.6 for Text 6.2 and 7.8 for Text 6.3) provides further evidence as to why Text 6.3 would be less accessible to a young child.

Activity 6.3 thus underlines the fact that there is a relationship between the context in which language is used and the types of grammatical structure and lexis that are appropriate and effective. Because both grammar and lexis are implicated when we examine the relationship between context and language, the term **lexicogrammar** tends to be the preferred term in SFG.

The use of specialised lexis and dense nominal groups may be effective in written texts aimed at a reasonably informed general public (as many Wikipedia texts generally are – the source of Text 6.3). However, it may not be the best choice in pedagogic texts aimed at young learners.

A similar point was made in relation to the dog text from Wikipedia in Chapter 3.

The notion of 'choice' is central to SFG theory: language is viewed as a system of resources which people choose from in order to make meaning. Viewing language in this way – as a set of options – requires a **system** perspective, a perspective that is central to SFG and one that differentiates it from many other approaches to grammar, including the formal and communicative approaches you worked with in Chapters 1–5. It is this aspect of SFG that will be the focus of the next section.

6.4 A systemic perspective on language

As stated previously, SFG is a theory concerned with how people use language in real-world situations to achieve their social goals and purposes. The focus therefore is on how language functions and how it makes meaning – hence the term *functional*. But why the word 'systemic'?

Look at the following:

(a)   School will be cancelled.

(b)   Will school be cancelled?

(c)   Cancel school!

If we analyse these clauses from the perspective of their formal structure, we can see that each follows a different structural order or pattern: each involves a different clause type.

Example	Mood
School will be cancelled. (the subject *school* is followed by the verbal group *will be*)	declarative
Will school be cancelled? (the auxiliary, *will*, is followed by the subject *school*)	interrogative
Cancel school! (the verbal group *cancel* is followed by the object, *school*)	imperative

We can also consider each of the clauses in examples (a)–(c) from the perspective of the set of clause types available in the English language, noting which type was chosen against the set of possible options. Mapping the set of options available in any given language provides a system perspective. Figure 6.1 illustrates the graphical conventions that are used in this type of mapping or modelling. The arrow represents the entry point into the system, and the brackets show that there are three choices available – declarative, interrogative, and imperative.

Figure 6.1

Clause types as a set of options

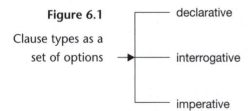

declarative

interrogative

imperative

Whereas the initial table provided a **syntagmatic** perspective on examples (a)–(c) by focusing on the sequential ordering of elements in each of the clauses, Figure 6.1 offers a **paradigmatic** perspective by setting out the options available. Traditional formal and communicative approaches tend to take a syntagmatic perspective, whereas systemic functional linguists hold the view that both perspectives are important in order to understand the meaning made by a clause (or any other language element). Activity 6.6 reveals the importance of a paradigmatic view.

Activity 6.6

Read the following (fictional) dialogue in which Lieutenant Columbo, a police detective (from a classic American TV series), informally asks a suspect for information.

(a) Underline the clauses which function to make questions. You will find that Columbo does not just use interrogatives to ask for information.

(b) Consider why Columbo might have chosen to use different clause types in order to ask questions.

Chapter 1 discussed how each main clause type is associated with a basic communicative function (known as 'speech function' in SFG). However, there is not always a one-to-one relationship between form and function. This will be explored further in Chapter 9.

Text 6.4 Columbo asks some questions

Lt. Columbo:	You don't mind if I ask you a personal question, do you?
Walter Cunnell:	No.
Lt. Columbo:	What'd you pay for those shoes?
Walter Cunnell:	I think about 60 dollars.
Lt. Columbo:	I stepped into some water yesterday and ruined mine. You don't know where I could find a pair that looks like that for around 16 or 17?

(http://en.wikiquote.org/wiki/Columbo (accessed 11 August 2008))

Columbo asks three questions using different options. He uses an interrogative, the clause type most obviously associated with the communicative function of asking a question:

What'd you pay for those shoes?

He uses a declarative – with intonation to show that it is a question:

> *You don't know where I could find a pair that looks like that for around 16 or 17?*

And he uses a declarative with a question tag:

> *You don't mind if I ask you a personal question, do you?*

From a system perspective we can now add in a second set of choices – whether to add a question tag or not to the declarative:

Figure 6.2

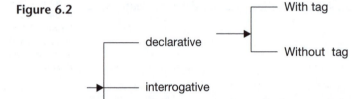

Why do you think Colombo made such choices? Without knowing the TV series or Colombo's character, this may be a difficult question to answer, but, given that a key skill for detectives is to extract important information from suspects (and ideally information that condemns them!), then catching people off guard may be an important criterion. In other words, asking questions directly may not always be an effective technique.

Activity 6.7

In the left-hand column is the original dialogue between Columbo and the suspect, Cunnell. In the right-hand column, the questions have been reworked. What effect do you think the use of different clause types might have?

	Original dialogue	Reworked dialogue
Lt. Columbo:	*You don't mind if I ask you a personal question, do you?*	*I want to ask you a personal question.*
Walter Cunnell:	*No.*	
Lt. Columbo:	*What'd you pay for those shoes?*	*Those shoes must have cost you a lot of money, mustn't they?*
Walter Cunnell:	*I think about 60 dollars.*	
Lt. Columbo:	*I stepped into some water yesterday and ruined mine. You don't know where I could find a pair that looks like that for around 16 or 17?*	*I stepped into some water yesterday and ruined mine. Where can I find a pair for 16 or 17?*

Although we cannot say definitively how in real life a suspect might react to the different style of questioning, it is quite likely that there would be advantages to a Columbo-style interrogation, using strange questions that the suspect is unlikely to have thought about the answers to, often expressed in an excessively polite manner. Such an approach may lull a criminal suspect into a false sense of security, whereas a more direct or coercive approach (as illustrated in the right-hand column) may lead to a defensive reaction.

Once we start to speculate as to why language users use one structure rather than another, we can begin to see how speakers (usually unconsciously) and writers (often more consciously) make different 'choices' in grammar and how these are influenced by the context of the interaction. In SFG, although structure is seen as important, it is not viewed as the defining characteristic of language. Rather, language is primarily conceptualised as a system (that is, a set of choices), and each act or instance of meaning derives its meaning from what could have been selected but was not.

Sometimes choices are effective, sometimes less so. As you will see in the rest of this book, the degree of effectiveness is partly a result of the relationship between choice and context.

6.5 What is the relationship between language choice and context?

So far we have explored some of the ways in which language varies in relation to context and we have explained the importance placed by SFG on viewing language as a system of choices rather than just as a set of structures. In order to bring these two aspects of the theory together, this section explores in greater detail the connection between context and language choice, and introduces the concept of register as a means of doing this. Register analysis makes it possible to systematically link aspects of the context with different patterns in language choice, such as modality, pronoun use, reference, etc.

Activity 6.8

Read and analyse the key language patterns in Text 6.5 by answering the questions that follow. The questions have been grouped together into three tables for reasons that will become clear.

Text 6.5 It looked like 9/11 . . .

Sarah:	It looked like 9/11 could have been happening all over again. Apparently the, I don't know, jets of some sort went whizzing into the building and everyone ran out or they had to be evacuated, I'm not quite sure what was going on.
Kevin:	No, no, no, no. It was, it was, it was a a little plane. It's called a Cessna or something like that. It wasn't jets as such, it was just a little plane. It didn't hit the White House though.

(Author's personal data)

206

What are the main lexical items in the text?

What kinds of subject, complement, or object are chosen?

What kinds of adjunct are chosen?

Complements and adjuncts were introduced in Chapter 1. Chapter 2 identified different types of adjunct: adjuncts of place, time, manner, purpose, and means.

Which clause types are used to communicate what communicative functions?

The main communicative functions at clause level (or speech functions) are asking a question, making a statement, and making a command – see Chapter 1.

Are the clauses evenly distributed across the participants?

Are there any examples of epistemic or deontic modality?

Epistemic and deontic modality were introduced in Chapter 5.

Is there any use of colloquial language or contractions?

Are there densely packed nominal groups (including embedding)?

Are there any minor clauses or other features of spoken language?

Anaphoric and exophoric reference were introduced in Chapter 3.

Is there any use of anaphoric or exophoric reference?

Having made observations about the language choices made in Text 6.5, we are now in a good position to speculate about the context in which the text occurred. The three groups of questions show how we can link our pieces of linguistic evidence with three main aspects of context, namely:

1   the social activity/topic (relating to the initial group of questions);

2   the social roles and status of the interlocutors (relating to the middle group of questions);

3   the channel of communication (leading to different degrees of interactivity and spontaneity) (relating to the final group of questions).

Organising evidence in this way avoids having to make a long list of disconnected points.

The use of *I* in subject position shows the text producers are personally reconstructing the event, i.e. they are exchanging their views on the incident.	**Social activity: an exchange of views on a news event**
Choices in lexis and in subjects, objects, complements, and adjuncts show that the main topic is a plane incident in the USA.	**Topic: a plane incident**

The direct contradictions (*no, no, no, it wasn't jets*) suggest the participants know each other reasonably well and are likely to be friends.	**Social roles: friend to friend**
Each participant in the exchange contributes a similar number of declarative clauses in which they make statements. This suggests there is no significant status differential. However, Sarah's use of epistemic modality and Kevin's lack of modality alongside his direct contradictions gives him a little more authority.	**Relative social status: equal status**

There are several features of conversational interaction: use of exophoric reference (the personal pronoun *I*) to refer to the speakers, repetition, and use of interrupted clause and minor clause.	**Interactivity: two way conversation**
There are very few nouns which have pre- or postmodifiers. The text is not lexically dense.	**Spontaneity: high – no evidence of pre-planning**

Activity 6.8 demonstrated that, even when we take short extracts out of their original context, we can make quite reliable predictions about some aspects of their original context of use. The fact that we can do this indicates that, in some way, context 'gets into' text. Activity 6.9 gives you further practice in using your knowledge of language patterns to make predictions about social context.

One further point to make here is that you will have noticed that, in some of the transcripts of spoken language used in this chapter (such as Text 6.4), conventions such as full stops and capitals are used. However, people do not talk in sentences. Systemic functional linguists therefore prefer not to use the term sentence but rather clause or, where more than one clause is linked to another, **clause complex**. The notation for showing the end of a clause complex (or complex sentence) is three parallel lines – |||.

Activity 6.9

Read through Texts 6.6–6.8 and then complete Table 6.1 by answering the questions at the top of each column. Make sure you identify and use linguistic patterns as evidence for your deductions. We have provided the answers for Text 6.6 in order to model the kind of answer expected.

Table 6.1: Linguistic analysis of Texts 6.6–6.8

Text 6.6

What is the social activity?	What are the social roles of the speakers/writers?	How interactive is the text?
News report: within headline absence of articles before subject and adjuncts	Writer to reader (probably news reporter to mass audience): the only communicative functions are statements expressed as declaratives	Non-interactive: there are no features of conversational interaction
What is the topic of the text?	**What is the status of the speakers/writers?**	**How spontaneous is the text?**
USA plane incident: main subjects, objects, and adjuncts refer to planes and associated items	Authoritative expert: there is no use of epistemic modality to express lack of certainty	Non-spontaneous: nominal groups are quite dense with both pre- and postmodifiers. High lexical density.

Text 6.7

What is the social activity?	What are the social roles of the speakers/writers?	How interactive is the text?

What is the topic of the text?	What is the status of the speakers/writers?	How spontaneous is the text?

Text 6.8

What is the social activity?	What are the social roles of the speakers/writers?	How interactive is the text?

What is the topic of the text?	What is the status of the speakers/writers?	How spontaneous is the text?

Text 6.6 Capitol cleared in plane alert

Fighter jets yesterday fired warning flares at a small plane that entered restricted airspace over Washington causing the White House and Capitol building to be evacuated.

The two-seater plane was forced to land at a small airport in Maryland and two men were taken into custody. Officials said later that the intrusion appeared to have been accidental and that no charges would be filed.

(Jamie Wilson in Washington, *The Guardian*, Thursday 12 May 2005)

Text 6.7 The Cuban Revolution

nf5085: . . . what i propose that we do is that we have a bit of a debate i think we should have a bit of a debate about whether the Cuban revolution was a success or a failure and we don't have to position this debate necessarily within the extreme polarities of the political debate that i talked about in the lecture between the people in Miami and the people in Havana you don't have to necessarily fit into that framework i think there's plenty of scope for us to look at the Cuban revolution in terms of both its successes and its failures without our necessarily having to take er sorry extreme political positions although you're certainly welcome to if you want to but that's what i'd like to do would that be how would would you be okay with that can you cope with that

    sm5086: yep

(The Cuban Revolution (Base Corpus))

Text 6.8 Some big news

There's some big news Caroline,

When we say big news, we mean big news. On July 2nd, Better Airlines, are to launch a new second route with the World's biggest passenger aircraft – the B222. They'll be flying direct from London to Hong Kong, so if you were ever in need of an excuse to experience Hong Kong, then here it is!

(Author's personal data)

By systematically examining different aspects of the context in which Texts 6.6–6.8 were produced you were, in SFG terms, conducting a **register** analysis. That is, you were making connections between different aspects of context and particular areas of language. Register is used by systemic functional linguists to bridge between context and language. In the remainder of this chapter we will explore register in more detail. We will show how, by 'slowing down' your response to texts, register analysis makes it possibly to identify problems, as well as raise and explore interesting questions about the different kinds of meaning made through language. In relation to Texts 6.5–6.8, for example, your analysis might have provoked the following questions:

- In Text 6.5 the first speaker (Sarah) uses epistemic modality in all of her statements about the plane incident while the second speaker (Kevin) does not. How do these different choices position each of the interlocutors?

- Why does the tutor in Text 6.7 appear to need the go-ahead from his/her group of students? What is the effect?

- Why has what otherwise appears to be an impersonal advertisement (Text 6.8) addressed the recipient by name? Is this technique effective?

6.6 The relationship between context and text: an SFG perspective

In SFG, any **context of situation** (the technical term for social situation) is seen as influencing the kind of language people use in reasonably predictable ways.

It is posited that there are three main **contextual variables** – **field**, **tenor**, and **mode**. We will show, step by step, how a systematic analysis of the context of a text enables us to make predictions about language use and vice versa. To do this we will revisit one of the texts used in the first part of the book. It is the one taken from a transcript of an emergency telephone call in which the operator is talking Leo through what he needs to do post delivery of their baby:

Text 6.9 Call 999!

Operator: Is the baby crying or breathing?

Leo: Yes, it's crying.

Operator: Right, what I want you to do is gently wipe off the baby's mouth and nose. And dry the baby off with a clean towel. Then wrap the baby in a clean, dry towel, OK.

Leo: OK.

Operator: Just wipe the baby's mouth and nose first. Yeah?

(*The Guardian*, Saturday 15 September 2007 (http://www.guardian.co.uk/family/story/0,,2169187,00. html))

Below, in brackets, is an analysis of the field, tenor, and mode in Text 6.9.

1   **Field covers the following aspects of a situation:**

- the social activity taking place (*the delivery of a baby*);

- the topic being discussed (*cleaning and wrapping the baby*);

- the degree of specialisation (*basic practical knowledge*);

- the angle of representation (*The baby is presented as an object to be acted upon. Leo is put in the position of agent responsible for carrying out the operator's commands*).

Angle of representation will be more fully explained in Chapter 8.

2   **Tenor covers the following aspects of a situation:**

- the social roles and relative social status in terms of power, expertise, or authority (*the operator has more power and authority than Leo in this particular situation*);

- the social distance, i.e. the degree of connection or closeness (*although Leo and the operator did not previously know each other, the situation reduces the social distance between them*);

- speaker/writer persona, i.e. general stance and assumed degree of alignment/agreement between interlocutors (*the operator assumes that Leo will comply with her commands*).

3   **Mode covers:**

- the degree of interactivity (*this is a highly interactive interaction*);

- the degree of spontaneity (*this is a highly spontaneous, unplanned interaction*);

- the communicative distance in time and space from the events discussed, i.e. whether language accompanies action or constitutes the text (*language is accompanying action so is close in time but since it is a phone call it is not close in space*);

- the role of language, i.e. the degree to which it interacts with other meaning-making (**semiotic**) resources such as visual images, gesture etc. (*there are no semiotic resources other than language involved*).

Together, the three variables of field, tenor, and mode make up the register of a text.

Field, tenor, and mode are referred to as **contextual** or **register variables**:

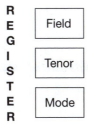

Figure 6.3

The register variables

It was these dimensions of context that were used in Table 6.1 to organise your linguistic analysis of Texts 6.6–6.8 (although at that point we did not use the technical labels). Such analyses show that information about the context can help to predict language use and patterns, and equally language patterns can help to predict context. In the next three sections we explore this relationship in more detail.

6.7 Field and language

One of the most noticeable influences of field on language lies in the choices of subjects, complements, objects, and adjuncts. The degree to which the

215

field is viewed through a personal, commonsense, as opposed to specialised or technical, lens also has a considerable impact, primarily on lexis. This difference in perspective is illustrated in the following texts. Both texts deal with the same topic – the Holocaust. The first, however, is a personal account, and the other is an extract from a textbook, so they reflect different social activities (*telling a personal story* as opposed to *teaching history*).

Activity 6.10

Read Texts 6.10 and 6.11 and then:

You saw in earlier chapters that subjects and objects are generally expressed through nominal groups.

(a)   underline the subjects and objects;

(b)   highlight the adjuncts;

(c)   compare the use of lexis in both the texts. Which text is more specialised?

Text 6.10 An account by a Holocaust survivor, Victor Greenberg

They punched me until I was in a state of collapse. I was eventually locked into a barrack full of people who had been selected to be taken to the gas chambers. Realising the consequences, I was determined to escape and managed to climb out at night through a narrow window with a colleague.

(Victor Greenberg Beechener, C., Griffiths, C., and Jacob, A. (2004) *Modern Times*, Oxford: Heinemann, p. 141)

Text 6.11 Hitler's Final Solution

After the outbreak of the Second World War the Nazis changed their policy towards the Jews. They wanted to get rid of as many Jews as possible, and began to make plans for how to deal effectively with what they called the 'Jewish problem'. In 1941 they came up with a plan which was known as the Final Solution. The Jews would be dealt with in two ways: they would either be worked to death or executed. Extermination and labour camps were therefore set up throughout Europe in order to exterminate the estimated eleven million European Jews.

(Victor Greenberg Beechener, C., Griffiths, C., and Jacob, A. (2004) *Modern Times*, Oxford: Heinemann, p. 138)

In the first text (Text 6.10), the writer, Victor Greenberg, uses everyday language to describe his first-hand, personal experience of the gas chambers. Events are recounted in everyday terms. He tells how he was *punched*, *locked into* a barrack, but *managed to climb out* (all concrete, physical processes). The majority of subjects and objects refer to Victor (through the personal pronoun *I* or *me*). Many of the adjuncts are to do with place and expressed through prepositional phrases – *he was locked <u>into a barrack</u>, he climbed <u>through a narrow window</u>* etc.

Text 6.11 is concerned with the same topic as Text 6.10 (i.e. the Holocaust), but a historical rather than personal perspective is developed. That is, the same events are now viewed through the eyes of a historian as part of a body of institutionalised knowledge. There is use of specialist terms such as *the 'Jewish problem', the Final Solution, policy, extermination*, and *labour camps*. The main subjects and objects are groups of people – *the Nazis, the Jews* – and the main adjuncts are to do with time – *after the outbreak of the Second World War, in 1941*.

Figure 6.4 summarises the connection between field and language. In Chapter 8 you will revisit and deepen your understanding of the relationship, and we will expand on the way that speakers' or writers' 'angle of representation' plays an important role in influencing their choices of subjects and objects.

Figure 6.4

The connection between field and language

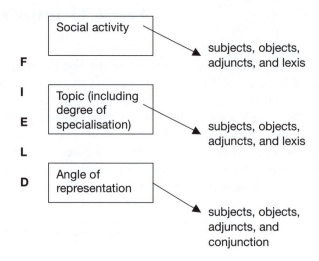

6.8 Tenor and language

Tenor also influences language use. The social roles (e.g. *friend/friend, interviewer/interviewee, teacher/student*) and how equal or unequal interlocutors are (e.g. *equal: professional/professional; unequal: expert/novice*) are likely to affect the distribution of communicative functions. For example, an interviewer asks many more questions than an interviewee, whereas among equal professionals there is more likely to be an even share.

How socially connected or distant interlocutors are is likely to influence the degree to which the language used is formal or informal, including the terms of address. For example, close friends or intimates are likely to use terms of endearment (e.g. *mate, darling, sweetie*), shortened names (e.g. *Caro* instead of *Caroline*), contractions (e.g. *I'm* rather than *I am*), and colloquial lexis (e.g. *cool, kinda, just joshing, awesome*).

Finally, in order to position, align, and negotiate (i.e. develop a stance), writers and speakers draw on modality and use evaluative lexis that expresses their attitudes and judgements (e.g. *that's good, it's a ground breaking book*). Such resources enable writers in particular to project certain textual personas, e.g. 'academic authority', 'technical expert', or 'social commentator'.

Activity 6.11

Read the following spoken interaction between P and K.

Complete the following steps:

(a)   Break the text up into clauses, including embedded clauses, and identify the clause type and communicative function of each clause/clause complex. Look at their distribution.
(b)   How formal or informal is the language?
(c)   Are there any patterns in the use of modality or evaluative lexis?
(d)   Use your linguistic analysis to describe the tenor of the text.

Text 6.12 Ok, everybody . . .

> P: Ok, everybody, now everybody if you can have a look at the overhead that's up there now (pause) Ali? (pause). We can see that, um, we have some of, what we have here, are aspects of warfare. In other words, the 'input'. So, for instance, first of all, we have an unavailability of goods here. That means that people couldn't get certain things at the end of the war. Now, how do you think that might have affected Australian Society at that time? What would the consequences be of that? Katina?
>
> K: They had to produce their own?
>
> P: Very good. They had to produce their own goods.

(Author's personal data)

Text 6.12 is an interaction between a teacher, P, and a student, K. The linguistic analysis provides evidence of:

- the teacher's status and authority (as evidenced in the asymmetrical distribution of commands (*now everybody if you . . .*), questions (*Now, how do you . . .*) as well as his lengthier turns;

- a degree of social connection (as indicated through the use of **terms of address** or **vocatives** *Ali, Katina*);

- a relatively open stance on the part of K towards the academic issue (i.e. the effect on Australian society of goods not being available). This is expressed through the use of the modal auxiliary in *how do you think that <u>might</u> have affected . . .?*;

- a desire for alignment on the part of K, as indicated by her tentative response to the teacher's question (note the rising intonation indicated by the question mark);

- the teacher's authority (as shown through his evaluation of the student's response – *very good*).

In conventional classrooms, linguistic patterns in teacher–student dialogue often resemble those illustrated there. Frequently, they indicate:

- the social roles of assessor and assessed (in addition to those of teacher and student);

- unequal status – the teacher is in a more powerful institutional position, both as subject expert and arbiter of classroom behaviour;

- regular contact – students and teachers meet regularly each week during school term;

- stance – teachers may often appear to take an open stance but frequently have in mind a preferred answer or response. Often students align their values with those of the authoritative teacher, as in this example (though this does, of course, depend on the nature of the pedagogic task and the age and attitude of the student).

Figure 6.5 summarises the connection between tenor and language, a connection that you will explore further in Chapter 9.

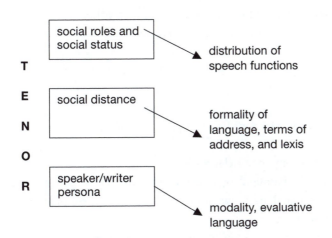

Figure 6.5

The connection between tenor and language

6.9 Mode and language

A third register variable that affects language use is mode. Mode is concerned with how a text is produced and transmitted and therefore how interactive or spontaneous it is. For example, casual conversation is interactive and spontaneous, whereas a political broadcast is usually monologic (non-interactive) and rehearsed (non-spontaneous). Interactivity affects the degree of interruption and overlap, as well as the clause structure. For example, in spontaneous spoken language, long clause complexes in which clauses are coordinated through conjunction are more common than in planned, written language. Minor clauses are also more common in spoken language, particularly in dialogue. Minor clauses include short words or phrases such as *yep*, *really*, or longer phrases where the verb is omitted, such as in Text 6.12 (e.g. *In other words, the 'input'*). Embedded clauses in postmodifiers, on the other hand, are less common in spoken language than in written.

The extent to which a text is spontaneously produced, as opposed to pre-planned or rehearsed, affects other aspects of language use, such as whether or not there are hesitations, repetitions, or false starts/mid utterance changes (in turn influencing clause structure). The spontaneity/non-spontaneity of a text's production is also closely correlated with the density with which the text packages its information (i.e. the lexical density).

Depending on whether language is accompanying action (as in a sports commentary) or constituting the text (as in a sports report), there are likely to be different patterns in the use of anaphoric and exophoric reference.

Finally, whether or not language interacts with other semiotic modes (such as visual images, music, etc.) also affects language use.

Activity 6.12

Read Texts 6.13–6.15 and then complete the following steps:

(a) Underline any minor clauses.

(b) Put brackets around any false starts/mid utterance changes or corrections.

(c) Double underline nominal groups where there are premodifiers and/or postmodifiers.

(d) Highlight any anaphoric or exophoric reference.

(e) Locate the communicative distance by placing each text more towards the spoken or written end of what can be referred to as a **mode continuum** in Figure 6.6.

Figure 6.6
Communicative distance: from action to reflection

(adapted from Martin 2001: 159)

Language as ACTION **Spoken**				Language as REFLECTION **Written**	
e.g. language used by players during football match	TV or radio sports commentary	email same day of match	newspaper report next day	newspaper editorial next day	book on football

Text 6.13 The batterings and the blows

It's worth dwelling on the batterings and the blows he takes to illustrate just how much Wilkinson sacrifices physically in defence of the English turf. His is essentially a creative role. He is the link between a monstrous pack and a back division that has become steelier and more dynamic over the past five unforgettable months. There is a fear that dare not speak its name. It is that England have become dangerously reliant on him in that playmaker's role. Charlie Hodgson, of Sale, has picked up a serious injury, and Grayson is generally thought of as a competent veteran who lacks Wilkinson's match-winning capability.

(Hayward (2003) 'Wilkinson throws doubts aside', *The Daily Telegraph*, 31 March 2003)

Text 6.14 They can go up in the air

Margaret:	Gosh they can go up in the air now
Jessica:	Oh, he just dropped it, that was rubbish . . . It's that nice looking guy again
Margaret:	don't let them
Jessica:	get the ball . . . oh look
Margaret:	go on, go on, go on
All:	hooraaaaaay
Madeline:	England's got a try!
Margaret:	He's been marvellous.
Chris:	Yes
Margaret:	I thought he was finished
Jessica:	Gosh he looked pretty happy about that
Chris:	Fantastic! I'd like to see that again.

(Author's personal data)

Text 6.15 Matt Dawson

A:	Matt Dawson was punching the air. They've got to try something out and . . . Greenwood reads it. Walking almost there. I don't think Jonny Wilkinson was very happy, the fact that he made him run into the corner for that but er . . .
B:	I don't think Jonny Wilkinson worries about that, does he?
A:	No, maybe not.
B:	There you have it. England strolling to the Grand Slam. Will Greenwood strolling to the line. Who thought that this would be such a stroll?

(BBC Sport (2003) Transcript from an extract of a live broadcast, Ireland v. England, 30 March 2003)

Activity 6.12 provides evidence of some of the effects that mode has on text. Text 6.13, as a sports editorial, was produced at some distance in time and space from the rugby match. Being non-interactive and non-spontaneous and at the written end of the spoken–written continuum in Figure 6.6, it features nominal groups that are packed with information in pre- and postmodifiers. The anaphoric references are all traceable to referents within the text. In Texts 6.14 and 6.15 (both sports commentaries), the clause structure is quite different to that of Text 6.13. Because they are both spoken texts, they feature more minor clauses and fewer dense nominal groups. The references are mainly exophoric, linking to people and places that would only be obvious if you had access to the immediate physical context.

In this section, we have seen some of the effects that the mode of a situation has on language use (as summarised in Figure 6.7). In particular, we have considered some of the differences between highly interactive, spontaneous modes (typified in casual, face-to-face conversation) and non-interactive, non-spontaneous modes (typified in formal writing). In each of these contexts, language packages and organises information in quite distinct ways. You might like to consider how the cartoon in Figure 6.8 exploits these differences to humorous effect. Chapter 10 will provide further explanation and exploration of the links between mode and language.

Figure 6.7

The connection between mode and language

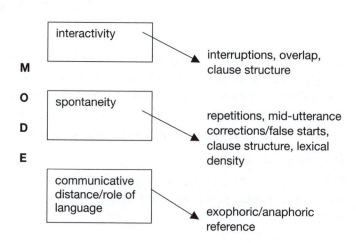

224

Figure 6.8

(http://headrush.
typepad.com/
creating_passionate
_users/2005/09/
conversational_.
html (accessed
30 March 2008))

6.10 Register, language, and meaning

So far, we have considered how the register variables of field, tenor, and mode have an impact on how people use language. In this section, we will show how, within the SFG model, register is used to systematically link the three aspects of social context we have now discussed with three general areas of meaning.

In order to explain what we mean by three *general areas of meaning*, we need to introduce another key theoretical principle underlying the SFG model – the notion that language has three main functional orientations that have evolved to represent three areas of meaning. Referred to as **metafunctions**, these three primary functions of language enable users to:

225

- represent the world – referred to as the **ideational** metafunction;
- engage interpersonally and exchange points of view – referred to as the **interpersonal** metafunction;
- create cohesive text – referred to as the **textual** metafunction.

Thus, in the following extract:

In addition it showed how unfairly the local people were exploited by the wealthy tourists.

we can say that language is simultaneously working to:

(a) represent past events: local people were exploited by the wealthy tourists (*ideational meaning*);

(b) present a point of view: the behaviour of the wealthy tourists was unethical (*interpersonal meaning*);

(c) link different parts of the message together: the connector *in addition* signals that the writer has previously drawn a deduction about the significance of the events alluded to (*textual meaning*).

Each of the three general areas of meaning (ideational, interpersonal, and textual, as represented by the metafunctions) is associated with the three register variables and with different language systems, as shown in Figure 6.9.

Figure 6.9

Register–metafunction–language relationship

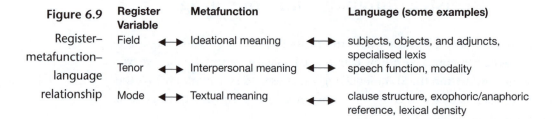

Register Variable	Metafunction	Language (some examples)
Field ←→	Ideational meaning ←→	subjects, objects, and adjuncts, specialised lexis
Tenor ←→	Interpersonal meaning ←→	speech function, modality
Mode ←→	Textual meaning ←→	clause structure, exophoric/anaphoric reference, lexical density

The SFG model posits that there is a two-way relationship between the social and cultural environment and linguistic choices. That is, the particular field, tenor, and mode 'configuration' affects the kinds of meaning we make and the language we choose to express those meanings. But equally, by making certain language choices (rather than others), we make different kinds of ideational, interpersonal, and textual meaning and thus have some influence over the particular field, tenor, and mode configuration that is created. Activity 6.13 illustrates this principle.

Activity 6.13

Compare the two emails below (Texts 6.16 and 6.17). Focus on how the changes in language affect your view of the relationship between the interlocutors.

Text 6.16 Hi there . . .

11th August 2009 12.55

Hi there

Had great time in IOW. Fantastic weather. Am at jazz thing on Sat and walking on Sun. Sunday eve might b back late depending on how long it takes . . . but if not what about then?

C

(Author's personal data)

Text 6.17 Dear Stephen . . .

Dear Stephen

I had an excellent holiday on the Isle of Wight. The weather was beautiful. Unfortunately, I am at a jazz concert on Saturday and on Sunday I will be doing a walk with friends. It is likely that, depending on how long the walk takes, I will be back late on Sunday evening. However, if I am back early, perhaps we could meet up at that point.

Best wishes

Christine

(Author's personal data)

Activity 6.13 illustrates the principle that there is a two-way relationship between the social context and language choices. The re-versioned text (Text 6.17) shows that, by making different language choices, the interpersonal meanings are altered: there is a distinct shift in tenor relations. Language therefore does not simply reflect a different relationship but helps to construct it. In the original email (Text 6.16) the writer constructs a close, familiar relationship with Stephen, whereas in the second version (Text 6.17) relations are more distant and formal. This shows how social reality can be differently interpreted and indeed (in some cases) consciously manipulated through its linguistic encoding.

6.11 Using register to explore real-world problems

How does register help in real-world problem solving? This section is designed to stimulate your thinking about possible applications of register analysis.

Activity 6.14

Consider the following letter in which Joe is pursuing the possibility of a job at John's shop. First, consider the letter from the perspective of tenor:

(a)   How many statements, questions, and commands are there?

(b)   How does Joe address John? How formal or informal is the language used?

(c)   Are there any patterns in the use of modality or evaluative language?

Next consider the letter from the perspective of mode:

(d)   Are the clauses connected through coordination or subordination?

(e)   Are there any patterns in the use of pre- and postmodifiers?

Text 6.18 Job application

John,

I'm looking for a job, and I've heard through the grapevine that you need a workhorse for your shop. Well, I'm the man of the hour, as I've got a lot to offer. I'm pretty hard-working, and I'm really good about being on time. I'm also used to working by myself. Anyway, tell me whether you want to get together for an interview, okay?

Joe

(http://www.wikihow.com/Avoid-Colloquial-(Informal)-Writing)

Your analysis will have revealed that Joe uses language that assumes a social closeness with John. His use of *okay* with a command assumes compliance, thus indicating greater social power. His use of coordination leads to fairly lengthy clause complexes that give the text a spoken feel. As a result, Joe creates a text that may not make a good impression. It is likely to be seen as inappropriate, particularly if he does not know John.

Activity 6.15

Now rework the letter, making changes to the linguistic choices in order to make the text more appropriate for a job application where the applicant and potential employer do not know each other. Compare your version with the one in the Answer key.

Finally, here are some possible problems/areas/issues in which register can play a role. From your own experience, can you add any that are of particular interest to you – either personally or professionally?

- Why do some people sound like a book and others write (even formal assignments) as they speak? In what situations might this be problematic? As a teacher or friend, what might your response be?
- What are some of the problems students have in producing successful essays across different disciplines or subjects (e.g. in school history, undergraduate sociology, laboratory report writing)? What might be the solution?
- In what ways is some news reporting biased? Can anything be done about it?
- Why are some speakers unsuccessful in engaging and persuading their audience?
- Why is it sometimes difficult to know how to pitch an email or a blog entry?

6.12 Summary

Our main goal in Chapter 6 has been to consider the overall 'architecture' of SFG and to provide an overview of its unique approach to language. By now you will have begun to see how it differs from the approach presented in the first half of the book. First, through the concept of register, SFG tightens up and systematises the relationship between grammar and social

230

context. It does not simply look at formal structures in relation to general communicative functions, but looks in detail at how certain aspects of the social context (the field, tenor, and mode) relate to particular areas of grammar (such as modality, reference, clause structure, etc.).

Second, SFG endeavours to understand how grammar enables humans to make meaning – both at the most obvious literal level and at the more abstract, often invisible, but communicatively significant, levels. The aim may be straightforward, but the account is necessarily complex! While we certainly do not intend, in this book, to give a full of account of systemic functional theory, the following four chapters are the start of a new phase in your journey that will take you deeper into grammar as the 'engine house' of meaning-making. As such, there will be a certain amount of reorientation as you learn to look at grammar from a new perspective. And, since you will be making different kinds of observation through a new theoretical lens, you will also need to acquire some of the terms and labels used in SFG. You will see that, rather than focusing on grammatical forms and asking what functions they are used for, we can directly label grammar functionally (by, for example, using terms such as agent instead of the more general term subject). We can also look at the way people make meaning in different contexts and for different purposes. At the same time, however, it is important to remain connected to the formal and communicative approaches to grammar we explored in Chapters 1–5. Although SFG adds new layers to these, they remain an important foundation for any exploration.

Here are just some of SFG's 'wide-angle' views and ideas on how language can be examined, described, and explained. Do not be concerned if they still seem somewhat abstract at this stage, as they will all be grounded and applied throughout the rest of the book.

- Language, rather than being a set of rules, is a set of resources for making meaning (which at a very general level can be referred to as ideational, interpersonal, and textual meaning).

- The forms and structures of language are organised with respect to ideational, interpersonal, and textual meaning.

- Meaning arises from the way that the choices which are made acquire value in relation to the choices that are not made.

- Language varies according to context (the field, tenor, and mode).

At this point on your grammatical journey we hope you will have seen that one of the most significant contributions of SFG is to provide a new way of organising grammar. Rather than setting out a vast reference inventory of structures and rules, or even a list of communicative functions (as some reference grammars do), it brings together those areas of grammar that have particular significance for meaning-making in the broadest sense (i.e. ideational, interpersonal, and textual meaning). For many users, this gives the endless sea of grammatical items a shape and coherence that make them manageable and meaningful, and, equally important, helps text analysis to be more systematic.

6.13 Answer key

Activity 6.1: Dear Mr Gallone

|| Hi my name is Raeesha. || My principal told me about the sports ground near my school || that there is going to be a big housing development there || and I want || to complain * about that. || If you put lots of houses there || we won't have anywhere to play sport || and there will be nowhere <<when it is hot and sunny>> to run around || and there will be too much people and cars, noise and no place for us to get fit ||.

> from
> Raeesha

*Note that *I want* is counted as a separate clause. In SFG it is said to 'project' the clause that follows. We will come back to this point in Chapter 8.

Activity 6.2

Demonstrators **disrupt** Olympic torch lighting (*The Daily Telegraph*, UK)

Protesters **disrupt** Olympic ceremony (*The Boston Globe*)

Olympics torch worries (*Bangkok Post*)

Olympic torch relay protests 'shameful': China (*The Times of India*)

China **vows** tight security for Games torch (*New Zealand Herald*)

Activity 6.4

|| Spiders look very distinctive ||. They have two body parts, the head and the abdomen. || They have eight legs. || Spiders can be colourful || but most are dark. || They have spinnerets [[that make silk]] ||

|| Spiders live everywhere. || They can live in hot desert areas or cool mountain areas. || Some spiders live in people's homes or gardens. ||

All spiders spin silk. || They use the silk for egg sacs, || to line their burrows || and to make webs. ||

|| Spiders are predatory invertebrate animals [[that have two body segments, eight legs, no chewing mouth parts and no wings]]. || They are classified in the order Araneae, one of several orders within the larger class of arachnids, a group [[that also contains scorpions, whip scorpions, mites, ticks, and opiliones (harvestmen).]] || The study of spiders is called arachnology. ||

|| All spiders produce silk, a thin, strong protein strand [[extruded by the spider from spinnerets [[most commonly found on the end of the abdomen]]]]. || Many species use it || to trap insects in webs,* || although there are also many species [[that hunt freely]].

|| Spiders are found all over the world, from the tropics to the Arctic, || living underwater in silken domes [[they supply with air]], and on the tops of mountains.

* Although in the first half of the book you did not analyse non-finite clauses (see Chapter 2), in this half of the book we will generally do so.

Activity 6.5

Words underlined are lexical (content-carrying) items. The words not underlined are non content-carrying words.

Other words are

Text 6.2	Text 6.3
Spiders look very distinctive. They have two body parts, the head and the abdomen. They have eight legs. Spiders	Spiders are predatory invertebrate animals that have two body segments, eight legs, no chewing mouth parts and no wings.

can <u>be</u> <u>colourful</u> but most <u>are</u> <u>dark</u>. They <u>have</u> <u>spinnerets</u> that <u>make</u> <u>silk</u>.

<u>Spiders</u> <u>live</u> <u>everywhere</u>. They can <u>live</u> in <u>hot</u> <u>desert</u> <u>areas</u> or <u>cool</u> <u>mountain</u> <u>areas</u>. Some <u>spiders</u> <u>live</u> in <u>peoples</u> <u>homes</u> or <u>gardens</u>.

All <u>spiders</u> <u>spin</u> <u>silk</u>. They <u>use</u> the <u>silk</u> for <u>egg</u> <u>sacs</u>, to <u>line</u> their <u>burrows</u> and to <u>make</u> <u>webs</u>.

They are <u>classified</u> in the <u>order</u> Araneae, one of <u>several</u> <u>orders</u> within the <u>larger</u> <u>class</u> of <u>arachnids</u>, a <u>group</u> that also <u>contains</u> <u>scorpions</u>, <u>whip</u> <u>scorpions</u>, <u>mites</u>, <u>ticks</u>, and <u>opiliones</u> (<u>harvestmen</u>). The <u>study</u> of <u>spiders</u> is <u>called</u> <u>arachnology</u>.

All <u>spiders</u> <u>produce</u> <u>silk</u>, a <u>thin</u>, <u>strong</u> <u>protein</u> <u>strand</u> <u>extruded</u> by the <u>spider</u> from <u>spinnerets</u> most <u>commonly</u> <u>found</u> on the <u>end</u> of the <u>abdomen</u>. Many <u>species</u> <u>use</u> it to <u>trap</u> <u>insects</u> in <u>webs</u>, although there are also many <u>species</u> that <u>hunt</u> <u>freely</u>.

<u>Spiders</u> are <u>found</u> all over the <u>world</u>, from the <u>tropics</u> to the <u>Arctic</u>, <u>living</u> <u>underwater</u> in <u>silken</u> <u>domes</u> they <u>supply</u> with <u>air</u>, and on the <u>tops</u> of <u>mountains</u>.

Lexical density of Text 6.2:	Lexical density of Text 6.3:
the number of lexical items = 47	the number of lexical items = 70
divided by	divided by
the number of ranking clauses = 13	the number of ranking clauses = 9
= 3.6	= 7.8

Activity 6.8

What are the main lexical items in the text?
9/11, jets, whizzing, evacuated, plane, White House

What kinds of subject, complement, or object are chosen?
Planes: the jets of some sort, a little plane, a Cessna, jets, the White House.
Pronouns: either referring to speakers (I) or people, planes (it, they).

What kinds of adjuncts are chosen?
Absence of adjuncts apart from place: into the building.

Which clause types are used to communicate what communicative functions?
All the clauses are declarative and are used to make statements.
There are some minor clauses used by Kevin to contradict Sarah.

Are the clauses evenly distributed across the participants?
Even distribution of declarative clauses. Only Kevin uses minor clauses.

Are there any examples of epistemic or deontic modality?
There is an absence of modality apart from Sarah's use of could (epistemic).

Is there any use of colloquial language or contractions?
Colloquial: whizzing, jets of some sort.
Contractions: it's, I'm, wasn't.

Are there densely packed nominal groups (including embedding)?
There are no densely packed nominal groups.

Are there any minor clauses or other features of spoken language?
There is the minor clause 'no'. Other features include repetition, false starts (apparently the, I don't know, jets of some sort) contraction, colloquial language.

Is there any use of anaphoric or exophoric reference?
Anaphoric: they, it.

Activity 6.9

Text 6.7

What is the social activity?	What are the social roles of the speakers/writers?	How interactive is the text?
A school or university debate: lexis – debate, two groups, failure/success	Teacher to students: speaker/teacher nf5085 makes majority of clauses. His communicative functions include commands	Interactive: There are features of conversational interaction through minor clause yep, interrupting clauses, and use of exophoric reference (the personal pronoun I, you, we to refer to the speakers)

235

What is the topic of the text?	What is the status of the speakers/writers?	How spontaneous is the text?
The Cuban revolution: a number of subjects and objects refer to revolution	Teacher has more status (e.g. students comply with his commands) but he tries to align students through openness to topic (high use of epistemic modality)	Spontaneous: There are repetitions, and changes mid-utterance. The text does not have a high lexical density.

Text 6.8

What is the social activity?	What are the social roles of the speakers/writers?	How interactive is the text?
Advertisement	Commercial org (Better airlines) to (potential) client: Status relatively equal through use of colloquial language (we mean it, then here it is!, contractions – there's, they'll).	Non-interactive: There are features of conversational interaction through use of minor and interrupting clauses and use of exophoric reference (the personal pronoun you, we to refer to the speakers.

What is the topic of the text?	What is the status of the speakers/writers?	How spontaneous is the text?
New airline route: main subjects, objects, and adjuncts refer to planes and travel routes	Close social connection (direct use of vocative Caroline and pronoun you). Authoritative – no use of modality	Semi-spontaneous: The text does not have a high lexical density.

Activity 6.10

Underlining = subjects and objects
Highlighting = adjuncts

Text 6.10

They punched me until I was in a state of collapse*. I was eventually locked into a barrack full of people who had been selected to be taken to the gas chambers. Realising the consequences, I was determined to escape and managed to climb out at night through a narrow window with a colleague.

* Note that although *in a state of collapse* is a prepositional phrase, in this clause it is being used as a complement, not an adjunct. You saw in Chapter 3 that complements are typically nominal groups or adjectival groups, but sometimes prepositional phrases are used as complements too.

This serves to illustrate that form does not map onto function: prepositional phrases are sometimes adjuncts, sometimes complements, and sometimes postmodifiers.

Text 6.11: Hitler's Final Solution

After the outbreak of the Second World War the Nazis changed their policy towards the Jews. They wanted to get rid of as many Jews as possible, and began to make plans for how to deal effectively with what they called the 'Jewish problem'. In 1941 they came up with a plan which was known as the Final Solution. The Jews would be dealt with two ways in: they would either be worked to death or executed. Extermination and labour camps were therefore set up throughout Europe in order to exterminate the estimated eleven million European Jews.

Activity 6.11

(Modality in bold)

|| Ok, everybody, now everybody if you **can** have a look at the overhead [[that's up there now]] || (declarative, command)

Ali? (minor clause, question)

||| We **can** see that, um, || we have some of *, ||what we have here are aspects of warfare. ||| (declarative, statement)

In other words, the 'input'. (minor clause – statement)

|| So, for instance, first of all, we have an unavailability of goods here. || (declarative, statement)

||| That means || that people couldn't get certain things at the end of the war. ||| (declarative, statement)

||| Now, how do you think || that **might** have affected Australian Society at that time? ||| (interrogative, question)

||| What **would** the consequences be of that? ||| (interrogative, question)

(Katina?) (minor clause, question)

|| They had to produce their own? || (declarative, statement)

(Very good.) (minor clause, statement)

|| They had to produce their own goods ||. (declarative, statement)

* this appears to be a false start.
Example of colloquial language: *get things*
Example of contraction: *couldn't*
Evaluative language: *very good.*

Tenor analysis

Social relations	Social connectedness	Persona
Teacher–student unequal status: asymmetrical distribution of communicative functions	Interlocutors are in regular contact: use of first name	Teacher has open stance: epistemic modality. The other interlocutor has a compliant stance. Teacher authoritative: uses attitudinal language.

Activity 6.12

Underlining = minor clauses
Double underlining = nominal groups with modifiers
Square brackets = mid utterance changes
Highlighting = anaphoric or exophoric reference

Text 6.13

It's worth dwelling on <u>the batterings and the blows he* takes</u> to illustrate just how much Wilkinson sacrifices physically in <u>defence of the English turf</u>. His** is essentially <u>a creative role</u>. He is <u>the link between a monstrous pack and a back division that has become steelier and more dynamic over the past five unforgettable months</u>. There is <u>a fear that dare not speak its name</u>. It is that

England have become dangerously reliant on him in that playmaker's role. Charlie Hodgson, of Sale, has picked up a serious injury, and Grayson is generally thought of as a competent veteran who lacks Wilkinson's match-winning capability.

* from the extract it is not clear whether he refers to a previous mention of Wilkinson or this is a forward (**cataphoric**) reference.
** this is ellipsis – his <role>.

Text 6.14

Margaret:	Gosh they can go up in the air now
Jessica:	Oh, he just dropped it, that was rubbish . . . It's that nice looking guy again
Margaret:	don't let them *
Jessica:	get the ball . . . oh look
Margaret:	go on, go on, go on
All:	hooraaaaaay
Madeline:	England's got a try!
Margaret:	He's been marvellous.
Chris:	Yes
Margaret:	I thought he was finished
Jessica:	Gosh he looked pretty happy about that
Chris:	Fantastic! I'd like to see that again.

* this utterance, started by Margaret, is completed by Jessica. This co-construction of clauses is common in spoken language

---

Text 6.15

A:	Matt Dawson was punching the air. They've got to try something out and . . . Greenwood reads it. Walking almost there. I don't think Johnny [Wilkinson was very happy], the fact that he made him run into the corner for [that but er . . .]
B:	I don't think Johnny Wilkinson worries about that, does he?

A: <u>No, maybe not</u>.

B: There you have <u>it</u>. <u>England strolling to the Grand Slam</u>. Will <u>Greenwood strolling to the line</u>. Who thought that this would be such a stroll?

Communicative distance of Texts 6.13, 6.14, and 6.15.

Language as ACTION				Language as REFLECTION	
Spoken				**Written**	
e.g. language during football match	TV or radio play by play or replay	email same day of match	newspaper report next day	newspaper editorial next day	Book on football
Text 6.14	**Text 6.15**			**Text 6.13**	

Activity 6.13

Text 6.17

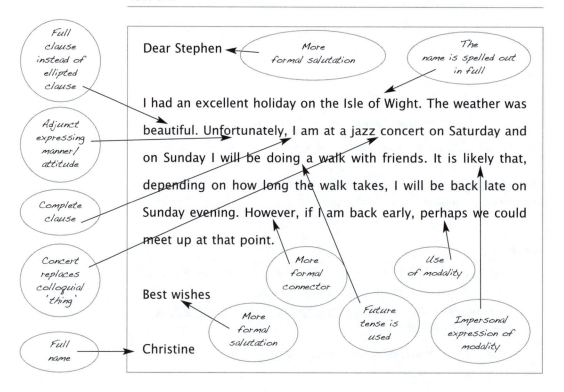

Activity 6.14

Tenor

1	Seven statements, one question, and one command
2	*John.* Generally the language is colloquial e.g. *the grapevine, workhorse, the man of the hour, got, pretty, anyway, get together okay.*
3	Absence of epistemic modality, one use of deontic modality (need). Evaluative language includes positive evaluation of writer – *the man of the hour, pretty hardworking, really good about being on time*

Mode

1	Two clauses are connected through coordination; one clause is connected through subordination.
2	The lexical density is low. Only one noun is modified – *the man of the hour.*

Activity 6.15

Dear Mr Krench

I understand that you are looking for a strong worker to assist you in your shop. I would like to apply for this position. I possess all the appropriate qualities – I am diligent, punctual, and accustomed to working with minimal supervision. I would be delighted if you would consider interviewing me.

Yours sincerely

Joe Townsend

seven

Shaping a text to meet social purposes: genre

7.1 Introduction

Scenario

In the text below Dr E makes a complaint in response to poor treatment by an airline company (which we will call Air X). In your opinion, are there any problems with the way Dr E has structured and organised the letter? Is it likely to have been successful?

Text 7.1 Letter of complaint

> Dear Sir
>
> I am one of a party of 35 Israeli tourists that were processed by employee Carla from Air X, on October 28, 2005, at 7.00 am, at terminal T2, counters 402–3.

Due to circumstances beyond our control, we only got to the counter at 7.00 am, while the flight was supposed to take off at 7:10. We are still investigating who is to blame, but this is NOT the subject of my complaint.

The subject is the incredibly rude behavior of your employee Carla. I politely asked her to call her supervisor, in order to delay the flight. After all, we were 35 people, without luggage (since we were in transit), and the time was 7 am.

Carla told me that 'the flight is already closed'. However, I told her, this is at least 1/3 of the plane capacity we are talking about (35 people), and the fact that the flight is closed is not an act of God, but a human decision – one that can, and should, be cancelled. After a brief consultation in Spanish with one of her colleagues, Carla turned to me and said: 'You don't understand – the plane is already in the air.' The time, by then, was 7:05, according to the airport clock. I asked Carla how come the plane is in the air 5 minutes early, and she only repeated, in an abrasive and impertinent way, that 'the plane is in the air'. At this point, I asked to speak to her supervisor, and she said there is none, since she is the highest in command. As she was not wearing the obligatory name tag, I asked her her name, and she only gave me the name Carla – when I asked for her last name, she told me 'she has none'.

I wish to say that we are a group of people who have travelled to every part of the world. We are doctors, lawyers, and business people. We're not stupid, and we're not ignorant. However, such an attitude of insult to the intelligence and to common civil behavior we have never seen. We strongly doubt we will continue using the services of Air X, if no measures are taken against problematic employees such as this young lady. Is she really the highest in command there? Was the plane early in its takeoff? Is she exempt from wearing a name tag? Does she really not have a last name?

I doubt it . . .

Please keep me informed about the measures taken regarding this employee. We all wish to avoid a lawsuit.

Best regards

Dr E

cell phone +972-xxx

(http://www.grumbletext.co.uk (accessed 5 February 2008))

In Text 7.1, the writer's purpose is to make a complaint and resolve the cause of his dissatisfaction by requiring the airline company to take measures regarding what he sees as a 'problematic employee'. However, in our opinion, the way he has structured the letter is likely to have reduced his chance of a successful outcome. The opening paragraph, for example, consists of material that he goes on to say is 'NOT the subject of my complaint'. There are other problematic aspects in the way the letter is organised, and we will return to look at these in more detail at the end of the chapter.

So far, in this book, we have set our exploration of language within meaningful texts as opposed to decontextualised fragments of language. Each chapter in the first half of the book was organised around texts with a broadly similar communicative function, such as *describing* (Chapter 2) or *predicting and hypothesising* (Chapter 5). We saw there that some grammatical features are more likely to occur in relation to certain communicative functions (for example, modal verbs frequently occur when making predictions, but do not occur so much when giving instructions); so organising the chapters around communicative functions enabled us to explore particular areas of grammar. The notion of communicative function is, however, rather loose. While communicative functions provide a context for a more meaningful exploration of grammar than would otherwise be the case, each one is linked to a diversity of types of text. Describing, for example, occurs in encyclopaedia entries, academic lectures and essays, classified ads, travel writing, and hotel reviews (among many other types).

Traditional formal grammar and communicative grammar do not provide a theoretical framework or analytical tools for making different types of text an object of study – in the sense of how they are structured and organised and how they differ one from another in terms of their lexicogrammatical patterns. In SFL, in contrast, the way writers and speakers use lexicogrammar to organise and stage whole texts and how this relates to their social purposes is an important dimension of the theory. While, in

In brief, field refers to the social activity, tenor to social relations, and mode to how a text is produced and therefore the degree of spontaneity and interactivity.

Chapter 6, we looked at the relationship between context and lexicogrammar from the perspective of field, tenor, and mode, in this chapter we will look at the relationship between context and lexicogrammar from the perspective of social purpose.

7.2 Social purpose and text structure: an SFL perspective

Whereas the founder of SFL, Michael Halliday, has tended to focus on clause level grammar (e.g. 2004) – albeit always in relation to text and context – another major SFL theorist, Jim Martin, has been primarily interested in text level meanings, including the way that texts are structured in relation to speakers' and writers' social purposes (Martin 1992; Martin and Rose 2007, 2008). In this chapter, we will show how social purposes such as *telling a story*, *explaining how something works*, or *arguing a point of view* affect the way a text is structured and the lexicogrammatical patterns that occur across its different stages. In particular, we will show how the shape and structure of a text are important aspects of a writer's or speaker's meaning: text structures are not simply arbitrary containers into which meaning is poured, but emerge in the course of a language user's pursuit of their social goal. For example, when writing about why the Second World War occurred, choosing to use an explanation rather than argument text structure means that the causes of the war are explained, without giving different perspectives on which causes were the most and least important. Choice in shaping and structuring a text is therefore as important to meaning as choice in shaping and structuring a clause.

Some of the social purposes mentioned above (*telling a story etc.*) relate to the communicative functions that you came across in the first half of the book. We saw there that communicative function is a label that can apply to any stretch of language, from clause to a complete text. Thus the communicative function of apologising can be carried out in a short, spoken utterance, such as *I'm sorry. I didn't mean to do it*, or in an extended text such as a letter of apology. In SFL, **social purpose** is used in a more rigorous fashion than communicative function. It relates to specific types of text, with distinct text structures and distinct lexicogrammatical patterns.

Activity 7.1

Below are three texts.

(a) Read through them and decide what overall social purpose each one is fulfilling, selecting from the following list:

- telling a story;
- classifying and describing;
- explaining how something works;

245

- giving instructions;

- arguing a point of view;

- discussing different perspectives on an issue.

(b) Identify any distinct lexicogrammatical patterns that distinguish one text from another (e.g. use of tense, modality, etc.).

Text 7.2 Rocks

There are three types of rock.

1 *Igneous*: these are rocks that solidified directly from molten silicates, which geologists call magma. Examples are: granite, basalt, pumice and flint (which is a form of quartz).

2 *Sedimentary*: these are formed when igneous rocks are eroded as a sediment under the sea. Fossils are often found in this layer. Examples are limestone, chalk, sandstone.

3 *Metamorphic*: these are made up of igneous and sedimentary rocks of all ages which have been subjected to intense pressure. Examples are: slate, marble, quartzite.

(http://www.zephyrus.co.uk/rocktypes.html (accessed 29 March 2007))

Text 7.3 British journalism

Message 1 – posted yesterday

Is British journalism really sloppy and morally bankrupt?

Message 2 – posted by Sunny yesterday

BBC journalism is especially prone to regular anti-American, anti-Israeli, anti-Conservative and anti-capitalist slants.

The BBC is the worst of the lot in terms of presenting news with a particular ideological slant

Message 3 – posted by Dave yesterday

Since I don't read every article written by every newspaper I can't speak for all of British journalism.

I can say that I feel the BBC is sloppy, particularly when it comes to scientific issues. Take the story below:

news.bbc.co.uk/1/hi/ . . .

The bit about extinction is written as a fact. But there is no universal agreement as to what caused the extinction event.

A less sloppy piece of journalism might have pointed out that a possible cause was an asteroid impact.

Message 4 – posted by Redwood, 25 October 2008

It's easy to just knock everything on these discussion boards, so on this occasion I will put the opposite point of view. I have a great deal of respect for British journalism. OK they may make mistakes and of course all journalists are biased to some extent.

But where would we be without the investigative work and news they have produced over the years?

(Author's personal data)

Text 7.4 The three magic arrows

Once upon a time in a little cottage in the forest, there was a little girl named Andrea who lived with her father, who was very good to her, and her two older brothers, who were, well, you know. One day the father went on a long journey, and told the children to stay at home, and the brothers to look after their sister.

Now, this forest was in the heart of the kingdom, and in the midst of the forest there was a mountain, and in the centre of the mountain was a cave, and in the centre of the cave was a well. In that well lived an evil Waterdragon, and one day the Waterdragon sent the King a message saying: 'It has been seven years since my last human meal. Send me the Royal Prince, sealed alive into a golden cask, for my dinner on the next Midsummer Day, or I will open my floodgates and destroy the whole kingdom.'

The King had no choice but to obey the Waterdragon. But before sending the Prince to the dragon's cave, he put out a proclamation to the whole kingdom, which said: 'Anyone who can rescue the Prince and deliver the country from this Waterdragon may have half the kingdom as a reward.'

'So,' Andrea said to her brothers as soon as she heard the news, 'what are we going to do about it?'

'About what?' said her oldest brother.

'About rescuing the Prince and saving the kingdom.'

They laughed at her. 'Nobody can do anything. Forget it. Dragons happen.' . . .

(http://www.rosemarylake.com/andrea.html (accessed 5 February 2008))

Comment

Chapter 3 looked at nominal groups and other grammatical resources for presenting information about qualities, features, and characteristics. Tense and temporal expressions were the focus of Chapter 4. Modality was introduced in Chapter 5.

In completing Activity 7.1, it is unlikely that you experienced any difficulty in working out the overall purpose of each of the texts – even without reading them in detail. This is partly because, as a competent language user, you can draw on your intuitive knowledge of the different ways in which texts are structured and grammatically patterned in line with their different purposes. Thus, Text 7.2 provides a classification of rocks, using generic nominal groups (e.g. *sedimentary rocks*) in which the heads are elaborated through pre- and postmodifiers (e.g. *rocks that solidified directly from molten*). The tense is present. In Text 7.3, there is some (though limited) use of modality (*can, might, may*) in order to negotiate different perspectives on British journalism. Text 7.4 is the beginning of a story and predictably uses the past tense (*was, lived*) and temporal adjuncts (*once upon a time, one day*) to locate the events in the past.

In SFL, the term **genre** has been adopted to refer to the way in which we construct texts in similar and recognisable ways according to our communicative goals and social purposes. Martin and Rose (2007: 6) define genre as follows:

> For us genre is a staged, goal-oriented social process. Social because we participate in genres with other people; goal-oriented because we use genres to get things done; staged because it usually takes us a few steps to reach our goals.

In SFL, the genres exemplified by Texts 7.2, 7.3, and 7.4 are called **taxonomic report**, **discussion**, and **narrative**, respectively. All three genres play a key role in everyday life. Narratives, for example, play an important role in transmitting cultural and social values, alongside their more transparent role of entertaining and creating pleasure, whereas discussions occur across a vast array of professional and social situations, ranging from parliamentary and local council debates to business meetings and dinner party conversations.

Outside linguistics and language studies, you may be familiar with the use of the term 'genre' to refer to various forms or types of literature, music, art, or film. (Typical film genres, for example, would be *romantic comedies*, *westerns*, and *fantasy*.) Within SFL, genre is viewed from a linguistic perspective: it refers to the overall structural organisation and grammatical features shared by texts that have a common social purpose, such as telling a story (narrative genre) or debating an issue (discussion genre).

Activity 7.2

Read Text 7.5 and note any grammatical patterns that stand out. Use these to help identify the writer's social purpose.

Text 7.5 Stan

Anne: Years ago I was, when I was married, about I don't know how long ago about ten or twelve years ago I lived in Mosman and I had a really nice neighbour called Stan. Sometimes he used to cut the grass outside our place and sometimes we'd cut the grass outside his place. And one weekend, I was away when this happened, but he'd told me about it much later. This weekend Stan cut the grass outside the front and was clipping along the edges of our garden with a little axe.

Jane: Mmm

Anne: And a funnel web spider jumped out and . . .

(de Silva, Joyce, and Burns (1999) *Focus on Grammar*, Sydney, National Centre for English Language Teaching and Research (NCELTR), Macquarie University, p. 94)

The following grammatical patterns feature in Text 7.5, which is an extract from a narrative genre:

Chapter 4 discussed the importance of both tense and aspect in narrating events. Often, past perfect is used to shift to a different time frame, and the progressive to provide background information to a narrative.

past tense (*was*, *had*);

past perfect and past progressive aspect (*he'd told me*, *was clipping*);

temporal adjuncts (*years ago*, *one weekend*);

dependent clauses (*when I was married*).

The repetitions and clause structure (among other features) indicate that Text 7.5 is a spoken text (in mode terms it is both spontaneous and interactive). It is important to recognise that there are spoken as well as written genres, even though it may be easier to see the shape of written genres – on the whole, they are more carefully planned and less fluid than spoken ones.

It is also important to recognise that, increasingly, partly due to the widespread use of new technologies, genres involve semiotic modes other than language. Visual images, animation, sound, and creative use of graphics are all becoming standard features of many twenty-first century texts.

Activity 7.3

Look at the following visual image, which accompanies a text on the Internet. Can you predict what kind of social purpose the text (including the image) might have?

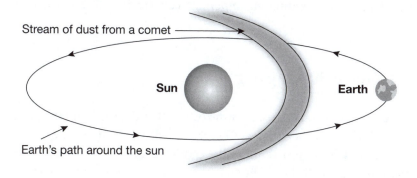

The image above is part of a text whose purpose is to explain how falling stars are formed. SFL classifies such a text as an explanation genre. If you look at the full text in the Answer key, you will see that one key grammatical pattern is the use of clauses of time, which set up the conditions for certain events to occur:

> || *and they occur* || *when the Earth passes through the trail of debris [[left by a comet* || *as it orbits the Sun]].*||

Clauses of time and cause, together with causal verbs, such as *cause* or *produce*, are key features of an explanation genre.

Where verbal text combines with visual (or any other non-verbal, meaning-making resources such as sound or animation), it is referred to as a **multimodal** text. The text in Activity 7.3 was taken from a website where the colour diagram is used to enhance the verbal explanation. On the Internet, animation and moving images are often used to enhance explanations (particularly scientific ones). For example, if you type into an Internet search engine *'types of rock' animation*, you will find some dynamic explanations of different types of rock. If you have access to the Internet, we suggest you take a look at a range of explanations and consider the effectiveness of any elements that are not written text. Consider, for example, whether they are necessary for the genre to make meaning. Do they replace written text (i.e. constituting the genre)? Or do they serve a more decorative function, with their purpose being to hook the viewer/reader in (i.e. accompanying the genre)? Or are they somewhere in between, neither constituting nor accompanying the written explanation, but reinforcing or elaborating an important concept that forms part of the explanation?

7.3 Generic staging

One of the key points about most texts, whether they are written, spoken, or multimodal, is that they are characterised by distinctive beginnings, middles, and ends. (Just think of the classic opening to a fairy tale – *Once upon a time* ... and the traditional closing of a prayer – *Amen.*) The SFL model proposes that, rather than view a text in terms of a beginning, middle, and end (which is a formal structure), its unfolding organisation can be more usefully viewed from a functional perspective. Such a perspective provides insight into how different genres enable language users to achieve their social purposes by moving through distinct functional stages. For example, the beginning stage of a narrative genre provides an orientation to a time or a place (the **orientation** stage), while the beginning of a discussion genre sets out a controversial issue (the **issue** stage).

Below, we have annotated Text 7.3 (*British journalism*), which is an example of a discussion genre, to illustrate how we can break up a genre into its different stages. The distinctive functional 'chunks' of text are called **generic stages**, and the combined set of stages is referred to as the **generic structure**. Sometimes, generic structure may also be called 'schematic structure' or 'generic structure potential'.

Annotation of Text 7.3

Functional labels are in *italics*.

Message 1 – posted yesterday – *Issue*

Is British journalism really sloppy and morally bankrupt?

Message 2 – posted by Sunny yesterday – *Argument 1 (for)*

BBC journalism is especially prone to regular anti-American, anti-Israeli, anti-Conservative and anti-capitalist slants.

The BBC is the worst of the lot in terms of presenting news with a particular ideological slant

Message 3 – posted by Dave yesterday – *Argument 2 (for)*

Since I don't read every article written by every newspaper I can't speak for all of British journalism.

I can say that I feel the BBC is sloppy, particularly when it comes to scientific issues. Take the story below:

news.bbc.co.uk/1/hi/ . . .

The bit about extinction is written as a fact. But there is no universal agreement as to what caused the extinction event.

A less sloppy piece of journalism might have pointed out that a possible cause was an asteroid impact.

Message 4 – posted by Redwood, 25 October 2008 – *Argument 3 (against)*

It's easy to just knock everything on these discussion boards, so on this occasion I will put the opposite point of view. I have a great deal of respect for British journalism. OK they may make mistakes and of course all journalists are biased to some extent.

But where would we be without the investigative work and news they have produced over the years

In the discussion genre there are typically four distinct functional stages:

Issue

Arguments for $(1-n^2)$

Arguments against $(1-n)$

(Position)

The final stage, position, is shown in brackets because it is optional.

In the example, a jointly constructed electronic discussion, there was no concluding position stage, where a writer or speaker puts forward an overall final perspective on the issue under debate. This is an important step in formal written discussions (such as a traditional academic essay), but less so in more informal, interactive contexts, where there are many authors rather than one, and the discussion remains open-ended.

In combination, the stages of a discussion genre function to achieve its overall social purpose – to discuss a range of perspectives on an issue. 'Arguments for' may be interwoven with 'arguments against', or 'arguments for' may be followed by 'arguments against' as a block. Ordering often depends on the strategic purpose of the writer, or is an outcome of the degree of spontaneity (compare a spoken or electronic multi-party discussion with a single-authored, written discussion essay).

Given its different social purpose, it is not surprising that the narrative genre has a very different structure to that of the discussion genre. So far we have only looked at incomplete examples (Texts 7.4 and 7.5), but typically a narrative moves through four stages, which can be glossed as follows:

Orientation	This orients the reader to what is to follow.
Complication	A usual sequence goes awry in some way, thus creating a problem for one or more of the characters.
Evaluation	This gives significance to the events through the narrator's or characters' reactions to them.
Resolution	The problem is resolved as a consequence of action taken by a character or the characters. 'Usuality' is restored at the end of the narrative.

Activity 7.4

Read the following abridged narrative genre, which was written by a thirteen-year-old girl. It has been divided into four generic stages, which have been jumbled. The notation [. . .] indicates an abridged section.

(a)   Decide on the correct order of the stages and place the labels for the generic stages of a narrative (see above) on the appropriate lines (A)–(D).

(b)   Identify the main grammatical patterns in the text.

Text 7.6 The Hero of Geduldig

(A) _____

Santina, as if in slow motion saw Eaon forcing the massive fireball down the hill into the raging torrent. With a final cry, he hit the fireball. They vanished together in a huge explosion of steam. Steam rose up clouding the whole of Geduldig, forming new, fresh clouds, to protect her world from the cruel heat of the sun. Geduldig was saved.

(B) _____

She [Santina] woke up and once again looked out of the window. She was horrified to see that the whole world was beginning to melt. Drip, drip, drip. CRASH, the cathedral spire had collapsed into a slushy mess. People everywhere were running, screaming, shouting, praying for the temperature to drop. Santina looked up and saw the ball of the sun getting ever closer, red, blazing, angry.
        [. . .]

(C) _____

She ran into her closest friend Eaon. He looked at Santina, saw her golden eyes staring fearfully out of that pale face, and they both understood. They knew that they had to do something. They ran out into the square, and looked at the remains of the cathedral. They stood in horror, their silver hair blowing in the strangely warm breeze.
        [. . .]

(D) _____

The snow began to fall, the winds began to howl and the temperature began to drop.

> Santina poked her head out of the window. Her face did not flinch when the snow rose to head height. This was not unusual weather on the planet of Geduldig; these snowstorms were about as common as rain is in England. Santina felt a flood of relief when she saw the temperature had dropped to −500°.
>
> [. . .]

(Author's personal data)

Activity 7.4 provides an illustration of the relationship between social purpose, text structure (generic stages), and lexicogrammatical patterns. Activity 7.5 provides further practice in analysing the relationship between context and lexicogrammar from the perspective of social purpose and genre.

Activity 7.5

Read the text segments A–F in Table 7.1 below. Consider the overall social purpose of the text to which the segment belongs, selecting from the following list (which also shows genre names in brackets).

- to discuss a range of perspectives on an issue (discussion)

- to make a judgement (case judgement)

- to retell a sequence of events in the narrator's life (personal recount)

- to give instructions (procedure)

- to explain a phenomenon (explanation)

- to tell a story (narrative)

- to record a sequence of events in a person's life (biographical recount)

- to classify and describe a phenomenon (taxonomic report)

Table 7.1

Text segments	Social purpose
Segment A	
On Thursday 25th September we went to the Tower of London. It took two hours to get there and it rained all the time.	
(Author's personal data)	
Segment B	
Therefore, there are a number of factors that can contribute to the outbreak of revolution. Leadership, to a certain extent is one, as is disillusionment with the monarchy or previous ruler (For example, the Provisional Government in Russia.) Other major factors are social and economic grievances. The discontent of the peasants and proletariat is also a contributor, but often, once their grievances are met they are no longer revolutionary. Thus, it is only to a small extent that the peasants and proletariat contribute to the outbreak of revolution.	
(Author's personal data)	
Segment C	
1482 Enters the service of Ludovico Sforza, Duke of Milan, and serves him for 17 years, until the duke's fall from power. It is during this time that he completes much of his greatest work, including paintings and weapons design for the duke.	
(Author's personal data)	
Segment D	
Message 1 – posted by discussion moderators. Gordon Brown told us this morning that 'politicians shouldn't moralise or lecture'. Is he right? If politicians don't moralise, who should? Or is all morality private and all moralising best left within the family?	
(Author's personal data)	

257

Segment E	Social purpose
Remove from heat and stir in the cold butter. Cool the syrup for 5 minutes. Whip the eggs in a bowl with a whisk to break the yolks, then whisk in the syrup and vanilla.	
(Author's personal data)	
Segment F	
The statutory basis for rectification Article 29(1) of the 1994 Order provides: 'If the court is satisfied that a will is so expressed that it fails to carry out the testator's intentions, in consequence – (a) of a clerical error; or (b) of a failure to understand his instructions, it may order that the will shall be rectified so as to carry out his intention.'	
(http://www.courtsni.gov.uk/NR/rdonlyres/801BBEC2-F291-43AD-8CB3-AEFAAB729066/0/j_j_GIRF3533.htm (accessed 8 February 2008))	

Activity 7.6

Each of the segments A–F in Activity 7.5 represent functional stages that help the genre to which they belong achieve its social purpose.

(a)   Using the list below, identify the functional stage represented by each segment:

- Orientation

- Position

- Relevant law

- Record of events

- Issue

- Steps

(b)   Note any lexicogrammatical patterns in relation to the functional stage
      (e.g. tense, adjuncts, pronouns, mood, nominal groups, use of modality)
      as illustrated in relation to segment (A).

Text segments	Functional stage of the text	Grammatical features associated with this stage.
Segment A	Orientation	Past tense
		Temporal adjuncts
		Use of personal pronoun *I*
		Declarative mood

Activity 7.6 suggests that, in order to achieve their purpose, genres
have distinctive stages. Although these are generally easily recognised by
members of a culture, you may have found segment F less familiar than the
others and therefore more difficult to categorise. This is not surprising since,
as an extract from a legal document, it requires greater expert, professional
knowledge than the other texts. If you were a member of the legal discourse
community or had specialist knowledge of the workings of English law,
however, the extract would be easily recognisable as forming a stage within
a written legal judgment, the 'relevant law' stage of a structure that contains
at least three parts:

• facts as found

• relevant law

• decision/ruling.

7.4 Genres and generic stages: a review

So far, we have examined eight different genres and examined some of the
stages that language users move through in pursuit of their social purposes.
Table 7.2 provides a complete overview. Note that the lexicogrammatical
features identified are those that have already been introduced in previous
chapters of this book. As you progress through the next three chapters you
will be introduced to functional grammatical terms that are more effective

for characterising genres and the stages that writers and speakers move through in performing them.

Table 7.2: Genres and generic stages

Genre	Social purpose	Generic stages	Lexicogrammatical features
personal recount	to retell a sequence of events in the narrator's life	• orientation • record of events • (reorientation)	• past tense • temporal adjuncts • declarative mood • personal pronoun *I*
biographical recount	to retell the events of a person's life	• orientation • record of events • (evaluation of person)	• past tense (present tense can be used for effect) • temporal adjuncts • declarative mood • third person pronoun *he/she*
narrative	to tell a story	• orientation • complication • evaluation • resolution	• past tense (present and past may occur in dialogue) • temporal adjuncts • declarative mood (other mood choices may occur, particularly in dialogue) • third person pronoun *he/she, they* • evaluative lexis
taxonomic report	to classify and describe phenomenon	• identification of phenomenon and classification • description of types or parts (1–n)	• present tense • declarative mood • generic nominal groups • third person pronoun *it, they*
procedure	to give instructions	• goal • material • steps (1–n)	• present tense • adjuncts of place • imperative mood

explanation	to explain how something works	• identification of phenomenon • explanation sequence	• present tense • declarative mood • generic nominal groups • causal and temporal connectors
discussion	to consider different perspectives on an issue	• issue • arguments for • arguments against • (position)	• present tense (and past where appropriate) • declarative mood (some use of interrogatives in spoken mode) • modality • generic nominal groups
legal judgement		• facts as found • relevant law • decision/ruling	• present tense • third person pronouns • declarative mood • use of conditional clauses • epistemic (*may*) and deontic (*shall*) modality

Activity 7.7

(a) Using Table 7.2, read through Texts 7.7–7.9 below and identify the social purpose and genre of each (using grammatical features as evidence).

(b) Analyse the generic structure of each text. (You may have already noticed from our analysis of Texts 7.3 and 7.6 that generic stages map onto relatively large chunks of text, so it is important to focus on the major stages a writer or speaker moves through rather than become too concerned with the detail of a particular text).

Text 7.7 The Cuban revolution

sm5087: you got to look you got to look at outcomes as well not what they set out not what they actually said that's not what you've got to judge the revolution on you've got to judge the revolution on the impact it's had on the people not what the impact it's had on the original aims you can't i mean yeah that's a useful historical exercise but the important thing to look at is the success in terms of outcomes not aims

sm5086: and those are

sm5087: the outcomes are very useful link there er i think we're looking at you know healthcare to start with now er you know healthcare in Cuba is free at the point of delivery which is true in this country but it's not true in America far from being free at the point of delivery now that's a it's actually a very helpful very very progressive er system and we've also got it's a net exporter of doctors which is quite an impressive statistic for such of a sort of a

sm5087: yes it's a net exporter of doctors and it's also a trainer of the rest of the Caribbean's doctors a lot of the other Caribbean countries don't have 'cause that's one of the strange things about Cuba it's Caribbean but Latin American at the same time and it actually takes medical students from other Caribbean countries and from some northern Latin American countries and trains them for those countries not asking for much in return you know maybe some trade [. . .]

sm5086: i think that leads us on to education the success of the education the scientific and technical success of the education system the literary success

sm5087: yeah we've got twenty to twelve per cent was the change in that three years in literacy rates in Cuba

sm5086: and now

sm5087: phenomenal

sm5086: i think i think there's ninety-five per cent

nf5085: illiteracy

sm5087: illiteracy rates sorry

sm5086: i think there's ninety-five per cent or ninety per cent or ninety-nine per cent it's in the nineties er literacy rates which is quite impressive i think it's comparable to like you know most western states it might even be higher than America but i can't not sure whether that's true

(BASE corpus, http://www2.warwick.ac.uk/fac/soc/al/research/projects/resources/base/citation/)

Text 7.8 Everything I needed to know about personality types I learned in Little League Basketball

There really are only about four kinds of basketball players:

1) The scrappy point guard who knows how to handle the ball and has his favorite players with whom he'll share it. If one of those players isn't open, he keeps the ball for himself until he drives himself into a corner with four opponents fighting him for it.

2) The obedient child strictly follows the coach's orders. 'The coach said this was my spot, so this is my spot. No dad, I have to stand right there . . . the coach said so.' The obedient child is so worried about staying in his little spot that he never runs out to meet the ball and rarely gets open. Yet, he just can't figure out why nobody will throw him the ball.

3) The hustler. This player doesn't hold back. If there's a ball out there, he's diving for it. He's racking up fouls. He's thinking with his heart. He acts first, thinks later and sometimes that means he's diving for a ball that an opponent just tipped out of bounds. He's so busy acting, he doesn't realize that some balls you just have to let go.

4) The natural is the child who makes basketball look effortless. He swishes shots from the outside and drives down the court to score the winning points. Of course, the scrappy point guard loves to pass him the ball. All goes right in the world of the natural.

These same types of players are the same types of people you'll encounter in life.

(http://marniep.typepad.com/gratitude/2008/01/everything-i-ne.html (accessed 29 March 2008))

Text 7.9 Analog and digital technology

Can you explain the basic difference between analog and digital technology?

In analog technology, a wave is recorded or used in its original form. So, for example, in an <u>analog tape recorder</u>, a signal is taken straight from the <u>microphone</u> and laid onto tape. The wave from the microphone is an analog wave, and therefore the wave on the tape is analog as well. That wave on the tape can be read, amplified and sent to a <u>speaker</u> to produce the sound.

In digital technology, the analog wave is sampled at some interval, and then turned into numbers that are stored in the digital device. On a <u>CD</u>, the sampling rate is 44,000 samples per second. So on a CD, there are 44,000 numbers stored per second of music. To hear the music, the numbers are turned into a voltage wave that approximates the original wave.

(http://entertainment.howstuffworks.com/question7.htm (accessed 29 March 2008))

While, in general, the labels for the generic stages adequately reflect what is occurring in the different parts of Texts 7.7–7.9, you may question whether 'issue' accurately captures what is going on in the opening stage of Text 7.7. The speaker (a university lecturer) is, in a sense, setting out a discussion task and advising students on how to approach the task, i.e. to focus on the outcomes rather than aims in order to judge the success of the Cuban Revolution. However, in so doing, he is setting up the controversial issue that he wants students to consider. The various speakers then proceed to provide evidence of (in this extract) success. In this particular discussion, the argument concerning health is quite protracted, and one could argue that there are two related but distinct dimensions of the healthcare argument: that it is, 1) free at the point of delivery, and 2) an exporter of doctors. Also note that, given the open-ended nature of the discussion (and the fact that this is merely an extract from a much longer text), there is no position stage.

In Text 7.9, notice that, because the question essentially required an explanation of two different phenomena, we have distinguished the two explanation sequences.

7.5 Generic stages and lexicogrammatical patterns

So far we have largely considered texts from the perspective of the different generic stages language users move through and their overall lexicogrammatical patterns. In a narrative genre, for example, a writer moves through the four stages of orientation, complication, evaluation, and resolution, and across all these stages key lexicogrammatical features are past tense, temporal adjuncts, and third person pronouns. In a taxonomic report genre, in contrast, a writer moves through the stages of identification of phenomenon and classification, and description of types, featuring present tense and generic nominal groups.

Lexicogrammatical patterns are also influenced by the different kinds of meaning that are made within generic stages: as one stage finishes and another begins, discernable shifts in meaning typically entail some change in the lexicogrammatical patterning. We began to explore this in Activity 7.6, where we identified the lexicogrammatical patterns of different genre stages. To explore this further, return to Text 7.7 (*The Cuban revolution*) and look at the movement from issue to argument 1 and the transition from argument 1 to argument 2. Equally, in Text 7.9 (*Analog and digital technology*), consider the shift from identification of phenomenon to explanation sequence. Do you notice any significant shifts in the language patterns as the writer moves from one stage to another?

In Text 7.7, in the issue stage, the nominal groups are abstract and at a high level of generality (*the success in terms of outcomes not aims*), whereas, in the argument stages, in order to provide evidence of outcomes, the nominal groups refer to more specific phenomena – *healthcare* and *education*. In turn, particular aspects of healthcare (e.g. *free system*, *export of doctors*) and education (e.g. *literacy levels*) are used as examples of successful outcomes. You may also have noticed that the arguments are staged, both through the use of verbs that have a temporal dimension, and through temporal adjuncts:

> *i think we're looking at you know healthcare <u>to start with</u>* (verb) <u>*now*</u>
> (temporal adjunct)
>
> *i think that <u>leads us on to</u>* (verb) *education the success of the education*

In Text 7.9, which comes from an Internet 'question and answer' site, the identification of phenomenon is expressed as a question reflecting other aspects of the text's context, namely the mode (interactive) and tenor (social roles: novice to expert):

Can you explain the difference between analog and digital technology?

The two explanation sequences consist of a series of declarative statements that explain how the two technologies work. The explanations are short, and so the temporal and causal connectors are minimal. Nevertheless, these are an important part of the explanation. They include *therefore, then, so, to* (implying *in order to*).

Shifts in meaning and therefore language patterns are helpful criteria for distinguishing generic stages. Let's consider this in relation to one more text – Text 7.3 (*British journalism*), the sample discussion genre, taken from a message board. What do you notice about the issue stage?

Is British journalism really sloppy and morally bankrupt?

Polar interrogative was first introduced in Chapter 1.

It consists of a question (expressed by a polar interrogative) that invites either agreement or disagreement. Of course, not all issue stages in all discussion genres use an interrogative to put forward an issue. However, it is often the case that the proposition to be debated is put forward in a way that opens up the topic for debate, through use of either modals or interrogatives.

In the arguments for and arguments against stages of a discussion genre, the claims put forward (in the form of declaratives) may be more or less modalised. In Text 7.3, some claims are tentative, with the contributors 'hedging' their views through the use of epistemic modality and other linguistic devices:

I can say that I feel the BBC is sloppy, particularly when it comes to scientific issues.

Other claims are quite categorical:

The BBC is the worst of the lot in terms of presenting news with a particular ideological slant

Some statements, but by no means all, are supported by evidence. The contributor below offers a hyperlink to a BBC news story as evidence of their sloppiness in scientific areas. Whereas, in a formal essay, the lexicogrammar generally makes explicit the relationship of exemplification between general claim and specific evidence, through formal connectors such as *for example* and *for instance*, owing to the more spoken-like mode of the message board, the writer uses the more informal *Take:*

> *I can say that I feel the BBC is sloppy, particularly when it comes to scientific areas. Take the story below:*
> **news.bbc.co.uk/1/hi/ . . .**

There are, of course, other lexicogrammatical features we could focus on, and we will return to the relationship of genre, generic stages, and lexico-grammar as we continue to build functional grammatical terms and explore language from a meaning-making perspective throughout Chapters 8–10.

7.6 Genre specialisation

So far we have considered a relatively small number of genres, which, for the most part, reflect social purposes forming part of many individuals' genre repertoires, no matter which culture they may be located in or indeed which language they speak (although there may be some cross-cultural variation in the staging and in the lexicogrammatical resources within the stages). In any one culture, however, there are a myriad of genres relating to the diverse range of communities that exist in that culture. How many of these a citizen needs to be familiar with depends very much on their professional goals and/or personal needs. For example, primary school teachers in a number of countries are expected to be familiar with a set of what are often referred to as 'elemental' (basic) genres that form part of the national or state literacy and language curricula. These comprise:

Cross-cultural variation in generic stages is an area we will explore in Chapter 8.

- personal recount
- narrative
- procedure
- explanation
- discussion
- argument.[3]

Some language observers (such as genre analysts, teachers, and vocational trainers) may need expertise in analysing more specialised genres (the 'legal judgement' in Section 7.3, for instance, or the 'patent' that you came across in Chapter 2). One useful way of capturing the specialised nature of genres is to create increasingly delicate classifications. That is, rather than simply classify a text as an explanation or procedure genre, it is possible to go a step further in delicacy by specifying the type of explanation or procedure. This is an area that is beyond the scope of this book. However, there has been considerable research into specialised genres (in a wide range of educational and workplace settings), which has involved the mapping of genre 'families' in order to look at similarities and differences within and among genre groupings (such as different types of recount). You may wish to use the 'Bookend: further reading' list at the end of the book to follow up on studies relevant to your professional or personal interests.

7.7 Using genre analysis to explore real-world problems

In this section, we return to the opening scenario in this chapter where we suggested that the letter of complaint was unlikely to be successful, partly because of the way it was organised. We will show how genre can be a useful tool for diagnosing and pinpointing problems that are to do with the way that a text is structured.

At this point we need to introduce two new conventions used in the analysis of generic stages – the use of angle brackets < > to indicate that a stage can occur more than once, and an asterisk* to indicate stages whose position in the text are not predictable. (Note that in the context of grammatical analysis these have different meanings: an asterisk refers to anything that is regarded as ungrammatical, and angle brackets indicate ellipsis.)

Typically, a letter of complaint moves through the following stages:

<contact details>

salutation

aim of letter

identification of complaint

elaboration of complaint

demand for action

<(compliment)>*

(recommendation)

conditional threat

salutation

(distribution of copies)

Activity 7.8

Use the generic structure set out above to analyse the following text. Consider whether the writer is likely to have been successful in obtaining compensation.

Text 7.10 A huge mistake

October 1, 2004

Mr S Brown
President
Brown Travel Agency
111 Main Street
Waston, PA 42111

Dear Mr Brown,

After successfully using your agency for many years, I recently experienced a terrible problem. I am writing to obtain compensation for a huge mistake for which I believe your firm is responsible.

On September 1, 2000, I used Brown Travel to book my honeymoon trip to Hawaii. Your agent, Caroline Drindale, made all of the arrangements for us. She booked my husband and I on the American Airlines flight to Honolulu (Flight 444) on September 14, which was scheduled to arrive at 6 am on the morning of September 15. Our timely arrival was essential, as we were scheduled to participate in a tour group which began its journey on the afternoon of September 15.

Upon our arrival at the San Francisco Airport, we discovered that our reservations had not been confirmed and the airline had overbooked the flight. Sadly, we were unable to get seats on the plane, which was the last American Airlines flight to Hawaii that day. We were reluctant to book seats on another airline, as we had already paid for this trip in full, using a Visa card (account #4494 2296 8939 7121). Our card was charged, yet we had no flight. Unfortunately, our credit limit was inadequate to book a different flight on another airline.

The bottom-line: we missed our flight to Hawaii, along with our tour group's departure in Honolulu. Instead of lying on a tranquil beach, we spent our first married days in the Airport Hilton in San Franciso, trying to sort out this mess. We were unable to speak with Ms Drindale until Monday, September 16, which was two days after our scheduled departure. She was extremely apologetic, but could not explain what had caused the problem. She was unable to book us on an alternative flight to Hawaii on such short notice, but did offer to clear our credit card of all charges. She offered us no further explanations or compensation.

My husband and I are both livid. We planned this trip for over a year and were excited about visiting Hawaii on our honeymoon. Ms Drindale's mistake cost us our once-in-a-lifetime chance to fulfill a significant personal dream. In fact, we not only missed the trip; we are still fighting to recover our deposits at the hotel in Honolulu!

Because your agency caused the problems, we expect you to work with us to obtain a satisfactory resolution. Specfically, we expect you to:

1)) Verify that our Visa card has been credited for the $4539 we paid for the aborted honeymoon trip
2) Reimburse us for the $560 in deposits we are unable to recover from the Honolulu Sheraton Islander Hotel
3) Reimburse us for the two nights we spent stranded at the San Francisco Airport Hilton ($347)
4) Provide us with two first class round-trip tickets on a flight to Hawaii which will be good for the next calendar year (dates of travel to be our choice)

Your agency can't give us back our wedding trip, but we expect you to provide a future trip comparable to the one we were denied because of your booking mistake. We also expect a full apology from Ms Drindale and assurance that she takes responsibility for her error.

From our experience, this situation was a dramatic let down from the superlative service that we usually receive from Brown Travel. In fact, we have always been loyal to your firm because of the exemplary treatment we have received from you and your attentive staff. We suggest that you coach Ms Drindale in proper booking procedures and in customer relations. Her behavior does not reflect positively on Brown Travel.

Please call me before October 15 with confirmation that our requests will be honored. If I don't hear from you, I will report you to the appropriate regulatory agencies in California and Hawaii.

Sincerely,

Jill Moor
111 Walnut Street
Avondale, PA 43211
717–555–7777

cc: Better Business Bureau
      American Society of Travel Agents
      US Department of Transportation: Consumer Affairs Division
      Federal Aviation Authority: Consumer Protection Division
      Office of Consumer Protection: State Office of the Attorney General

(http://www.savvychicks.com/samplecomplain.html (accessed 10 January 2008))

Although it could be argued that Text 7.10 is longer than would normally be recommended for a letter of complaint, a genre analysis reveals that the letter writer worked through a number of stages that, in combination, increase the chances of a successful outcome. In fact, according to information on the website where the complaint letter was posted, the author received everything she asked for (items 1–4 above)!

Activity 7.9

Using the set of labels provided on pages 268–9 (for the generic structure of a successful complaint letter), carry out an analysis of Text 7.1 (*Letter of complaint*). You will find that you will not be able to use all the labels, and there will be some parts of the letter that do not seem to match any of the labels. In this way, you will be able to diagnose some of the problems with the letter's text structure and consider how its organisation could be improved.

The analysis in the Answer key reveals that there are a number of stages missing in the letter. There is no *aim of letter*, no *demand for action*, no *compliment*, and no *recommendation*. The absence of these stages represents a serious weakness – without a demand for action or recommendation, what the writer hopes to achieve is not sufficiently specific. Therefore it would be possible for the recipient not to act, or to act in a way that was not satisfactory to the letter writer. The absence of a compliment stage is less problematic, although, as you will see in Chapter 9, the interpersonal dimension of human interactions often plays a pivotal role in the success and effectiveness of a text.

Aside from missing stages, there is also the inappropriate inclusion of a recount of events stage that serves no clear purpose in relation to the overall goal of the writer. Its positioning as first stage in the letter also distracts from the main purpose.

The ability to write an effective complaint and obtain some kind of resolution or compensation is an important aspect of living in a society where citizens have some control over events around them. If you are a teacher, making explicit to students the way such a letter (or indeed any genre) is structured and organised can help support and guide their writing. Below are some other areas in which genre analysis may play a useful role. From your own experience, can you add any of relevance to your professional or personal context?

1   What are some of the problems students have in producing well-structured essays or other types of written text across different subjects or disciplines (e.g. in school history, undergraduate sociology, business report writing)?

2   Why are some letters of complaint or application ineffective? Do organisation and structure play a role? Is there a cross-cultural dimension?

3   Why do some discussions lack direction?

7.8 Summary

In this chapter we have looked at the relationship between context and grammar from the perspective of social purpose. You have seen how social purposes such as *telling a story*, *explaining how something works*, or *discussing an issue* affect the way a text is structured and the lexicogrammatical patterns that occur across and within its different stages. Within SFL, these differences are systematically identified and described through genre names and genre stages. Although it is beyond the scope of this chapter to cover all the genres that have been researched to date, we have explored most of the elemental genres, as well as one or two of the more specialised academic and workplace/ professional genres. You may like to elaborate the following list in the manner of Table 7.2 by way of review:

Elemental genres

personal recount

narrative

taxonomic report

procedure

explanation

discussion

More specialised academic genres

biographical recount

More specialised workplace genres

legal judgement

Others

letter of complaint

7.9 Answer key

Activity 7.3

The purpose of the image and the text it belongs to (see below) is to explain how falling stars are formed.

What causes a falling star?

At certain times of year, you are likely to see a great number of meteors in the night sky. These events are called meteor showers and they occur when the Earth passes through the trail of debris left by a comet as it orbits the Sun. [. . .]

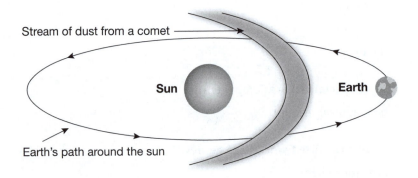

The dust and rocks that cause meteor showers come primarily from the Earth passing through the debris stream left behind by a comet as it orbits the Sun. Usually, the Earth's orbit and the comet's orbit are slightly tilted relative to one another. So the paths only intersect on one side!

(http://starchild.gsfc.nasa.gov/docs/StarChild/questions/question12.html (accessed 17 August 2007))

Activity 7.4

(A)   Resolution

(B)   Complication

(C)   Evaluation

(D)   Orientation

Grammatical patterns:

*   past tense (*began, was, ran*, etc.)

*   past perfect and progressive aspect (*had dropped, was beginning*)

*   dependent clauses of time (*when the snow rose to head height, when she saw the temperature had dropped*)

*   third person pronouns (*she, he, they*)

Activity 7.5

Text segment	Genre
A	personal recount
B	discussion
C	biographical recount
D	discussion
E	procedure
F	case judgement

Activity 7.6

Text segment	Stage of text	Grammatical evidence
B	position	present tense
		absence of pronouns apart from *their* (third person possessive pronoun)
		declarative mood
		dense nominal groups with pre- and postmodifiers
C	record of events (1–n)	temporal adjuncts
		use of third person pronoun – *he*
		declarative mood

		note the use of historic present rather than the more typical past tense (to give immediacy to events even though they are set in the past)
D	issue	mainly present tense
		first and third person pronouns
		mainly interrogatives
		deontic modality *should/n't*
E	steps	present tense
		(implied) second person reference
		imperative mood
F	relevant law	present tense
		third person pronouns
		declarative mood
		use of conditional clauses
		epistemic (*may*) and deontic (*shall*) modality

Activity 7.7: Analysing generic structure

Text 7.7

Discussion genre (*perspectives on whether the revolution was successful*)

Grammatical features: modality (e.g. the modal verb *might* and other phrases such as *I think, not sure, maybe*, which indicate degrees of certainty and uncertainty – an area discussed further in Chapter 8).

Generic structure

Issue (*i.e. the success of the Cuban revolution*)

sm5087: you got to look you got to look at outcomes as well not what they set out not what they actually said that's not what you've got to judge the revolution on you've got to judge the revolution on the impact it's had on the people not what the impact it's had on the original aims you can't i mean yeah that's a useful historical exercise but the important thing to look at is the success in terms of outcomes not aims
sm5086: and those are

Argument 1 (*i.e. the health system as evidence of success*)

sm5087: the outcomes are very useful link there er i think we're looking at you know healthcare to start with now er you know healthcare in Cuba is free at the point of delivery which is true in this country but it's not true in America far from being free at the point of delivery now that's a it's actually a very helpful very very progressive er system and we've also got it's a net exporter of doctors which is quite an impressive statistic for such of a sort of a

sm5087: yes it's a net exporter of doctors and it's also a trainer of the rest of the [. . .]

Argument 2 (*i.e. the education system as evidence of success*)

sm5086: i think that leads us on to education the success of the education the scientific and technical success of the education system the literary success

sm5087: yeah we've got twenty to twelve per cent was the change in that three years in literacy rates in Cuba [. . .]

Text 7.8

Taxonomic report genre

Grammatical features: present tense, generic nominal groups (e.g. *basketball players*) in which the heads are elaborated through pre- and postmodifiers (e.g. *The <u>scrappy</u> point guard <u>who knows how to handle the ball and has his favorite players with whom he'll share it</u>*).

Generic structure

Identification of phenomenon and classification

There really are only about four kinds of basketball players:

Description of type 1

1) The scrappy point guard who knows how to handle the ball and has his favorite players [. . .]

Description of type 2

2) The obedient child strictly follows the coach's orders. 'The coach said this was my spot, so this is my spot. [. . .]

Description of type 3

3) The hustler. This player doesn't hold back. If there's a ball out there, he's diving for it. He's racking up fouls. [. . .]

Description of type 4

4) The natural is the child who makes basketball look effortless. [. . .]

(http://marniep.typepad.com/gratitude/2008/01/everything-i-ne.html (accessed 29 March 2008))

Text 7.9

Explanation genre

Grammatical features: temporal and causal connectors (e.g. *therefore, then, so, to* (implying *in order to*), present tense, low frequency of personal pronouns.

Generic structure

Identification of phenomenon

Can you explain the basic difference between analog and digital technology?

Explanation sequence 1

In analog technology, a wave is recorded or used in its original form. So, for example, in an <u>analog tape recorder,</u> [. . .]

Explanation sequence 2

In digital technology, the analog wave is sampled at some interval, and then turned into numbers that are stored in the digital device. [. . .]

(http://entertainment.howstuffworks.com/question7.htm)

Activity 7.8

Generic structure

October 1, 2004

Contact details
Mr S. Brown
President
Brown Travel Agency
111 Main Street
Waston, PA 42111

Salutation
Dear Mr Brown,

Compliment
After successfully using your agency for many years,

Aim of letter
I recently experienced a terrible problem. I am writing to obtain compensation for a huge mistake for which I believe your firm is responsible.

Identification of complaint
On September 1, 2000, I used Brown Travel to book my honeymoon trip to Hawaii. Your agent, Caroline Drindale, made all of the arrangements for us. She booked

my husband and I on the American Airlines flight to Honolulu (Flight 444) on September 14, which was scheduled to arrive at 6 am on the morning of September 15. Our timely arrival was essential, as we were scheduled to participate in a tour group which began its journey on the afternoon of September 15.

[. . .]

Elaboration of complaint

My husband and I are both livid. We planned this trip for over a year and were excited about visiting Hawaii on our honeymoon. Ms Drindales's mistake cost us our once-in-a-lifetime chance to fulfill a significant personal dream. In fact, we not only missed the trip; we are still fighting to recover our deposits at the hotel in Honolulu!

Demand for action

Because your agency caused the problems, we expect you to work with us to obtain a satisfactory resolution. Specifically, we expect you to:

1) Verify that our Visa card has been credited for the $4539 we paid for the aborted honeymoon trip
2) Reimburse us for the $560 in deposits we are unable to recover from the Honolulu Sheraton Islander Hotel

[. . .]

Compliment

From our experience, this situation was a dramatic let down from the superlative service that we usually receive from Brown Travel. In fact, we have always been loyal to your firm because of the exemplary treatment we have received from you and your attentive staff.

Recommendation

We suggest that you coach Ms Drindale in proper booking procedures and in customer relations. Her behavior does not reflect positively on Brown Travel.

Conditional threat

Please call me before October 15 with confirmation that our requests will be honored. If I don't hear from you, I will report you to the appropriate regulatory agencies in California and Hawaii.

Salutation

Sincerely,

Contact details

Jill Moor
111 Walnut Street

Avondale, PA 43211
717–555–7777

Distribution of copies
cc: Better Business Bureau
[. . .]

Activity 7.9

Generic structure

(Notice non-typical stages are in capitals)

Salutation
Dear Sir

RECOUNT OF EVENTS

I am one of a party of 35 Israeli tourists that were processed by employee Carla from Air X, on October 28, 2005, at 7.00 am, at terminal T2, counters 402–3.

Due to circumstances beyond our control, we only got to the counter at 7 am, while the flight was supposed to take off at 7:10. We are still investigating who is to blame, but this in NOT the subject of my complaint.

Identification of complaint

The subject is the incredibly rude behavior of your employee Carla.

Elaboration of complaint

I politely asked her to call her supervisor, in order to delay the flight. After all, we were 35 people, without luggage (since we were in transit), and the time was 7 am.

Carla told me that 'the flight is already closed'. However, i told her, this is at least 1/3 of the plane capacity we are talking about (35 people), and the fact that the flight is closed is not an act of God, but a human decision – one that can, and should, be cancelled.

[. . .]

Conditional threat

We strongly doubt we will continue using the services of Air X, if no measures are taken against problematic employees such as this young lady. Is she really the highest in command there? Was the plane early in its takeoff? Is she exempt from wearing a name tag? Does she really not have a last name?

I doubt it . . .

Conditional threat

Please keep me informed about the measures taken regarding this employee. We all wish to avoid a law suit.

Salutation

Best regards

Dr E

Contact details

cell phone +972-xxx

Notes

1   Bear in mind that you may find the same genres called by other names in other contexts. For example, in some educational contexts, the terms **description** or **classification** may be used rather than taxonomic report.
2   1–n means that a stage can be repeated any number of times.
3   Aside from the argument genre, this chapter has examined all the elemental genres. The argument genre is a one-sided argument in which an overarching thesis stage is supported through a series of supporting argument stages and optionally reinforced through a reinforcement of position stage.

eight

Representing the world

8.1 Introduction

Scenario

Below, an adult man talks about a holiday he particularly enjoyed on the Gold Coast (a famous beach resort in Queensland, Australia). How would you characterise his description of the holiday?

You will probably have viewed the speaker's description as somewhat incoherent, and you may have been surprised by the absence of any detailed description or opinion (particularly given that this was a holiday the speaker had particularly enjoyed). The verbs he uses are relatively simple. In some clauses, the choice of verb is puzzling (*I'd like the kids out*), and the tense often switches, seemingly for no reason, from past to present. The nominal groups are relatively unelaborated, with virtually no pre- or postmodification, although determiners (either articles or quantifiers) are used (*the pool, the kids, some fun*). In some cases, it is not clear what pronouns such as *it* are referring to, and in other cases the noun seems to be 'made up', e.g. *kelevans*,

Text 8.1 The Gold Coast

That (–) up the Gold Coast . . . good one yeah . . . pick on that one . .
. what we did with the kids . . . Mum did . . . went and played . . . we
did things . . . uh . . . went to . . . the pool went swimming and walks .
. . get into things . . . we'd get I'd like the kids out and make 'em like
kelevans . . . kids on kids . . . and they like to get out and make junks
. . . make things make a giant (–) . . . gotta get out and do it . . . kids
(–) we get away by ourselves . . . go out and uh . . . play silly buggers
and play around a lot . . . we have some fun that way

(Armstrong, E., Ferguson, A., Mortensen, L., and Togher, L. (2005) 'Acquired language disorders: some
functional insights', in Hasan, R., Matthiessen, C., and Webster, J.J. (eds) *Continuing Discourse on
Language: A functional perspective*, vol. 1, pp. 383–413, p. 387)

junks. The repeated use of *things* does not help to clarify or give precision to
the actions and events being discussed.

All the problems identified above arise in a type of brain injury referred
to as aphasia. Aphasia has particular consequences for how speakers
represent the world around them, in other words how they make ideational
meanings. In the scenario above, the speaker suffered a stroke one month
prior to the recording and, as a result of aphasia, had considerable difficulty
in producing a description of his holiday.

Difficulties in producing clear and effective representations of the
world are not restricted to those suffering from brain injuries. They could
be connected to problems in acquiring a first language, as with Paul in
Chapter 1, or in learning a second one, or simply (for whatever reason) not
having sufficient control over linguistic resources for representing events
effectively. By the end of the chapter, you will see how SFG analysis can be
used as a diagnostic tool to identify some of the difficulties speakers may
experience in using language to represent the world around them, and we
will return to Text 8.1 to do a more systematic analysis.

In particular, we will focus on the linguistic resources that function,
at clause level, to represent 'who does what, to whom, where'. Rather than

The SVOCA clause
elements were
introduced in
Chapter 1.

simply use the traditional labels of SVOCA to break up clauses, we will introduce some of the functional terms used within SFG and see how they illuminate language users' representations of the world. Given SFG's focus on lexis as well as grammar, we will also consider the role of specialised terms in building less common-sense representations.

8.2 Ideational meaning: a systemic functional perspective

One reason for using functional labels is that they can help to reveal language users' particular ways of viewing the world – their 'angle of representation'. A formal analysis would not reveal this. In order to see how functional labels can provide this type of illumination, consider the following sentences:

(a)   Traditionally, fishermen used to catch 100,000 tons of fish per year in the North Sea.

(b)   The North Sea used to provide 100,000 tons of fish per year.

These are two representations of the same 'slice' of reality, i.e. *fishing in the North Sea*. In sentence (a) you can see that there is an action initiated by *fishermen*, the subject in traditional grammar, which functions as the agent in this example, i.e. the person or people doing the action. You can also see that the natural world is referred to in a prepositional phrase – *in the North Sea* – functioning as what is called a **circumstance** in SFG. Sentence (b), in contrast, provides a representation where the natural world is the agent. Here, the natural world is <u>not</u> relegated to the role of circumstance, and there is no human agent.

The two sentences illustrate how grammatical choices may be related to different ways of viewing the world and how functional labelling makes this prominent. Sentence (a), for example, could readily be tied to a perspective where people operate on nature, where nature is somehow separate from humans. Such a perspective could help to legitimise humans' domination of nature, taking 'resources' from it. Nature is just a 'place' where people obtain what they need. Representations such as sentence (b), in contrast, place nature instead of humans in a focal position and move away from the idea that humans dominate and exploit nature. With the first representation, questions may arise such as: *Why don't fishermen catch so much fish anymore? Is it something to do with the fishing industry? Are there fewer fishermen these days?* With the second representation, questions are perhaps more likely to be focused on nature rather than humans; for example: *What's the problem with the North Sea? Why doesn't the North Sea yield so much fish anymore?* These questions show concern over the effects of the domination and consumption of nature. Different representations thus provide different orientations to the natural world.

As we discussed in Chapter 6, one of the three primary functions of language is to enable users to represent the world. Within SFG, this function is referred to as the ideational metafunction. In Chapter 6 we discussed the relationship between the ideational metafunction and the contextual variable of field. Figure 8.1 serves as a review. You will note in the diagram the inclusion of conjunctions (e.g. *so*, *then*). Although they are not a major focus of this chapter, you should note that conjunctions serve to express very general logical relations, such as time or cause, and are an aspect of ideational meaning.

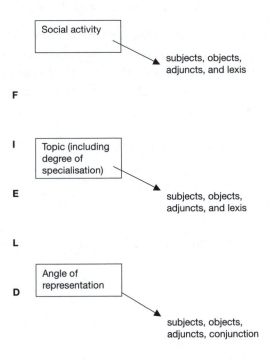

Figure 8.1

Resources for representing the world

8.3 Representing the world: who does what to whom in what circumstances

Activity 8.1

A person suffering from aphasia (whom we shall call Mr X) wrote a 'picture description' genre in response to a task set by a speech therapist. The picture he was asked to describe, together with his description (with clauses numbered 1–8), is shown in Figure 8.2. Such a task is commonly used by speech therapists/ pathologists to assess a patient's language abilities.

Read Mr X's description and consider what insights it offers into his ability to represent what is going on. In order to guide and systematise your observations, use the table below to analyse each numbered clause using the following functional labels. These labels, which replace the traditional ones of subject, verb, object, and adjunct, will be explained in Section 8.5:

(a) **Participants:** Who or what is involved in the event or situation? (Use your knowledge of subjects and objects to help you.)

(b) **Processes:** What is the action or event or relationship presented in the clause? (Use your knowledge of verbal groups to help you.)

(c) **Circumstances:** What kind of information are we given about the situation surrounding the process, e.g. Where is the event occurring (location in space)? When is it occurring (location in time)? Why did it occur (cause)? And how did it occur (manner)? (Use your knowledge of prepositional phrases to help you.)

If a process is missing, mark it with a dash, as in the examples already shown below.

Table 8.1

	Circumstance/s	Participant	Process	Participant	Circumstance/s
1		a cat	–		on shelf in wall (location)
2					

	Circumstance/s	Participant	Process	Participant	Circumstance/s
3					
4					
5					
6					
7					
8	*on a low shelf* (location)		–		*loudspeaker and stereo*

Text 8.2 Picture description

Figure 8.2

Picture description task

1   A cat on shelf in wall.
2   The cat . . . goldfish in the disk
3   The cat . . . books
4   A man is sleeping in a armchair
5   His feet on the table
6   A book on shelf
7   A boy on the floor carry a dinky car
8   On a low shelf there loudspeaker and stereo.

(Swinburn *et al.* (2004); unpublished data, Black (2008), personal communication)

In some ways Activity 8.1 is relatively straightforward. Despite the fact that some clausal elements are missing (namely the verbal groups) and some lexical items inaccurate (e.g. *disk* for *dish*), you were probably able to pick out most of the participants, processes (where they occurred), and circumstances. In so doing you were conducting what is referred to in SFG as a **transitivity analysis**. That is, you were analysing the components of language that function to represent 'who does what, to whom, where, when, and how'. A transitivity analysis thus reveals how the world is represented.

Based on your analysis you will have seen that some patterns emerge:

- the majority of processes are missing;
- the majority of clauses have only one participant;[1]
- most circumstances provide information about spatial location.

These patterns indicate that one of the main problems with Mr X's description is that participants and circumstances are disconnected from one another. Thus, while the circumstances provide relatively precise information about spatial location (e.g. *on a low shelf*), there are no processes (such as *are placed*) to relate these circumstances to the different entities (e.g. the *loudspeaker and stereo*). Similarly, there is an absence of processes linking participants. For instance, the writer does not create a connection between the cat and the goldfish, or the cat, the books, and the man who is sleeping. The picture that emerges is a static one – the situation remains unchanged because, although entities exist, they are not connected to one another and do not act on one another. The question arises as to why the writer does not create more explicit connections between things. Why does he fail to build a more dynamic model of the world by, for example, representing participants (such as *the cat*) acting on (*trying to catch*, for instance) other participants (*the goldfish*)? Why does he break up and categorise events in the way that he does?

Such questions are hard to answer in the case of language disorders such as aphasia (they require some understanding of complex neurological processes for a start). They do, however, get us thinking about the choices we have for breaking up and categorising experience, how people typically do this, and the kinds of problem that occur when they don't or can't. Mr X's relatively ineffective representation, for example, gives us insights into the role (and significance) of processes.

In many ways, the process is the most important component of the clause: the hub around which other information clusters. As you have seen, without processes there is little sense of anything going on. However, most processes require at least one participant in order to occur at all, and so participants are also important. Circumstances, on the other hand, are more peripheral. They are often not essential to an understanding of what is occurring, although they always contribute to an overall framing of the event under discussion. Figure 8.3 illustrates this point.

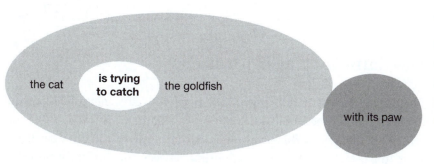

the cat **is trying to catch** the goldfish

with its paw

Figure 8.3

Representing an experience: processes, participants, and circumstances

In sum, we can see that, in combination, processes, participants, and circumstances are key components in allowing us to break up and categorise events. They enable English speakers, as Halliday puts it, 'to build a mental picture of reality, to make sense of what goes on around them and inside them' (1994: 107). All experienced English users, in other words, decompose the constant and continuous flow of events into a process + participant form when they want to communicate it. As Halliday explains:

Imagine that we are out in the open air and that there is movement overhead. Perceptually the phenomenon is all of a piece; but when we talk about it we analyse it as a semantic configuration – something which we express as, say, *birds are flying in the sky*. This is not the only possible way of organizing such a fragment of experience; we might have turned it into a meaning structure – 'semanticized' it, so to speak – quite differently. We might have said something like *it's winging*; after all, we say *it's raining*, without analysing the process into components, although it would be quite possible to do so – many languages represent the phenomenon of rain as 'water is falling' and there is in fact one dialect of Chinese which represents the phenomenon of rain as 'the sky is dropping water'. In English, there are a few processes, like raining, which are left unanalysed; but more typically the English language structures such experience as a semantic configuration on the principle illustrated above, consisting of process, participants and (optionally) circumstantial elements. So in this instance we have a process *are flying*, a participant *birds*, and a circumstantial element *in the sky*. In this interpretation of what is going on, there is a doing, a doer, and a location where the doing takes place.

(2004: 175)

8.4 Function and form

In carrying out Activity 8.1, you may have noticed something about the relationship between functional categories and grammatical form. If you did not, look again at the table you produced and see if you can now detect one. In particular, notice the relationship between the formal categories of nominal groups, verbal groups, and prepositional phrases, and the functional categories of participants, processes, and circumstances.

All the participants map fairly closely on to the traditional categories of subject and object, and are encoded or **realised** by nominal groups (e.g. *a man*, *a boy on the floor*). The processes (where they occur) are realised by verbal groups (e.g. *is sleeping*). The circumstances (e.g. *in an armchair*) are realised by prepositional phrases. These forms (nominal groups, verbal groups, and prepositional phrases) are the most straightforward, natural, or **congruent** way to express the functional elements.

As you gain more practice in analysing language, you will find that breaking a clause into participants, processes, and circumstances will help you to identify the formal structures of nominal and verbal groups and prepositional phrases. Equally, you may find these formal categories helpful when trying to identify participants, processes, and circumstances. Either way, the most important point is to recognise that clauses are made up of chunks that can be separated out – either functionally, if the meaning-making dimension is of primary interest, or formally if the structural dimension is the focus. In SFG, it is, of course, the functional dimension that takes priority, but, as we have pointed out elsewhere, form still plays an important role. A clause analysis can bring the two together as follows:

The cat	is trying to catch	the goldfish in the bowl	with its paw
det. noun	finite + non- lexical finite verb verb	det. noun postmodifier	prep. det. noun
Nominal group	Verbal group	Nominal group	Prepositional phrase
Subject	Verb	Object	Adjunct
Participant	Process	Participant	Circumstance

You may be somewhat surprised that *in the bowl* is not categorised as a circumstance, given that it provides information about location. The test question is, however, whether it gives information about the situation surrounding the process, e.g. where the process is occurring.

In the bowl is in fact a postmodifier in the nominal group, with *goldfish* as the head noun. It is telling us more about the goldfish. Therefore it is part of the participant. To help distinguish circumstances from postmodifiers that form part of a participant, it is helpful to use the following tests:

Is the prepositional phrase (in this case, *in the bowl*) telling us more about the event or situation <u>as a whole</u> (e.g. the event in which the cat is doing something to the fish)? Or, is it telling us more about a participant (in this case *the goldfish*)?

Is it mobile, i.e. can it be detached from the nominal group?

Clearly, *in the bowl* is telling us more about the goldfish and therefore cannot be detached. If it was telling us more about the event as a whole, the cat would have to be wearing scuba gear!

Activity 8.2

Using the clause analysis above as a guide, draw a table to show the formal and functional components of the following four clauses.

He shot the stag with a rifle.
He shot the stag with the biggest antlers.
She bought a handbag with a black patent finish.
She bought a handbag with her last few euros.

8.5 Creating an angle on the world: participants, processes, and circumstances

Participants and processes

Activity 8.3

Look at Figure 8.2 again and, this time, write your own description. When you have finished, compare it with ours (in the Answer key). What do you think are the key differences in how the patient described the picture, how you described it, and how we did?

While we cannot predict the detail of your description, it is likely that it differed from ours in the choice of processes, participants, and circumstances. This is an important point. Essentially you, we, and the patient, all described the same piece of reality but made different language choices to do this. As discussed earlier, different choices in type (and number) of processes, participants, and circumstances create different 'angles on the world'. In our description, we used four different kinds of process, to encode action, physiological behaviour, relationships, and existence. SFG categorises such processes as follows:

Process type	Concerned with	Example
Material	doing and happening	*the books hit a man* . . .
Behavioural	physiological and psychological behaviour	*a man is sleeping* . . .
Relational	identifying and classifying	*the music system is rather old fashioned.*
Existential	things existing	*there is a child*

In our description, partly as a result of our choices in processes, we have drawn on different types of participant. Whereas, in traditional formal grammar, the terms subject and object cover all possible types of participant, SFG makes distinctions. Each process type is accompanied by different types of subject and object. For example, in material processes, there are participants that do things to other participants (known as agents, or sometimes as 'actors'):

> *He is pushing a car*
>
> agent

There are also participants who have things done to them (the **affected**, sometimes referred to as 'goal'):

> *He is pushing a car*
>
> affected

In behavioural processes, there are participants who engage in physiological behaviour (**behavers**):

> *A middle aged man is sleeping in an armchair*
>
> behaver

Finally there are participants that are related to one another (in relational processes)[2]:

_He_	_is_	_quite little_.
participant		participant

While participants in relational processes are generally realised as nominal groups, they may sometimes be expressed by an adjectival group, as in the example above – _He is quite little_. In traditional grammar, _quite little_ would be termed the complement.

Complements are
discussed in
Chapter 3.

The examples below show the range of participants associated with each of the process types we have encountered so far. Participants may be either human (_a child_) or non-human (_the music system_), and either generic (_the books_) or specific (_the man_).

In general (for the purposes of this introductory book), you need only be concerned with the central participants (you will find additional participants in more advanced SFG text books).

Processes	Central participants	Example
Material (action, doing)	agent, affected	_the books_ hit _the man_. agent affected _killer tiger_ bit _arm of zoo worker_ agent affected
Behavioural (physiological, psychological)	behaver	_a man_ is sleeping. behaver _the tiger_ sniffed at him behaver that night _the tiger_ roared. behaver
Existential (there is, there are)	existent	_there_[1] is _a child._ existent

	there remain only <u>*a few Caspian tigers*</u>
	existent
Relational	<u>*the music system*</u> *is* <u>*rather old*</u>
(having, being)	participant participant
	sometimes <u>*tigers*</u> *are* <u>*white*</u>.
	participant participant

Material clauses

By systematically identifying the processes and participants within a text, we begin to have a sense of how different choices in these linguistic resources create different world-views. For example, in our picture description (compared with the earlier one by Mr X), entities are linked together, and there is more 'going on'. In particular, the presence of material clauses means that people or things are 'doers' (i.e. agents): they act and do and, as a consequence, there are changes: the emerging account feels more dynamic. As Halliday (2004: 179) puts it:

> a material clause construes a quantum of change in the flow of events as taking place through some input of energy ... the source of the energy bringing about the change is typically the agent.

In some material clauses (i.e. clauses in which there is a material process), there may be only one participant, and the change (or 'happening') is confined to the agent; e.g.

<u>*the books*</u>   *fell down*

agent   material process

In traditional terms these are intransitive (SV) clauses.

Alternatively, the change may extend to the affected; e.g.

The books *hit*   <u>*a man.*</u>

agent   material process affected

The terms intransitive and transitive were briefly introduced in Chapter 2.

295

Using traditional terminology, this is a transitive (SVO) clause. Conceptually, the affected is the thing to which the process is directed.

Behavioural clauses

Aside from several material processes (all of which are transitive), our picture description also features a behavioural process:

> *The man*   *is sleeping.*
> behaver   behavioural process

Behavioural clauses represent processes of (typically human) physiological and psychological behaviour, such as *yawning, sneezing, laughing, dreaming,* and *staring.*

Relational clauses

Behavioural and material clauses are distinct from relational clauses in that relational clauses model experience in terms of *being* rather than *doing*, allowing us to characterise and identify. They enable us to generalise – to relate one fragment of experience to another: *this is one kind of x, this is the same as that.* For example:

> *The tiger (Panthera tigris)*   *is*   *a member of the Felidae family.*
> participant   relational process   participant

> *The tiger*   *is*   *the largest of all the cats.*
> participant   relational process   participant

Existential clauses

The fourth type of process in our picture description is existential. Existential processes typically use the verb *to be* and in this sense resemble relational clauses. However, unlike in relational clauses, there is only one participant – the existent.

| There | is | a *young child* . . . |
| | existential process | existent |

| There | is | *another shelf* . . . |
| | existential process | existent |

Now compare your choices of processes and participants and consider the effect of your choices and the particular 'angle on the world' that they represent.

Circumstances

So far, we have considered some different process types and their associated participants. We said earlier that circumstances are less central to the meaning of an event but nevertheless help to frame it. However, in certain genres, circumstances play a significant role. Can you think of any genres where this might be the case?

Activity 8.4

Text 8.3 is an example of a procedure genre and comes from a website that provides guidance, in the form of animated diagrams, on tying different types of knot. The goal of the text is to show viewers how to create the 'masthead knot mat', as illustrated in Figure 8.4. We have removed the circumstances from the text (and added in the clause boundaries). Consider the effect. Would you be able to tie the knot?

Figure 8.4

(for source, see Answer key)

Text 8.3 The masthead knot mat

||| Lay three loops . . . ||| Overlap them || and weave them . . . || so that each step locks the loops . . . ||| Pass the end . . . || using an over and under sequence. ||| Follow the end . . . || to complete the mat |||.

(For source, see Answer key)

Without the circumstances of location that are present in the full text (see the Answer key), this particular procedure would not achieve its goal. In other genres too, circumstances may play a key role in contributing to the text's meaning. Activity 8.5 provides further illustration.

Activity 8.5

The following two texts come from an Australian secondary school context, where eleven-year-old history students were learning how to write about the key events in their lives. Taking into account the context (particularly the field and social purpose) and focusing in particular on the use of circumstances of time, diagnose the strengths and weaknesses of each text.

Text 8.4 I was born . . .

I was born in a hospital in Burma. I was born at 9.00 am on Wednesday. I remember when all of my relatives were all crowding around me when my parents brought me home. they were saying how cute I was. I remember when my sister was born I use to always fight with her. I also remember my first birthday. I remember when I was 5 and I had to come to Australia. I was crying because I didn't want to leave my relatives. I also remembered that I had a big brother and sister but they had both died. My brother died when he was 7 because he had a car crash and my sister died when she was just born. I also remember when I started kindergarten I was so excited I was jumping up and down.

298   (Author's personal data)

Text 8.5 My Life by Virginia A

My Name is Virginia A. I was born in Burma at 9.00 am on Wednesday 9th April 1980. The following recount is about the most important events that happened in my life.

My earliest memory was the death of my brother and my sister. My brother died when he was seven in an car accident. My sister died when she was just born.

In 1985 it was a sad time for me because I left my relatives behind and came to Australia. I remember when they were all crying when we were at the airport. When we got on the plane I waved to them and started crying.

One year later I started kindergarten at Glebe Primary school. I was excited and was jumping up and down.

(Author's personal data)

You probably deduced that both the texts were written by the same child, Virginia. Whereas Text 8.4 was a first draft, Text 8.5 was produced as the final version of an assessment task after some intensive 'literacy-in-history' work by the class teacher and a literacy consultant. The purpose of the text was to record some important events in the writer's life, and so it can be classified as an autobiographical recount genre (with the generic structure of orientation, record of events, and reorientation). Within school history, a particularly important pedagogic use of autobiographical recounts is to introduce students to the historical use of time, time lines, and the chronological sequencing of events.

In Chapter 7 we came across two other types of recount genre – the personal recount and the biographical recount.

Given that the target genre was an autobiographical recount, the topic was history, and the social activity 'learning about history', you would probably judge the final version, Text 8.5, as more effective. One important reason is that, in the earlier draft, Virginia uses memory to project from the present into the past, and the main grammatical structure is _I remember_ plus what is called a projected clause (we will discuss this further in Section 8.6):

I remember <u>when all of my relatives were all crowding around me . . .</u>
projected clause

299

> *I remember <u>when my sister was born</u>*
>   projected clause

> *I remember <u>when I was 5</u>*
>   projected clause

In the final draft, in contrast, Virginia organises her text through circumstances of time (with several placed in first position in the clause – a point we will come back to in Chapter 10). As we noted earlier, circumstances are generally realised as prepositional phrases:

> *at 9.00 am on Wednesday 9th April 1980*

Temporal meanings can appear, not only as circumstances <u>within</u> a clause, but also as dependent clauses, with their own process and participant configuration; e.g.

> *My sister died when she was just born.*

> ||| *My sister died* || *<u>when</u>*   *<u>she</u>*   *<u>was just born</u>.* |||
>   temporal connector   participant   process
>   dependent clause

Dependent clauses are 'secondary' with respect to a main clause: they serve to supply supportive, background, or elaborating information. Those that function in similar ways to circumstances are sometimes referred to as **circumstantial dependent clauses**.

The circumstances (underlined below) and the circumstantial dependent clauses (in italics) give a strong sense of events unfolding along a time line:

My Life by Virginia A

My Name is Virginia A. I was born in Burma <u>at 9.00 am on Wednesday 9th April 1980</u>. The following recount is about the most important events that happened in my life.

My earliest memory was the death of my brother and my sister. My brother died *when he was seven in an car accident*. My sister died *when she was just born*.

In 1985 it was a sad time for me because I left my relatives behind and came to Australia. I remember when they were all crying *when we were at the airport. When we got on the plane* I waved to them and started crying.

One year later I started kindergarten at Glebe Primary school. I was excited and was jumping up and down.

Another important point about the use of circumstances in Text 8.5 is that they comprise culturally shared calendar references (*at 9.00 am on Wednesday 9th April 1980, in 1985*). Such an orientation is central to history as a field of study and many other contexts. This contrasts with Text 8.4, in which time references are relative to the writer – *when my sister was born, when I was 5, when I started school* – and are expressed as dependent clauses.

The use of circumstances of time and circumstantial dependent clauses of time to manage the record of events in Text 8.5 helps to explain why it would be more successful than Text 8.4, given the context in which it was produced. This does not mean, however, that Text 8.4 is ineffective in general terms. Perhaps, in an English lesson, for example, it would be compared favourably with Text 8.5. Can you think why? We will come back to this point later in the chapter.

Activity 8.6

So far, we have considered particular patterns of circumstances with reference to procedure genres and autobiographical genres. Circumstances of location in space are salient in the case of procedures, and circumstances of location in time are central to autobiographical genres. If we return to the picture description genre, we can see that, both in Mr X's description and our own, most of the circumstances were to do with location in space.

Aside from circumstances of location, there is, however, one other kind of circumstance in our description. See if you can identify it. If it helps, use the examples below, which illustrate the main types of circumstance. Consider, too, whether there are any particular patterns in your own description. Do you use, for example, mainly circumstances of location, or a variety of different types?

Circumstance type	Subcategory	Question/test to identify type of circumstance	Example
extent	distance	how far?	*I went <u>35 miles</u> after the tank light came on.*
	duration	how long?	*It lasted <u>from June 11 to September 21.</u>*
	frequency	how many times?	*You have to shuffle a deck of cards <u>about seven times</u> in order to mix them reasonably well.*
location	space	where?	*You must go <u>to the doctor.</u>*
	time	when?	*Meet me <u>at midnight.</u>*
manner	means	how? what with?	*Fix dry and frizzy hair <u>with hair wax.</u>*
	quality	how?	*You go to my head <u>like a sip of sparkling burgundy.</u>*
cause	reason	why?	*<u>Because of you</u> I find it hard to trust anyone.*

You will probably have identified *rather clumsily* as the only circumstance in our picture description that is not location in place. It is a circumstance of manner.

8.6 A return to processes and participants

We said earlier that Virginia's first draft might be positively valued within the field of school English but less so in school history. One reason for this is that the final version (Text 8.5) may seem somewhat detached and impersonal compared with the more 'immediate' and direct first draft. We will explore this point in the following activity.

Activity 8.7

Without looking back to Text 8.4 (I was born . . .), try to fill in the missing processes, using auxiliary and lexical verbs as necessary. Then, compare them with the original.

I was born in a hospital in Burma. I was born at 9.00 am on Wednesday. I _____ when all of my relatives were all crowding around me when my parents brought me home. they _____ _____ how cute I was. I _____ when my sister was born I use to always fight with her. I also _____ my first birthday. I _____ when I was 5 and I had to come to Australia. I was crying because I _____ _____ to leave my relatives. I also _____ that I had a big brother and sister but they had both died. My brother died when he was 7 because he had a car crash and my sister died when she was just born. I also _____ when I started kindergarten I was so excited I was jumping up and down.

The missing processes above cannot be classified as one of the four types encountered so far. *Remember* and *want* are **mental** processes, concerned with the world of consciousness rather than the external, material world. *Saying* is a **verbal** process. In total, there are seven mental processes and one verbal process in the draft text, and Virginia, the writer, is the sole participant doing the remembering and wanting. This pattern helps to account for its more personal feel. The final version (Text 8.5) has only one mental process and no verbal processes.

Mental clauses

With mental processes, the process of sensing may be construed as either flowing from a person's consciousness (*I remember*) or impinging on it (*this reminds me . . .*). The person (or entity) who does the thinking, feeling, wanting, or perceiving is the **experiencer** (sometimes referred to as 'senser'), and that which is thought, felt, wanted, or perceived is the **phenomenon** (or 'experience').

303

> *I also remember <u>my first birthday</u>.*
> experiencer   phenomenon
>
> *<u>The tiger</u> smelled <u>the blood trail</u>*
> experiencer   phenomenon

Verbal clauses

Verbal processes involve a **sayer** (any person or entity that can emit words or signal meaning) and often a quote or report of what is said:

> *<u>They</u> were saying <u>how cute I was</u>.*
> sayer   report
>
> *<u>They</u> were saying <u>'how cute you are'</u>*
> sayer   quote

Verbal clauses may also include the addressee or **receiver** of the process of saying:

> *They told <u>me</u> how cute I was.*
>   receiver

Processes of saying are interpreted in a broad sense to include various kinds of symbolic exchange of meaning, such as

> *My laptop clock <u>says</u> it's 2:32*

or

Document <u>Says</u> Oil Chiefs Met With Cheney Task Force.

These examples show that sayers (*my laptop clock* and *document*) need not be conscious beings).

Mental and verbal clauses and projection

Both mental and verbal processes are unlike other process types in that they can set up another clause that represents what is said or thought. Clause 1 below, which includes the sayer and the verbal process, is said to 'project' the quote or report in Clause 2.

they were saying || how cute I was.
Clause 1   Clause 2
projecting   projected report

they were saying || 'how cute you are'
Clause 1   Clause 2
projecting   projected quote

The content of what is being said may not always be projected through a clause. Instead, it can be a participant within the clause – the **said** (sometimes referred to as 'verbiage'):

He told her <u>a story</u>
         said

They asked him <u>lots of questions</u>
         said

Activity 8.8

Look at the following classic Peanuts comic strip (Figure 8.5).

(a)   There are two types of bubble used in the cartoon. One type has two smaller bubbles attached. What do you think these conventions indicate?

(b)   Rework the following clauses to go inside each of the four bubbles. Observe what grammatical changes take place.

He agreed that it would be right for father's day.

He was thinking that he'd just found out he was now retired and living in Florida.

He remembered there had been eight of them in the litter.

He knew he would appreciate getting the card.

Figure 8.5 Peanuts comic strip

(http://www.peanutscollectorclub.com/rumors.html (accessed 3 April 2008))

In cartoons, bubbles are used for speech and for thought (thought bubbles have two smaller bubbles attached), and these are the sorts of meaning that can be located in projected clauses:

He agreed || '*that's right . . . for father's day . . .*'
clause 1   clause 2
(projecting)   (projected)

He remembered || '*there were eight of us in the litter*'
clause 1   clause 2
(projecting)   (projected)

When sayings or thoughts are projected reports rather than (as in the examples above) projected 'quotes', there are often different uses of tense. Compare the different uses of tense below:

	Projected quote	Projected report	
past simple present simple	He was thinking '*I just <u>found out</u> that he<u>'s</u> retired now and living in Florida*'	*He was thinking that <u>he'd just found out</u> he <u>was</u> now retired* *NB: retired is adjective here, not verb	past perfect past simple
present simple	He thought '*That<u>'s</u> right . . . for father's day.*'	*He thought that it <u>would be</u> right for father's day.*	past modal

There are also differences in the use of pronouns (first person in the projected quotes, third person in the projected reports). These differences in projected reports and quotes are captured in the traditional terms **indirect** and **direct speech**, although, as we see here, they apply equally to thought.

8.7 Processes, participants, and circumstances: angle of representation

Distinguishing process types

An important test for distinguishing mental, material, and relational processes is to check the selection of aspect typically used in representing present time. Is it the simple present or the present progressive? Only material clauses favour present progressive:

> *Right now my cat <u>is catching</u> mice.* (material clause)
>
> *My cat <u>is</u> always hungry at the moment.* (relational clause)
>
> *For now, my cat <u>likes</u> you.* (mental clause)

Another important test is whether a clause can project another clause or not. If it can, it is not material, but rather verbal or mental.

Activity 8.9

By way of revision, complete Table 8.2, which is a summary of the main process and participant types in English.

(a)   Name the central participants in relation to each of the six process types.

(b)   Select which of the examples below belong to which process type.

(c)   Annotate the examples to identify the different types of participant (as we have done in the case of material processes).

(d)   Make observations about the form of the participants. Are they all realised by nominal groups? Are there premodifiers and postmodifiers?

Examples

I left my relatives behind

My earliest memory was the death of my brother and my sister.

I also remember my first birthday.

they were all crying

There[1] is a child.

They were saying how cute I was.

Table 8.2

Processes	Central participants	Example
Material (action, doing)		*I left* <u>*my relatives*</u> *behind* agent affected NG NG
Behavioural (physiological, psychological)		
Existential (there is, there are)		
Relational (having, being)		

Processes	Central participants	Example
Verbal (saying, telling)		
Mental (thinking, knowing, feeling, desiring)		

So far, we have looked at the main types of process, participant, and circumstance that language users regularly choose from in order to represent the world about them. These choices vary in relation to the contextual variable of field, that is, the type of social activity and topic. They also vary in relation to the different 'angles on the world' that different users of language invariably hold. As the North Sea example in Section 8.2 demonstrated, the same piece of reality can be represented from a different angle. The following anecdote and subsequent activities explore this further.

At a conference on the use of technology in education, Ewan McIntosh, a presenter, reported on a comment made by a teacher during a workshop he had given. The workshop concerned the use of computer games as a stimulus for creative writing. This was the teacher's comment:

> *Why would I start students writing by playing a computer game? I know nothing about that and it would be easier for me to show a film.*

The presenter, Ewan, interpreted the teacher's comment in the following way:

> *She couldn't care two hoots about the young people in her classroom.*

His evidence for such an interpretation was:

> *I did a little word count – 'why would I do this', 'why would I do that' . . . 'for me'. It was all about her.*

He then went on to comment:

Really, what she should have been saying was 'My students need to start writing by playing a computer game. They know everything about computer games and it's easier for them than watching a film'.

(The future, our lives, our technology and our learning (http://naaceconferences.blip.tv/#783496))

Whether you agree or not with Ewan's response, what we found interesting was his awareness of a transitivity pattern in the way the teacher represented herself, her 'angle on the world' in which she appeared as agent and experiencer. His preferred vision for the teacher would be for her to represent the students as agents and experiencers.

This short anecdote serves to illustrate how transitivity patterns provide a window into the way people see and position themselves in relation to others. In the following three (linked) activities, we will look at two different applications for the same job and examine how each applicant's language choices, including their choices of processes and participants, position them differently in relation to the post they are applying for. Activity 8.10 considers the effect of cultural context, while Activity 8.11 recycles and extends the work you did on genre in Chapter 7. Activity 8.12 focuses on transitivity patterns.

Activity 8.10

The following job applications for a teaching assistant position in Jordan were produced by two different applicants with different language and cultural backgrounds. The writer of Text 8.6 had English as a first language while the writer of Text 8.7 had Arabic as a first language.

In your view which letter would be more successful?

Text 8.6 English speaker application

Dear Mr X

I would like to be considered as a candidate for the teaching assistant position advertised in the Jordan Times on the 2nd of January 2000. I have finished my degree in English for specific purposes (ESP) with an average 'excellent'. I have taken all the ESP courses offered in the department; thus, I have solid background knowledge in ESP teaching.

My knowledge of ESP courses materials goes beyond my formal classroom education. For the past two years I have worked part-time in Jordan broadcasting and TV, where I have gained experience in teaching mass media courses. Also on my own initiative, I designed a teaching programme for the radio and developed a TV course.

In short, I believe I have the up to date ESP background and professional drive needed to contribute to your institution. I have enclosed a copy of my CV to give you further details about my qualification and experience. Sometime next week, I will plan to give you a call to see whether I can come in for an interview at your convenience.

I look forward to speaking with you then.

Sincerely,

Signature

(Mohammed Al-Ali, 2004)

Text 8.7 Arabic speaker application

In the name of Allah the most Merciful and the most Gracious
Professor Doctor, President of XX University
Peace, Mercy and Blessing of Allah be upon you.

I have read the advertisement in XX newspaper issued on the 2nd of January 2001, regarding the teaching assistant positions at X University. Since I am very interested in securing a job in an honourable institution like your university where I can participate and serve my country, I hereby submit my application for the position of 'teaching assistant' in the Department of Arabic Language, Faculty of Arts.

And I am very pleased to tell you that I graduated with the degree of Bachelor of Arts in Arabic from XX University in 2000 with the grade of 'excellent' (Attached are the required credentials).

I am also glad to inform you that while I was studying at the university, I worked for several private and evening schools where I gained valuable experience.

Based on what has been mentioned, I would kindly beseech your gracious and generous kindness to take my application into consideration and support me. I am quite sure that you will spare no effort to inform me, in due time, of your decision regarding my application.

With best wishes and respect, and may Allah reward you.

(Mohammed Al-Ali, 2004)

Texts 8.6 and 8.7 were collected and analysed as part of a research study by Mohammed Al-Ali (2004). The study concluded that different strategies in writing letters of application are effective in different cultures. The implication of this for Activity 8.10 is that, whichever letter you judged to be more effective, it might only be so in relation to a particular set of cultural values: an English or American interview panel would probably respond positively to Text 8.6, but a Jordanian interview panel would be likely to respond positively to Text 8.7.

So, what are the main differences? Activity 8.11 will consider differences in generic staging, and Activity 8.12 will explore differences in transitivity patterns. The purpose of both these activities will be to demonstrate how initial judgements and impressions of what is or is not effective can usually be explained by systematic linguistic analysis.

Activity 8.11

The generic stages of job applications include the following. Some stages are more likely to occur in Western-oriented cultures and others in Middle-Eastern culture. Read the two letters to see which generic stages are present and whether they occur in the same order.

- Salutation
- Referral to source of information
- Offer of candidature/Application for position
- Glorification of institution
- Promotion of candidature
- Reference to documents
- Invocation of compassion
- Solicitation of response
- Request for interview

The genre analysis suggests that there are a number of cultural differences in what is considered appropriate generic staging. The English applicant, for example, includes a 'request for interview' stage. Al-Ali explains that such a component does not reflect the way that employment works in the Arab world, where the use of a 'wasta' – a protagonist intervening on behalf of a job applicant – may make interviews redundant. Another difference is that, whereas invoking compassion and glorifying the institution would be generally inappropriate in English-speaking cultures, Al-Ali suggests that, in the Arab world, use of praise may be an important politeness strategy, and invoking compassion a way of motivating the addressee to offer a favour or give help to the applicant.

So far, analysis of the letters of application has revealed that the generic structure of job applications may differ from one culture to another. But what about the even less transparent meanings that lie below our conscious awareness? By conducting a transitivity analysis of the two letters, you will find some revealing differences in their linguistic patterns. This is the aim of Activity 8.12.

Activity 8.12

Use the following tables to guide an analysis of the transitivity patterns in each application letter. Each row indicates the number of examples in each text. Where rows are shaded there are no examples.

(a) List the mental processes where the job applicant is experiencer.

Text 8.6	Text 8.7
like	

(b) List the material processes where the job applicant is agent. Include any examples of participants in the affected role (noting down the whole nominal group) where they exist.

313

Text 8.6	Affected	Text 8.7	Affected
have finished	my degree	have read	the advertisement

(c)   List the relational processes where the applicant is one of the participants.

Text 8.6		Text 8.7	
have	solid background	am	very interested
	knowledge in ESP teaching		

(d)   List the verbal processes where the applicant is sayer

Text 8.6	Text 8.7
	tell

(e)   What participant role does *me* play?

Text 8.6	Text 8.7
	inform me (receiver)

(f)   What participant role does *you/your* play?

Text 8.6	Text 8.7
to give you (affected)	*tell you* (receiver)

(g)   Using the completed tables, consider the following questions:

- Which of the applicants is more often in the role of agent?
- Which of the applicants is more involved in material processes where there are participants in the affected role?
- Are there any differences in the grammatical form of the participants in affected roles across the two texts?

- What tense is mainly used in the material processes in Text 8.6? And in Text 8.7?
- What attributes and values are related (through relational processes) to the Text 8.6 applicant? And the Text 8.7 applicant? Are there any differences in the grammatical form?

Based on a detailed analysis of process and participant roles in relation to the two applicants, we can see that each writer creates quite a distinct angle on their suitability for the post. The applicant in Text 8.6, for instance, is an agent in a slightly larger set of material processes than the Text 8.7 applicant. Because, in addition, there are a larger number of participants in the role of affected in these processes, he positions himself as a more dynamic agent: his actions carry in them the process of change (interpreted in the most abstract sense). Also, because the participants in the affected role are primarily focused on areas of relevance to the advertised post, he represents himself as a highly appropriate candidate. Whereas, in Text 8.6, the participants in the role of affected are realised through complex nominal groups (e.g. *experience in teaching mass media courses, a teaching programme for the radio*) and give precise information, in Text 8.7 the participants in the affected role are relatively undefined (e.g. *valuable experience*). Finally, because the processes are largely in the past tense, the Text 8.6 writer presents evidence of what he has already achieved, as opposed to what he hopes to achieve. In contrast, the applicant in Text 8.7 is connected to fewer participants in the role of affected, and they do not relate to the requirements of the job. Several of the material processes are also in present tense, referring more to what the candidate hopes to do than what he has done. Similarly, the attributes and values that relate through relational processes to the Text 8.7 candidate are general rather than job-focused. They concern the writer's feelings (expressed as adjectival groups) rather than the skills he possesses (e.g. *I am very pleased, I am also glad*). The Text 8.6 candidate uses more complex nominal groups in which the pre- and postmodifiers clearly delineate his qualities (e.g. I have *the up to date ESP background and professional drive needed to contribute to your organization*).

Most significantly, the institution to which the candidates are applying is construed as potentially supporting and informing the Text 8.7 candidate (*take my application into consideration and support me, you will spare no effort*

317

to inform me). This places him in a passive role – a beneficiary of the institution rather than a contributor. In Text 8.6, in contrast, the pattern is reversed – it is the institution that the candidate acts upon (*give you, contribute to your institution*).

We hope that, if you are involved in preparing people for the world of work (or are yourselves engaged in applying for a post), the previous sequence of activities has revealed how useful it is to develop conscious awareness of text structure and transitivity patterns. If the aim of a letter of application is to open the door for an interview or obtain an offer of a post, then lexicogrammatical choices need to create the right impression. Job applications are a critical gate-keeping genre.

8.8 From commonsense to specialised fields

In the previous set of activities we looked at processes, participants, and circumstances, and how choices in these are related to the component of field known as the angle of representation. Another key aspect of field is topic. The degree to which a topic may be treated from a more commonsense or more specialised perspective (an area that we explored rather briefly in Chapter 6) is the focus of Section 8.8. You will see that, in this section, the focus is primarily on the lexical rather than grammatical end of lexicogrammar.

Activity 8.13

Read Texts 8.8–8.10.

(a)   Identify their social purpose.
(b)   Using the information in the texts complete the three diagrams that follow. You will need to decide which diagram best fits with which text.
(c)   Once you have completed the diagrams, decide which is the most and least specialised of the three texts.

Text 8.8 Spiders 1

Spiders are sometimes scary but they are sometimes useful because they eat pests. There are lots of different spiders.

Some of them have sharp fangs. The worlds most dangerous spiders are Funnel webs. But Daddy long legs have the deadliest venom but they can't use it because they're fangs aren't long enough.

Text 8.9 Spiders 2

Within Araneomorphae (and Araneae in general) Araneoclada is where the action is hottest and some observations of descriptive trends within this grouping (note that four genera account for well over 10% of all new spider species described) have prompted my proposal for a series of awards suggested below. The newly verified group Haplogynae (16 families) shows five new genera and 120 new species (nearly 90 of which are in the two dysderid mega-genera Dysdera and Harpactea). Entelegynes, of course, account for all the rest. Most activity was registered in Araneoidea (11 families) with nearly 130 new genera and 1060 new species. Paramount in this superfamily are the linyphiids with over 80 new genera (many of which are monotypic) and nearly 560 new species. This accounts for close to half of all new genera and over one quarter of all new species in the entire order Araneae. Other notables within Araneoidea include the synotaxids (10 new genera, 50 new species), theridiids (3 and 52), anapids (21 and 60) and araneids (6 and 300). Fully two-thirds of the araneid new species are in the two mega-genera Araneus and Alpaida. One can only hope that with this level of activity we must be getting close to resolving the familial relationships within Araneoclada.

Text 8.10 Spiders 3

Spiders are Arachnids.

Spiders look very distinctive. They have two body parts, the head and the abdomen. They have eight legs. Spiders can be colourful but most are dark. They have spinnerets that make silk.

Spiders live everywhere. They can live in hot desert areas or cool mountain areas. Some spiders live in peoples homes or gardens.

All spiders spin silk. They use the silk for egg sacs, to line their burrows and to make webs.

The webs are used to catch their food.

Some spiders are venomous and can kill people if they bite them. But most spiders are harmless and help people by catching and eating insect pests.

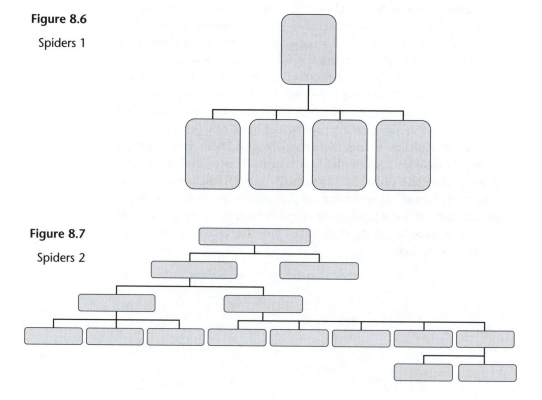

Figure 8.6

Spiders 1

Figure 8.7

Spiders 2

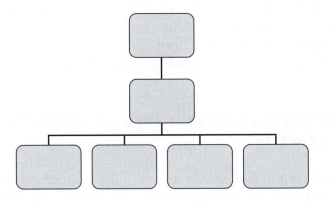

Figure 8.8

Spiders 3

The purpose of Texts 8.8 and 8.10 is to classify and describe phenomena. They can therefore be categorized as taxonomic report genres. Both texts move through the stages of identification of phenomena and classification, and description of types. They feature generic nominal groups (e.g. *spiders, funnel webs, Daddy long legs*). In the description stage, the NG heads are elaborated through determiners (*two*) and pre- and postmodifiers to provide precise information about different features of spiders, e.g. *two sharp* fangs, spinnerets *that make silk*, *two body* parts).

Text 8.9 is an extract from a longer text, and therefore it is more problematic to identify its overall social purpose and the genre to which it belongs. In fact, it is an extract from an academic book review where the writer discusses and evaluates new spider taxonomies. Scientific taxonomies are ordered, systematic classifications of phenomena based on the fundamental principles of either (a) superordination (where something is a 'kind of' or 'type of' something else) or (b) composition (where something is a part of something else).

The taxonomies in Texts 8.8 and 8.10 are neither particularly sophisticated nor systematic in that they were both written by non-expert school children. However, they both have elements of an everyday 'common-sense' taxonomy. Text 8.10, for example, uses colour and degree of harm/venom to classify spiders into groups and has taken a significant step by using the technical term *arachnids*. As students progress through the science curriculum, such simple taxonomies would generally be extended and developed. How deep into the taxonomy a student goes will depend on the level of schooling and degree of specialisation. It is unlikely, for example, that anybody apart from a world expert would need to develop the detailed taxonomies revealed in Text 8.9. What Text 8.9 does show, however, is the role played by specialised lexis in enabling the distinctions to be made: technical terms are crucial for building up sophisticated taxonomies.

8.9 Bringing together form and function: a review

So far, we have demonstrated how different lexical choices build either more technical or more commonsense representations of the world. We have also explored how different choices in types of process, participant, and circumstances can create different angles of representation, and we have shown that the use of functional labels enables us to see this particularly clearly.

From the perspective of form, we have observed that each functional component tends to be grammatically expressed, as follows:

- Participants tend to be realised by nominal groups.

- Processes tend to be realised by verbal groups.

- Circumstances tend to be realised by prepositional phrases.

For example:

They	*can live*	*in hot desert areas*
Participant	Process	Circumstance
Nominal group	Verbal group	Prepositional phrase

Participants may, however, also be realised by adjectival groups or even an entire clause:

Spiders	*can be*	*colourful*
Participant	Process	Participant
Nominal group	Verbal group	Adjectival group

To tread on a funnel web	*is*	*dangerous*
Participant	Process	Participant
Clause	Verbal group	Adjectival group

Circumstances can also be expressed by grammatical forms other than prepositional phrases, namely nominal groups or adverbial groups:

Many spiders	*live*	*only a few months*
Participant	Process	Circumstance
Nominal group	Verbal group	Nominal group

Joe	*lives*	*dangerously*
Participant	Process	Circumstance
Nominal group	Verbal group	Adverbial group

In order to bring together function and form in a systematic fashion, it may at times be useful to adopt a mode of analysis that shows the relationship between the functional components and the formal structure at the rank of group and word:

A cat	*is sitting*	*on a shelf*
Participant	Material process	Circumstance of location
Nominal group	Verbal group	Prepositional phrase
Determiner Noun	Finite + Lexical verb	Preposition Determiner Noun

Activity 8.14

Below, you can see the clauses from the picture description we produced (from Activity 8.8), divided into functional elements. Complete a form and function analysis of these clauses. Specify the type of process, participant, and circumstance as in the example above. Note that some cells have already been completed. In the third row, use a + sign between the labels for each of the words. Where there is shading there is no need to do an analysis.

And	*a middle aged man*	*is sleeping*	*in an armchair*
logical relation	behaver	behavioural process	
	nominal group		prepositional phrase
conjunction	determiner + adjective + noun	finite + lexical verb	preposition + determiner + noun

* * *

There	*is*	*a young child*	*on the floor.*

* * *

He	*is*	*quite little*

* * *

| He | is pushing | a toy car |

* * *

| There | is | another shelf with a music system | in the left-hand corner of the room. |

* * *

| The music system | is | rather old fashioned. |

* * *

| The cat | is dipping | her paw | into a goldfish bowl |

* * *

| in order to | try to catch | some goldfish. |

Verbal group
complex

* * *

| Rather clumsily | she | knocks over | some books. |

* * *

| The books | hit | the man who is asleep in the armchair. |

Activity 8.15

(a) Complete an analysis of Text 8.2 (*Picture description*) in Activity 8.1 from the perspective of both form and function. Where you can, specify the type of participant, process, and circumstance. Where language is missing you may also want to indicate the likely process or participant or language form, adding a question mark to indicate lack of certainty.

(b) Compare your analysis in this activity with the analysis in Activity 8.14. What do the analyses reveal about the two texts?

A cat		*on shelf in wall*
Participant	(relational?)	circumstance of location?
nominal group		prepositional phrase
determiner + noun		preposition + (missing determiner) + noun + inappropriate preposition (*in*) + (missing determiner) + noun

*   *   *

The cat	*goldfish*	*in the disk*

*   *   *

The cat	*books*

*   *   *

327

a man   is sleeping   in a armchair

*   *   *

His feet   on the table

*   *   *

A book   on shelf

*   *   *

A boy on the floor   carry   a dinky car

On a low shelf	there		loudspeaker and stereo.

By comparing the two picture descriptions, it becomes clear that, in our text (from Activity 8.14), participants are more varied and more 'filled in'. This is because the nouns in the nominal groups are both pre- and postmodified, giving shape and detail to the entities. The world created is further enriched through the use of verbal groups that realise more complex processes, and through the presence of logical causal meaning (*in order to*). In Mr X's text (analysed in Activity 8.15) it is often difficult to see how the component parts relate to one another. This is largely because the missing processes make the elements quite ambiguous in terms of their functional role. As a result, the representation is reduced in functional meaning and therefore has reduced representational power.

In carrying out this activity you will also have probably noticed that, from the perspective of form, there are several missing verbs and determiners (both definite and indefinite articles and quantifiers), as well as a number of inappropriate prepositions. There is also the lexical choice of *disk* rather than goldfish bowl. All these structural problems are just as indicative of a disorder as are the missing functional meanings.

8.10 Laying out an analysis

There are many different ways of laying out a transitivity analysis. As the previous two activities show, it can be done clause by clause and can combine form and function (if appropriate). Equally, it can be set out in tables highlighting various transitivity patterns, as in Activity 8.12. The important point is that texts should always be analysed systematically, so as to gain an overall sense of salient patterns of processes, participants, and circumstances (including absences as well as presences).

Activity 8.16

We now return to the problem scenario set out at the beginning of this chapter to see what patterns are revealed in Text 8.1.

(a) Identify the topic of Text 8.1.

(b) Analyse the types of process used.

(c) In the case of material processes, analyse who or what the agents and affected are.

(d) Count the number of circumstances and classify them.

Use the following two tables as a guide (although you will need to expand them to account for all of the examples).

Material	Behavioural	Mental	Relational	Verbal
did				
did				

Agent	Material	Affected
We	*did*	/
(ellipted *we?*)	*went*	/
(ellipted *we*)	went swimming	

From the analysis of the man's description of his holiday, a striking picture emerges: aside from material processes (which are all common, everyday realisations), there is almost a complete absence of any other process type. While it could have been predicted that material processes would be the dominant type chosen, it is perhaps somewhat surprising (given that the speaker is describing a holiday that he particularly enjoyed) that there is little evaluation through mental processes, or description through relational processes. It is also striking that the agents of the material processes are largely absent or ellipted, with consequent ambiguity in some clauses, and uncertainty as to who did what. Similarly, there are very few participants in the affected role, and the ones that are present are vague ('things') or appear to be invented (*junks, 'em like kelevans*). With regard to circumstances, there are surprisingly few circumstances of location. Instead, the presence of two circumstances of **accompaniment** suggest that company and family relationships take priority for the speaker.

Although you have insufficient data (or contextual information) to make any real interpretation of this fragment, it is interesting to note that the research study for which it was collected found that the aphasic speakers in the study used fewer relational and mental processes than their non-brain-damaged counterparts, who were matched for gender, age, and education. The 'aphasic speakers' choices resulted in more materially action-based texts with little description, self-reflection or evaluation on the events recounted' (Armstrong 2001). Such studies may therefore have important implications for post-stroke therapy and language treatment.

8.11 Using ideational analysis to explore real-world problems

In this chapter, we hope that the scenarios that you have encountered have given some insight into the power of transitivity analysis to reveal under-lying patterns of meaning that may not be obvious to the casual reader or to the speaker engaged in a fast-flowing interaction.

From an analyst's or practitioner's point of view, particularly revealing in carrying out such an analysis are the 'choices' people make in repre-senting reality. It should, of course, be remembered that in SFG choice is not seen as a necessarily conscious act, and is, in any case, always con-strained by the categories made available by the particular language we are speaking and, in most cases, the social context we are operating within. Transitivity analysis, nevertheless, makes it possible to see abstract patterns of meaning that go beyond more transparent literal meaning. You may like to consider how these patterns of meaning can be restricted or expanded by factors such as a person's stage of language acquisition or learning or an injury or illness that affects their control of the language system.

We hope that you have begun to see that developing a conscious knowledge of such patterns may be of considerable use to language professionals when communication goals are not achieved. It may be worth reviewing some of the uses to which the analysis of ideational meaning (particularly transitivity patterns) can be put by listing any particularly important areas that you have come across in this chapter and adding any other areas relevant to your own professional or personal context.

8.12 Summary

In this chapter, we explored the relationship between clause level grammar and the ideational metafunction, by examining how processes, participants, and circumstances combine with lexical choices to build a representation of the world. The ideational metafunction relates to the contextual variable of field, and therefore we took into account how the three main aspects of field – the social activity, the topic (including degree of specialisation), and the angle of representation – influence and, in turn, are influenced by, lexicogrammatical choices. Although we have not covered all the processes, participants, and circumstances identified in SFG, and we have not included in any detail logical relations in our discussion, this chapter has nevertheless set out the basic grammatical resources. Figure 8.1 and the table below summarise these.

Processes	Participants		Circumstances
Material	agent/affected		extent
Behavioural	behaver		location
Mental	experiencer/phenomenon		manner
Verbal	sayer/receiver/said		cause
Existential	existent		

Figure 8.9

Resources for representing the world

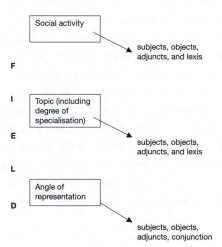

8.13 Answer key

Activity 8.1

	Circumstance/s	Participant	Process	Participant	Circumstance/s
i		a cat			on shelf in wall (location)
ii		the cat		goldfish in the disk*	
iii		the cat		books	
iv		a man	is sleeping		in a armchair (location)
v		his feet			on the table (location)
vi		a book			on shelf (location)
vii		a boy on the floor	carry	a dinky car	
vii	On a low shelf (location)			loudspeaker and stereo.	

*You may have analysed *in the disk* or *on the floor* as a circumstance. We will look at this issue in Section 8.4.

Activity 8.2

He	shot	the	stag	with	a	rifle
Pronoun	Verb	Determiner	Noun	Preposition	Determiner	Noun
Nominal group	Verbal group	Nominal group		Prepositional phrase		
Subject	Verb	Object		Adjunct		
Participant	Process	Participant		Circumstance		

He	shot	the	stag	with	the	biggest	antlers
Pronoun	Verb	Determiner	Noun	Preposition	Determiner	Adjective	Noun
Nominal group	Verbal group	Nominal group					
Subject	Verb	Object					
Participant	Process	Participant					

She	bought	a	handbag	with	a	black	patent	finish
Pronoun	Verb	Determiner	Noun	Preposition	Determiner	Adjective	Classifier	Noun
Nominal group	Verbal group	Nominal group						
Subject	Verb	Object						
Participant	Process	Participant						

She	bought	a	handbag	with	her	last	few	euros
Pronoun	Verb	Determiner	Noun	Preposition	Determiner	Determiner	Determiner	Noun
Nominal group	Verbal group	Nominal group		Prepositional phrase				
Subject	Verb	Object		Adjunct				
Participant	Process	Participant		Circumstance				

Activity 8.3

A cat is on a shelf and a middle aged man is sleeping in an armchair. There is a young child on the floor. He is quite little. He is pushing a toy car. There is another shelf with a music system in the left-hand corner of the room. The music system is rather old fashioned. The cat is dipping her paw into a goldfish bowl in order to try to catch the fish. Rather clumsily she knocks over some books. The books hit the man who is asleep in the armchair.

Activity 8.4

Lay three loops side by side. Overlap them and weave them into each other in an over and under sequence so that each step locks the loops together. Pass the end through the middle using an over and under sequence. Follow the end round to complete the mat.

Activity 8.8

Missing thought bubbles in sequence

1 That's right . . . for father's day.

2 I just found out that he's retired now and living in Florida.

3 There were eight of us in the litter.

4 I know he will appreciate getting this card.

Activity 8.9

Processes	Central participants	Example
Material (action, doing)	agent affected	*I left my relatives behind* agent affected
Behavioural (physiological, psychological)	behaver	*they were all crying* behaver
Existential (there is, there are)	existent	*there*[1] *is a child.* existent

Relational (having, being)	participants	*my earliest memory was*
		    participant
		
		the death of my brother and my sister.
		        participant

Verbal (saying, telling)	sayer	*they were saying how cute I was.* sayer
Mental (thinking, knowing, feeling, desiring)	experiencer, phenomenon	*I also remember my first birthday.* experiencer phenomenon

All the participants in the examples above are realised by nominal groups, apart from the adverbial group – *how cute I was*. Some of the nominal groups are of the simplest kind, being made up of pronouns (*I*, *they*) or determiner plus noun (*a child, my relatives*), while others are more complex and involve both pre- and postmodifiers (e.g. *My earliest memory* was *the death of my brother and my sister*).

335

Activity 8.11

Generic stages

Text 8.3	Text 8.6
• Salutation	• Salutation
• Offer of candidature/Application for position	• Referral to source of information
• Referring to the source of information	• Glorification of institution (Arabic letter only)
• Promotion of candidature	• Offer of candidature/Application for position
• Reference to documents	• Promotion of candidature
• Request for interview (English letter only)	• Reference to documents
• Salutation	• Promoting candidature
	• Invocation of compassion (Arabic letter only)
	• Solicitation of response
	• Salutation

Activity 8.12

(a) Mental processes

Text 8.3	Text 8.6
like	
believe	
look forward	
I (implied) to see	

(b) Material processes and affected

Text 8.3	Affected	Text 8.6	Affected
have finished	my degree	have read	the advertisement
have taken	all the ESP courses offered in the department	can participate	

have gained	experience in teaching mass media courses	(can) serve	my country
have worked		submit	my application for the position of . . .
have designed	a teaching programme for the	graduated	radio
developed	a TV course	was studying	
have enclosed	a copy of my CV	worked	
will plan to give	a call	gained	valuable experience
you (recipient) can come in			
my knowledge of ESP courses			
goes[3]			

(c) Relational processes

Text 8.3		Text 8.6	
have	solid background knowledge in ESP teaching	am	very interested
have	the up to date ESP background and professional drive needed to contribute to your organisation	am	very pleased
		am	also glad
		am	quite sure

(d) Verbal processes

Text 8.3	Text 8.6
	tell
	inform
	beseech

(e) Role of 'me'

Text 8.3	Text 8.6
	support me (affected)
	inform me (receiver)

(f) Role of you/your

Text 8.3	Text 8.6
to give you (affected)	*tell you* (receiver)
will plan to give you (**recipient***) *a call*	*inform you* (receiver)
speaking with you (reciever)	*you will spare no effort* (agent)
your institution (affected)	*your gracious and generous kindness* (receiver)
at your convenience (circumstance)	*your decision* (said)
	may Allah reward you (receiver)

* the **recipient** is a non-central participant in a material process who is a beneficiary, i.e. the one for whom the process is said to take place.

Activity 8.13

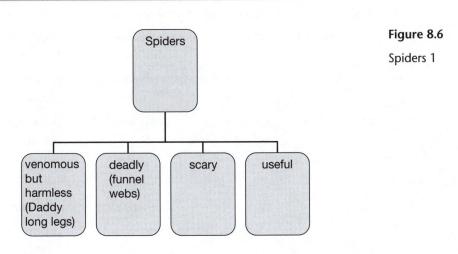

Figure 8.6

Spiders 1

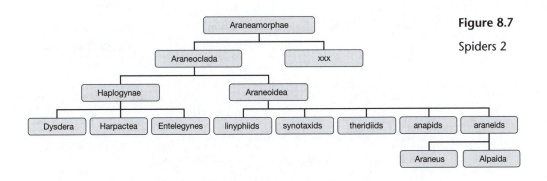

Figure 8.7

Spiders 2

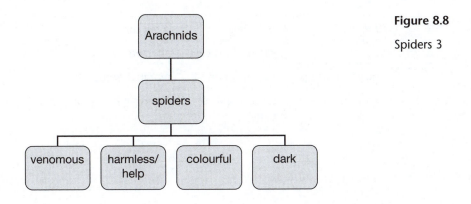

Figure 8.8

Spiders 3

Activity 8.14

And	a middle aged man	is sleeping	in an armchair
Logical relation	behaver	behavioural process	circumstance of location
	nominal group	verbal group	prepositional phrase
conjunction	determiner + adjective + noun	finite + lexical verb	preposition + determiner + noun

There	is	a young child	on the floor.
	existential process	existent	circumstance of location
	verbal group	nominal group	prepositional phrase
	finite lexical verb	noun	preposition + determiner + noun

He	is	quite little
participant	relational process	participant
nominal group	verbal group	adjectival group
pronoun	finite lexical verb	degree adverb + adjective

He	is pushing	a toy car
agent	material process	affected
nominal group	verbal group	nominal group
pronoun	finite + lexical verb	determiner + noun + noun

There	is	another shelf with a music system	in the left-hand corner of the room.
	existential process	existent	circumstance of location
	verbal group	nominal group	prepositional phrase
	finite lexical verb	determiner + noun + postmodifier	preposition + determiner + adjective + noun + postmodifier

The music system	is	rather old fashioned.
participant	relational process	circumstance
nominal group	verbal group	adjectival group
determiner + noun + noun	finite lexical verb	degree adverb + adjective

The cat	is dipping	her paw	into a goldfish bowl
agent	material process	affected	circumstance of location
nominal group	verbal group	nominal group	prepositional phrase
determiner + noun	finite + lexical verb	determiner + noun	preposition + determiner + noun + noun

in order to	try to catch	some goldfish.
logical relation	material process	affected
connector	verbal group complex	nominal group

	non-finite lexical verb	determiner + noun

Rather clumsily	*she*	*knocks over*	*some books*
circumstance of manner	agent	material process	affected
adverbial group	nominal group	verbal group	nominal group
adverb of degree + adverb	pronoun	finite lexical verb	determiner + noun

The books	*hit*	*the man who is asleep in the armchair*
agent	material process	affected
nominal group	verbal group	nominal group
determiner + noun	finite lexical verb	determiner + noun + postmodifier

Activity 8.15

A cat		*on shelf in wall*
participant (relational?)	relational?	circumstance of location?
nominal group		prepositional phrase
determiner + noun		preposition + (missing determiner) + noun + (inappropriate) preposition + (missing determiner) + noun

The cat		*goldfish in the disk*
participant (agent?)	material?	affected?
nominal group	verbal group	nominal group

determiner + noun	verb	(missing determiner) + noun + postmodifier

The cat		*books*
agent?	material?	affected?
nominal group	verbal group	nominal group
determiner + noun	verb	noun

a man	*is sleeping*	*in a armchair*
behaver	behavioural process	circumstance
nominal group	verbal group	prepositional phrase
determiner + noun	finite + lexical verb	preposition + determiner + noun

His feet		*on the table*
participant?	relational?	circumstance of location?
nominal group	verbal group	prepositional phrase
determiner + noun	verb	preposition + determiner + noun

A book		*on shelf*
participant?	relational?	circumstance of location?
nominal group	verbal group	prepositional phrase
determiner + noun	verb	preposition + (missing determiner) + noun

A boy on the floor	carry	a dinky car
agent	material process	affected
nominal group	verbal group	nominal group
determiner + noun + postmodifier	finite lexical verb	determiner + adjective + noun

on a low shelf	there		loudspeaker and stereo.
circumstance of location		existential?	existent
prepositional phrase		verbal group	nominal group
preposition + determiner + adjective + noun		verb	noun + conjunction + noun

Activity 8.16

Topic – beach holiday

Material	Behavioural	Mental	Relational	Verbal
did		like	have	
did				
went				
played				
did				
went				
went swimming				
get into				

get	
make	
get out	
make	
make	
make	
get out	
do	
get away	
go out	
play	
play around	

Agent	Material	Affected
we	did	/
Mum	did	/
/	went	/
/	played	/
we	did	things
(ellipted we?)	went	/
(ellipted we)	went swimming	
(ellipted we)	get into	things
We	get	
(ellipted I)	make	
They (kids)	get out	
?	make	'em like kelevans
ellipted they	make	junks
ellipted they	make	things
ellipted they	make	a giant (–)

ellipted they	get out	
ellipted they	do	it
we	get away	
?	go out	
?	play	
	play around	

Circumstances:

Accompaniment: with the kids, by ourselves;

Location: to the pool;

Extent: a lot.

Notes

1   In *on a low shelf <u>there</u> loudspeaker and stereo, there* has no representational meaning and is not counted as a participant. Nor is it a circumstance in this particular clause because it does not refer to a location. It is present in the clause simply because all English declarative clauses require a subject.

2   Although SFG has specific labels for participants in relational processes (like the specific labels 'agent' and 'affected' in material processes), in this introductory book we use only the more general term 'participant' in order to keep things simple.

3   The writer is implicated here even though the agent is *my knowledge of ESP courses* rather than 'I'.

nine

Interacting and taking a position

9.1 Introduction

With language, we do more than represent our experience of the world. We also interact with others. Representation and interaction occur simultaneously throughout the language we use. In the last chapter, we explored the grammatical systems that are deployed in representing experience – collectively known as the ideational metafunction. In this chapter, we explore the grammatical systems that are deployed in interacting with others – collectively known as the interpersonal metafunction. The difference is one of focus. The same clauses, clause complexes, or texts can be explored from both an ideational perspective and an interpersonal one. The difference in perspective brings into focus different language items, or different aspects of the same language items.

Although there is an interpersonal dimension to all communication, in certain contexts the interpersonal becomes particularly evident. Email communication provides some striking examples. While email can result in quicker and easier communication, it can also lead to dramatic communication breakdowns.

Scenario

The following emails were written after a telephone call in which a UK-based investment banker was invited to apply for work with a US-based one. Instead of resulting in a job offer, the correspondence ended in a trading of insults.

Read through the emails and identify what triggers the conflict that develops. Do you think one of the participants is more responsible for the conflict than the other? Is one the 'winner' and one 'the loser' in the conflict? Without doing a detailed analysis at this stage, can you explain any of your evaluations in terms of the grammar of the emails – particularly the use of modal forms?

Modal forms were
introduced in
Chapter 5.

Text 9.1 **An international email exchange**

Mail 1

From: Alan L
To: Daniel B

March 22

Daniel, thanks for calling earlier today. Enclosed is my CV for your review. I look forward to following up when you have more time.

Best regards, Alan.

Mail 2

From: Daniel B
To: Alan L

March 28

What are your three best current European ideas?

Mail 3

From: Alan L
To: Daniel B

March 28

Daniel, I am sorry but it does not interest me to move forward in this way.

If you wish to have a proper discussion about what you are looking to accomplish in Europe, and see how I might fit in, fine. Lesson One of dealing in Europe: Business is not conducted in the same informal manner as in the US.

Best regards, Alan.

Mail 4

From: Daniel B
To: Alan L

March 28

One idea would suffice.

We are an aggressive, performance-oriented fund looking for blood-thirsty competitive individuals, who show initiative and drive, to make outstanding investments . . .

We find most Brits are a bit set in their ways and prefer to knock back a pint in the pub and go shooting on the weekends rather than work hard. Lifestyle choices are important, and knowing one's limitations with respect to dealing in a competitive environment is too. That is Lesson One at my shop. It is good that we learned about this incompatibility early in the process, and I wish you all the best in your career in traditional fund management.

Mail 5

From: Alan L
To: Daniel B

March 28

Daniel, I guess your reputation is proved correct . . . I did not achieve the success I have by knocking back a pint, as you say. I am aggressive, and I do love this business.

I am half-American and half-French, and having spent more than half my life on this side of the pond, I think I know a little something about how one conducts business in the UK and Europe.

There are many opportunities in the UK and Europe; shareholder regard is only beginning to be accepted and understood. However, if you come here and handle it in the same brash way you have in the US, I guarantee you will fail. Things are done differently here. Yes, place in society still matters, where one went to school etc. It will take tact and patience (traits you obviously do not have) to succeed in this arena.

Good luck!

Alan.

Mail 6

From: Daniel B
To: Alan L
Cc: Patrick C

March 28

Well, you will have plenty of time to discuss your 'place in society' with the other fellows at the club. I love the idea of a French/English unemployed guy, whose fund just blew up, telling me that I am going to fail. At [my company], 'one's place in society' does not matter at all. We are a bunch of scrappy guys from diverse backgrounds (Jewish, Muslim, Hindu, etc) who enjoy outwitting pompous asses, like yourself, in financial markets globally.

Your 'inexplicable insouciance' and disrespect is fascinating; it must be a French/English aristocratic thing. I will be following your 'career' with great interest.

I have copied Patrick so that he can introduce you to people who might be a better fit. There must be an insurance company or mutual fund out there for you.

Dan B

Mail 7

From: Alan L
To: Daniel B

March 28

Hubris.

Mail 8

From: Daniel B
To: Alan L

March 28

Laziness.

(*Financial Times*, 1 April 2005, http://search.ft.com/ftArticle?queryText=Daniel+Loeb&page=3&y=4&aje=false&x=9&id=050401000995&ct=0)

Your evaluation of responsibility for the breakdown in this exchange will, to some extent, depend on your own values. You might hold Daniel responsible for triggering the breakdown with Mail 2, or Alan with an over-assertive Mail 3. It is unlikely that Daniel perceived his own Mail 2 as the trigger for conflict, but he probably did see Alan's Mail 3 as such. In some social and national cultures, Daniel's direct style in Mail 2 would be seen as reasonable, and Alan L would therefore be held responsible for his confrontational response in Mail 3.

Both men could be seen as losers, since Alan L failed to obtain a new job, and Daniel B failed to obtain a new staff member. However, there is more at stake. One aspect of many exchanges is the idea of 'face' and how far interlocutors save, threaten, protect, or lose face. Winning may depend on how much respect people emerge with from an interaction.

In order to manage interactions, a wide range of highly flexible and delicate language resources are available to language users. Language observers need grammatical terminology sensitive enough to describe these resources and explain how they are used. In order to begin considering this grammar, the next activity focuses on the role of modality in Mail 2.

Activity 9.1

The text below is a rewritten version of Mail 2, designed to be more inter-personally effective. Changes have been made to the generic structure of the text and the grammatical forms. Which changes can you identify?

Text 9.2 Mail 2

Original version

From: Daniel B
To: Alan L

March 28

What are your three best current European ideas?

Revised version

Dear Alan,

Thank you for sending me your CV as arranged.

I am interested in finding out more about what you would bring to our trading in Europe. Could you tell me what you consider to be the three most important issues in European trading at the moment?

Yours, Daniel

(Original version from *Financial Times*, 1 April 2005, http://search.ft.com/ftArticle?queryText=Daniel+Loeb&page=3&y=4&aje=false&x=9&id=050401000995&ct=0)

In the context of the whole email exchange, Mail 2 functions to acknowledge receipt of the CV and to obtain further information. From a genre perspective, the staging of the two versions of the mail can be represented as follows:

Genre stages

Original mail	Revised mail
	Salutation
	Acknowledgement of provision of goods and services in previous mail
	Rationale for request
Request for information	Request for information
	Complimentary close

The writer of the revised version moves through more stages, and does more interpersonal work, than the writer of the original one-line mail thought necessary. The email now explicitly functions as a turn in a dialogue, with the first sentence acknowledging the turn taken previously by the other participant. The second sentence prepares the reader for a request. This is the most likely function of a statement about what 'I am interested in'. Only after this is the request for information itself made.

In the request for information stage, rather than the direct *wh*-question of the original mail (*What are your . . .?*), the writer of the revised mail uses the modal verb, *could*, in combination with several other lexicogrammatical features (*Could you tell me what you consider to be . . .?*). As noted in Chapter 5, modal auxiliaries can be used to communicate indirectness; this indirectness helps to moderate the exercise of power that is implicit in a direct request for information.

In previous chapters, it has been pointed out that a *wh*-interrogative clause functions as a request for information. However, as this email exchange demonstrates, it does more than that. A request for information positions the speaker and listener in particular roles – one as requester, the other as giver. In order to manage this relationship, interlocutors have choices they can make from linguistic systems that constitute the interpersonal metafunction of the language, in particular mood and modality.

See Chapter 2 for mood and Chapter 5 for modality.

The mails also show how the functional values of lexicogrammatical choices at clause or sentence level need to be seen in the context of the genre in which these choices are made and the situation in which that genre is being performed. Managing interpersonal relationships depends on the participants' understanding of these. Understandings can vary, however, and it is possible that, for Daniel, a *wh*-interrogative was completely appropriate to the nature of the relationship as he perceived it, whereas for Alan it was not.

Thus, from an interpersonal perspective, a communicative situation is one of roles and relationships, identity, perspectives, and power. These constitute the <u>tenor</u> of the situation. In this chapter, we will explore how tenor is created through lexicogrammatical choices, mainly from the mood and modality systems. These lexicogrammatical forms realise the following three aspects of the situation:

These three aspects of the situation were introduced in Chapter 6.

- participants' social roles and relative social status;
- the social distance between participants;
- speaker/writer persona, i.e. general stance and assumed degree of alignment with others.

Figure 9.1 below was first introduced in Chapter 6. In this chapter, the ways these lexicogrammatical systems realise tenor will be explored in more depth.

Figure 9.1

The connection between tenor and language

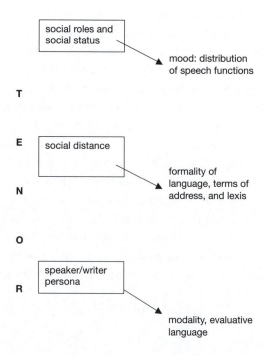

354

9.2 Interpersonal resources

The next activity focuses on mood, in the context of an accidentally recorded conversation between the former UK prime minister, Tony Blair, and US president, George Bush. The conversation was picked up by a microphone that had been left turned on at a G8 summit conference in Russia in 2006. At the time, three years after the invasion of Iraq, there was much speculation about the two men's relationship.

Activity 9.2

Text 9.3 is the first half of the entire transcript. From an initial reading, what does it tell you about Bush and Blair's relationship?

Text 9.3 Blair–Bush dialogue

(1)	Bush:	Yo, Blair. How are you doing?
(2)	Blair:	I'm just . . .
(3)	Bush:	You're leaving?
(4)	Blair:	No, no, no not yet.
(5)		On this trade thingy . . . [indistinct]
(6)	Bush:	Yeah, I told that to the man.
(7)	Blair:	Are you planning to say that here or not?
(8)	Bush:	If you want me to.
(9)	Blair:	Well, it's just that if the discussion arises . . .
(10)	Bush:	I just want some movement.
(11)	Blair:	Yeah.
(12)	Bush:	Yesterday we didn't see much movement . . .
(13)	Blair:	No, no, it may be that it's not, it may be that it's impossible.
(14)	Bush:	I am prepared to say it.
(15)	Blair:	But it's just I think that we need to be an opposition . . .

355

(16) Bush: Who is introducing the trade?

(17) Blair: Angela [Merkel, the German Chancellor].

(18) Bush: Tell her to call 'em.

(19) Blair: Yes.

(20) Bush: Tell her to put him on, them on the spot.

(21)   Thanks for the sweater – it's awfully thoughtful of you.

(22) Blair: It's a pleasure.

(23) Bush: I know you picked it out yourself.

(24) Blair: Oh absolutely – in fact I knitted it!!!

                (laughter)

(BBC News 24 website, http://news.bbc.co.uk/1/hi/world/americas/5188258.stm (accessed 10 April 2008))

This does not look like an exchange between two of the most politically powerful men in the world. Public dialogue between nations is typically carried on in different language, roles are more formal, and relationships are more distant. This much is obvious, without grammatical knowledge to guide us. However, grammatical knowledge can guide us in examining this conversation. We will first look at the function of mood.

9.3 Mood

As you know, a clause can be seen as a structure made up from the following elements: subject, verb, object, complement, and adjunct.

For example:

I	*just*	*want*	*some*	*movement.*
Subject	Adjunct	Verb	Object	
Nominal group	Adverbial group	Verbal group	Nominal group	
Pronoun	Adverb	Verb	Determiner	Noun

For a clause to be an independent one, capable of standing on its own, the verb must have a finite element. As explained in Chapters 1 and 2, the finite element is the part of the verbal group that signals tense, polarity, modality, and agreement between the verb and the subject. It may be contained within the lexical verb:

I	just	want	some	movement.
Subject	Adjunct	Verb	Object	
Nominal group	Adverbial group	Verbal group	Nominal group	
Pronoun	Adverb	Finite lexical verb	Determiner	Noun

Or it may be realised by a separate auxiliary verb:

Yesterday	we	didn't	see	much	movement.
Adjunct	Subject	Verb		Object	
Adverbial group	Nominal group	Verbal group		Nominal group	
Adverb	Pronoun	Finite auxiliary	Lexical verb	Adjective	Noun

The subject is the nominal group that interacts most closely with the finite verb; it has been chosen by the speaker to take 'responsibility' for the finite.

Because most of the grammatical terms used to talk about the interpersonal metafunction are familiar from formal grammar, it is important to recognise the differences in the way they are used in systemic functional grammar. In SFG, 'subject' identifies the particular nominal group that is 'responsible' for the finite, and this is seen as part of the interpersonal metafunction. From the perspective of the ideational metafunction, the same nominal group is named differently, as a participant in a process. In the clauses above, for example, *I* and *we* are experiencers. The same nominal

Chapter 8 showed that sometimes the subject can be a whole clause, not a nominal group.

Chapter 8 introduced the terms for different types of participant.

357

group seen from the perspective of the textual metafunction is again named differently. *I* is the theme of the first clause above, and *we* is part of the theme of the second.

Theme will be examined extensively in Chapter 10.

This proliferation of names for the same item may seem unnecessarily complicated. However, the separation of subject, participant, and theme serves communicative purposes and so needs to be recognised in the grammar. Consider how meaning is affected by the movements illustrated below.

Yesterday	*we*	*didn't*	*see*	*much movement.*
Adjunct	Subject	Finite	Lexical verb	Object
Circumstance	Experiencer	Mental process		Phenomenon
Theme				

Not much movement	*was*	*seen*	*yesterday.*
Subject	Finite	Lexical verb	Adjunct
Phenomenon	Mental process		Circumstance
Theme			

The first clause seems natural for a conversation. In contrast, the wording of the second clause seems more suitable for a public announcement, perhaps to the world's television cameras. The increased formality and reduced intimacy that are achieved by moving the phenomenom (*not much movement*) into subject position and the experiencer (*we*) out of the clause completely are an illustration of why mood is regarded in SFG as a central resource for the realisation of interpersonal meaning. In SFG, subject is a functional term, not simply a formal one.

The pattern of subject and finite establishes the clause as either declarative, interrogative, or imperative (see Table 9.1), and, together, the subject and finite are known as the **mood element**. Notice that it is the finite element rather than the entire verbal group that is part of the mood element, so, from now on, we will refer to finite rather than to verb when discussing the mood element.

Table 9.1: Mood element and clause type

Example	Mood element	Clause type
Subject Finite *I just <u>want</u> some movement.*	Subject-Finite	**Declarative**
Finite Subject *<u>Are</u> <u>you</u> planning to say that?*	Finite-Subject	**Interrogative:** polar interrogative
Finite Subject *How <u>are</u> <u>you</u> doing?*	Finite-Subject	*wh*-interrogative
Finite *<u>Tell</u> her to call 'em.*	Finite	**Imperative**

As pointed out previously, clause types are functional categories. They realise three primary speech functions. A fourth basic speech function is achieved by combining a modal form with the interrogative mood. This clause type is referred to as **modal interrogative**. The set of four speech functions is illustrated below, with variations on a clause from the Blair–Bush dialogue.

See Chapters 1 and 6 for more on communicative functions (including the four basic types referred to as speech functions in SFG).

Table 9.2: Clause type and basic speech functions

Clause type (mood of clause)	Speech function	Example
Declarative	Statement	*Yesterday we didn't see much movement.*
Interrogative	Question	*Did we see much movement yesterday?*
Modal interrogative	Offer	*Would you like me to move?*
Imperative	Command	*Move.*

The four speech functions performed by these clause types provide a basis for the entire range of communicative functions available to language users.

Activity 9.3

Refer to Text 9.3, which has been reproduced below for convenience:

(a) Identify nine full declarative clauses, three interrogatives, and two imperatives.

(b) Label the subject and finite parts of each of these, using S for subject and F for finite.

(c) In the case of the interrogative clauses, identify whether they are polar interrogative or *wh*-type interrogatives.

(d) Identify the speech function of each of these clauses.

Text 9.3 Blair–Bush dialogue

(1)	Bush:	Yo, Blair. How are you doing?
(2)	Blair:	I'm just . . .
(3)	Bush:	You're leaving?
(4)	Blair:	No, no, no not yet.
(5)		On this trade thingy . . . [indistinct]
(6)	Bush:	Yeah, I told that to the man.
(7)	Blair:	Are you planning to say that here or not?
(8)	Bush:	If you want me to.
(9)	Blair:	Well, it's just that if the discussion arises . . .
(10)	Bush:	I just want some movement.
(11)	Blair:	Yeah.
(12)	Bush:	Yesterday we didn't see much movement . . .
(13)	Blair:	No, no, it may be that it's not, it may be that it's impossible.
(14)	Bush:	I am prepared to say it.
(15)	Blair:	But it's just I think that we need to be an opposition . . .

(16) Bush: Who is introducing the trade?

(17) Blair: Angela [Merkel, the German Chancellor].

(18) Bush: Tell her to call 'em.

(19) Blair: Yes.

(20) Bush: Tell her to put him on, them on the spot.

(21) Thanks for the sweater – it's awfully thoughtful of you.

(22) Blair: It's a pleasure.

(23) Bush: I know you picked it out yourself.

(24) Blair: Oh absolutely – in fact I knitted it!!!

(laughter)

(BBC News 24 website, http://news.bbc.co.uk/1/hi/world/americas/5188258.stm (accessed 10 April 2008))

This analysis of clause types and speech functions may already have begun to reveal something about the relationship between Bush and Blair. However, we have not yet considered the complete range of speech functions available to the two men. The next section does this.

9.4 Speech functions

The reason that there are four basic speech functions is because:

- The <u>items</u> that are exchanged in an interaction can be **goods and services** or **information**.

- The <u>roles</u> of the speakers in the interaction can be **giving** or **demanding**.

Table 9.3: Speech roles, items exchanged, and speech functions

	ITEM	
SPEECH ROLE	information	goods & services
Giving	*Yesterday we didn't see much movement.* (Statement)	*Would you like me to move?* (Offer)
Demanding	*Did we see much movement yesterday?* (Question)	*Move.* (Command)

However, speakers' roles can be extended in terms of whether they are **initiating** or **responding** and, if they are responding, whether they are **supporting** or **confronting**. The total set of twelve speech functions is presented in the following table.

Table 9.4: Speech functions: initiating and responding

	Initiation	Response	
		Supporting	Confronting
Giving information	Statement *Yesterday we didn't see much movement.*	Acknowledgement *No we didn't*	Contradiction *Yes we did*
Demanding information	Question *Did we see much movement yesterday?*	Answer *We saw some*	Disclaimer *No idea* *I don't know*
Giving goods and services	Offer *Would you like me to move?*	Acceptance *Yes, that would be good*	Rejection *No thank you*
Demanding goods and services	Command *Move.*	Supply *Ok*	Refusal to supply *No*

Activity 9.4

Use the table below to count each of the speech functions Bush and Blair perform in Text 9.3. For each speech function, write the number of the clause from the transcript in the appropriate cell of the table. When you have completed the analysis, consider whether it tells you anything about the relative status of the two men in this interaction.

	Speech function	Bush	Blair
Initiating the exchange: giving information	Statement		
Initiating the exchange: giving goods and services	Offer		
Initiating the exchange: demanding goods and services	Command		
Initiating the exchange: demanding information	Question		
Responding: supplying information	Answer/ disclaimer		
Responding: supplying goods and services	Supply/refuse supply		
Responding: receiving goods and services	Acceptance/ rejection		
Responding: receiving information	Acknowledge/ contradict		

Despite the apparent ease with which the two men communicate, the speech function analysis above can be seen to indicate a difference in status. Bush's utterances fall more significantly in the Initiation section of the table and Blair's in the Response section; and Bush makes two commands. In simple terms, these features suggest that Bush is the more powerful of the two. Of course, no conclusions of that sort can actually be based on such a fragment of talk. But, in general, attention to who initiates turns and what speech functions each participant performs can be used to explore interpersonal relations in communication.

9.5 Lexicogrammar of the speech functions

We have seen that, for the initiating speech roles, the typical lexicogrammatical forms correspond to four basic clause types: declarative, interrogative, modalised interrogative, and imperative.

For the response speech roles, as illustrated in Table 9.4, the typical clause type tends to be an elliptical declarative clause or a minor clause. Elements that have been presented in the initiating clause may be ellipted in the response, e.g.

Yesterday we didn't see much movement.   *No we didn't <see much movement>*

Sometimes, this means that the mood element is ellipted, e.g.

Move.   *No <I won't move>*

Minor clauses were
introduced in
Chapter 2.
Minor clauses, however, do not have a mood element, even an ellipted one. In the exchange below, *Okay* is a minor clause:

Move   *Okay*

Activity 9.5

Look back at the Bush–Blair dialogue and identify which clause types are used in the response functions of the two men.

To summarise, lexicogrammatical choices (e.g., *You're leaving?*) realise speech functions (e.g., question), which in turn realise communicative functions (e.g., initiating a conversation) that play a role in constructing a text with a social purpose (e.g., a conversation). However, adult language users do not always use typical lexicogrammatical forms to achieve their social purposes. What you probably noticed is that the lexicogrammatical mood of *You're leaving?* is declarative; that is, it is a clause type that typically realises a statement. However, as the question mark in the text shows, it actually performs the speech function of a question. This ambiguity on Bush's part is likely to be functional. There is a difference between starting the conversation with a statement functioning as a question and starting it with a typical question such as, *Are you leaving?* Such manipulation of the interpersonal grammar is central to interaction.

Chapter 6 showed a range of different ways of realizing questions.

9.6 Modality

The second important interpersonal system is modality. The dialogue between Blair and Bush shows two speakers with the resources to:

• make **propositions** – i.e, say something IS or ISN'T

• make **proposals** – i.e., tell somebody, DO something or DON'T DO something

However, as Blair shows on two occasions, speakers may want to take up positions that lie between IS/ISN'T or DO/DON'T.
Speakers may want to say:

• something MIGHT, COULD, MAY, MUST, or WILL BE

as Blair does in this slightly adapted version of (13):

It *may* be impossible to move.

Or speakers may want to say:

• somebody SHOULD, MIGHT, CAN, or NEEDS TO DO something

as Blair does in this slightly adapted version of (16):

We *need* to be an opposition.

Modalisation enables a speaker to grade the strength of their commitment to a proposition or proposal. This permits a considerable range of refinement to the basic speech functions of statement and command.

See Chapter 5 for epistemic modality (propositions) and deontic modality (proposals).

When modalising a proposition or a proposal, speakers intrude into the text in a more or less obvious way and position themselves and their interlocutor. In this way, modality combines with mood to constitute the tenor of the relationship between participants in a communicative context.

In order to make the proposition and proposal quoted above, Blair chose to modalise them in the ways he did by selecting from the range of options available to him:

13) It _may/could/might/will_ be impossible to move.

16) We _need to/ought to/should/must/will_ be an opposition.

And, in fact, the range of options is considerably wider. From an SFG perspective, modal lexicogrammatical resources are seen to range from the familiar modal auxiliaries, to lexicogrammatical forms that are not traditionally seen as modal at all. The table below presents some of these resources.

Table 9.5: Some of the range of modalising forms

1.	Verbs:	
a)	modal auxiliaries	_can, could, will, would_, etc.
b)	semi-modals	_need to, dare to_, etc.
c)	lexico-modal auxiliaries	_have got to, be bound to_, etc.
2.	Modal adjuncts	_probably, possibly, surely, perhaps_, etc.
3.	Modal adjectives	_possible, probable_, etc.
4.	Modal nouns	_the possibility, likelihood_, etc.
5.	Mental process verbs	_think, believe_, etc.
6.	Verbal process verbs	_suggest, propose_, etc.
7.	Material process verbs	_allow, guarantee_, etc.
8.	Vague language	_a bit, any, rather_, etc.

When a speaker or writer uses a mental, verbal, or material process verb in order to modalise a proposition or proposal, they are using **interpersonal grammatical metaphor.** In other words, they are using a lexicogrammatical form for a purpose other than the one it typically has. An example of this occurred in a later part of the Bush–Blair dialogue (not presented here):

Bush: *I think Condi is going to go pretty soon.*

The mental process, *think*, projects the statement *Condi is going to go pretty soon*. The effect, however, is similar to these more typical modals:

Probably Condi is going to go pretty soon

It's likely that Condi is going to go pretty soon

Condi should be going pretty soon.

A question-tag test can be used to reveal the modalising function of *I think*.

I think Condi is going to go pretty soon, isn't she?

The subject that the tag test picks up is *Condi*, not *I*. *I think* is not the subject-finite mood element for the sentence. In fact, *I think* contributes to the mood element in the same way as the more obvious modals in the examples above.

Such interpersonal grammatical metaphor will be seen to be an important means of realising the interpersonal metafunction.

9.7 Social roles and relative social status

From an SFG perspective, social roles and power relationships are signalled by:

- who performs which speech functions, who makes statements, asks questions, gives directives, and so on;
- who takes turns in the interaction, how they take them, and how much of the time they use in doing so;
- who selects topics for discussion.

Text 9.1 illustrated how relationships can break down even when participants appear to have a shared goal. Text 9.4, by contrast, shows two people successfully collaborating in their pursuit of a shared goal.

Activity 9.6

Read through Text 9.4 and answer the following questions:

1   What is the situation?

2   What roles are the two participants performing?

3   Do you have the impression one of them is more powerful than the other? Why?

4   What features suggest that this exchange is successful?

5   What are the dominant clause types?

Text 9.4 Equality/inequality in a planning meeting

A: But I think, I think what we need to do as a way forward, I think probably between us now we want to get a list of questions that I need to ask him when he phones me. And then perhaps arrange a meeting of perhaps me and you to go out and, and see him.

B: Yeah, why don't we play it along the lines of erm, it's no use, it's almost no use saying 'Here is a list of questions', I think what we need first of all, are some more facts. A bit like the meeting we had in that hotel where it was, we knew a bit, obviously because of our involvement in the past but there was a lot of information gathering and searching and asking them really and, really asking them to define what they wanted out of all of this erm, although we didn't offer, you know, it wasn't an up-front asking the sort of the open question, to see what came back, and then asking it a different way around. Erm, so we need I think we, for you to have a list of questions, you could find that you get shot out of the water at stage one . . .

A: Because he's . . .

B: . . . because he's after something totally different. And what I would suggest is you, you try and say 'Look we'll come and talk to you know, no no commitment either side or you can come and talk to us or we can meet you half way, whatever you like erm, no commitment, we'll talk you through it, erm, but we need some more facts just beforehand erm, to go on, so we can start thinking about some of the issues that we may or may not want to discuss with you'.

A: What if, if the issue of fees are raised in terms of what ball park figures are we talking about. I mean, obviously the response to that would be we need to know . . .

B: Yeah.

A: . . . in more detail what we are doing, but I suspect in terms of establishing whether they can get retirement relief, and perhaps doing a, a valuation of intellectual property within the company.

B: Well . . .

A: That in itself would be, well . . .

B: The first bit is there's the smaller of those two items.

A: Exactly, yeah.

(Extract from Nelson, M., *The Business English Corpus (BEC)* (details available at http://users.utu.fi/micnel/business_english_lexis_site.htm))
(Extract adapted by omission of some language)

Most of the clauses in this dialogue are declaratives. As the typical function of declaratives is to make statements, it would seem that the role of each of the participants in the dialogue is simply to give information. However, this does not take into account the use of interpersonal grammatical metaphor in making suggestions.

Activity 9.7

(a)   Underline the four suggestions B makes in Text 9.4.

(b)   Below is a range of grammatical forms that could be used for presenting an imperative as a suggestion. Which of these does B use in the four suggestions you have underlined. Why?

Table 9.6: Interpersonal metaphors

Example clauses	Lexicogrammatical form
Make a list of questions.	Imperative
You should make a list of questions.	Modalised declarative (high obligation)
Let's make a list of questions.	Imperative with *let us*
Why don't we make a list of questions?	Negative interrogative
You could make a list of questions.	Modalised declarative (low obligation)
What about making a list of questions?	Non-finite interrogative
I would suggest you make a list of questions.	Modalised verbal process, projecting an imperative, declarative, or interrogative*
I think you need to have a list of questions.	Mental process projecting a declarative clause modalised as necessity
I think we could make a list of questions.	Mental process projecting a declarative modalised as possibility

* The projected clause could in fact be a reported version of any of these.

B can be seen as the dominant participant in this exchange and makes more suggestions than A. Despite this, the two participants maintain a productive working relationship in which they continue to collaboratively pursue their goal. This can probably be attributed in part to B's use of grammatical metaphor in the demands he makes.

9.8 Social distance in speaking

The following grammatical forms for making suggestions and proposals are taken from an English for Business Purposes teaching book. How many of them were used in the meeting in Text 9.4?

Text 9.5 Proposals, recommendations, suggestions

Proposals, recommendations, suggestions – strong:

> *I strongly recommend that . . .*
>
> *I suggest most strongly that . . .*

Proposals, recommendations, suggestions – neutral:

> *I propose that . . .*
>
> *My proposal is that . . .*

Proposals, recommendations, suggestions – tentative:

> *I would propose that . . .*
>
> *If I may make a suggestion, we could . . .*
>
> *I wonder if I might suggest . . .*
>
> *Wouldn't it be a good idea to . . .*

(Goodale, M. (1987) *The language of meetings*, USA: Thomson Learning, pp. 80–81)

The lexicogrammatical forms above are suited to a more formal business context than the one in Text 9.4. They signal a greater degree of social distance. Social distance is the second dimension of the tenor of the situation.

In order to understand social distance, it is useful to look at the language of casual conversation, which is a situation of reduced social distance. The following text is an extract from the conversation of a US family round the dinner table.

Activity 9.8

(a)   Which features of Text 9.6 tell you it is a conversation?

Text 9.6 Dinner table conversation

M = mother, F= father, C= 20 year old son, D= 17 year old son.

C   Mom, I, give me a rest, give it a rest. I didn't think about you. I mean I would rather do it <unclear> some other instance in my mind.

M   Yeah, well I can understand you know, I mean <unclear> Hi I'm Chris's mother, try to ignore me.

C   I went with a girl like you once. Let's serve this damn chili.

D   Okay let's serve the chili. Are you serving or not dad?

F   Doesn't matter.

M   Would you get those chips in there David, could you put them with the crackers?

F   Here, I'll come and serve it honey if you want me to.

M   Oh wait, we still have quite a few.

C   I don't see any others.

M   I know you don't.

C   We don't have any others.

M   Yes, I got you the big bag I think it will be a help to you.

F   Here's mom's.

. . .

M   Dave, put all the water in here. Well, here we are.

F   What?

M   Will y'all turn off the TV?

C   <to the dog> Pie, I'll kill you, I said I'd take you to the bathroom.

M   Man, get your tail out of the soup.

(Biber, D., Conrad, S., and Leech G. (2002) *Longman Student Grammar of Spoken and Written English*, England: Longman, p. 428)

(b)   The following is a list of the lexicogrammatical features that signal reduced social distance. The illustrations are from Text 9.3 (Blair–Bush dialogue). Identify additional examples from the conversation in Text 9.6 and add them to the list.

Contractions of the subject-finite mood element:
I'm, we <u>didn't</u>

First and second person pronouns:
thoughtful of <u>you</u>; <u>I</u> just want some movement.

Ellipsis:
On this trade thingy; If you want me to

Colloquial language or dialect:
Yo; awfully thoughtful; oh absolutely

Vocatives (terms of address):
Blair (as opposed to Tony, or Mr Blair)

Formulaic utterances:
It's a pleasure

Lexical and grammatical inaccuracies:

No, no, it may be that it's not, it may be that it's impossible.

Independent clauses with short nominal groups (in longer turns often connected by coordinating conjunctions):

Yesterday we didn't see much movement.

Non-technical/non-specialist lexis (or low frequency of specialist lexis):

trade thingy

To some extent, much of the less effective writing that has been considered throughout *Exploring English Grammar* has reflected the challenge of transferring from situations of familiarity like this, where the spoken mode has been developed, to more public contexts of written language. The next section examines this more closely.

9.9 Social distance in writing

In part, social distancing entails moving from the more fluid and fluent language of conversation towards the more planned language of academic or administrative writing. University writing, for example, is expected to construct uncommonsense knowledge and does this in part by moving away from the familiarity of conversation. This can be a challenge for students entering university, particularly those with less experience of such written English.

Activity 9.9

The two texts below are extracts from two first year university film-students' essays responding to the assignment title: In what ways does *mise-en-scène* construct meaning in film noir, with particular reference to the first fifteen minutes of *Red Rock West*?

Apply the categories presented above describing spoken language to the writing, bearing in mind the different social purposes of a conversation and an essay – in other words, you might expect an absence or reduction of conversation features in an essay. Which essay do you think was judged the most successful?

Text 9.7

[Paragraph 3]

I will be studying and discussing the first fifteen minutes of the film Red Rock West. The film starts off with an establishing shot of a road which disappears into the distance, I think this shot was used to give you the idea that it's the middle of nowhere. The next shot you see the main character, Nicholas Cage, emerging from a bad nights sleep, he was sleeping in his car. He then starts preparing himself for the long day ahead. He puts on his jeans then starts doing one handed press ups, this could be done for a couple of reasons.

1) He wants to stay fit

or

2) This shows how he prepares himself for the day ahead (like in Taxi Driver)

My opinion is option two. The fact that his home is a beaten up rusty Cadillac and he has a damaged leg also he has no money, life can't be that good for him. After the press ups he shaves then puts on a white cow boy looking shirt and looks at himself in a mirror and say, 'Nice to meet you . . .'.

[Concluding paragraph]

I think that the mise-en-scene was used very well in 'Red Rock West'. The zooming in and shading kind set the mood for the film but also the characters emotions. Mise-en-scene to me is important to all films but referring it to film noir mise-en-scene is important. Film noir is a complex genre it has many elements which splits it up from all the other types of genre, it's a mystery with twists and turns the subjects covered are money, love, betrayal, murder. In the reading given to the class by John Orr 'The road to nowhere', he describes film noir as a deadly

---

triangle: Love – passion – money. The thing I like the most about the old film noir was that in the beginning you're left in mystery until the end. I also like the low key-lighting I think that it sets the mood and adds to the suspense.

(Author's personal data)

Text 9.8

[Paragraph 3]

Costume and props play an essential role in creating verisimilitude and conveying different meanings within the context of a film's genre. Costume worn by Wayne and Michael contributes significantly to the generic verisimilitude of the film. Audiences expect to see characters in contemporary American West settings wearing denim, cowboy boots and cowboy style shirts. Their costumes also visually convey meanings to the audience about their respective characters. The protagonist is dressed in light serene colours, stone washed denim and a white cowboy style shirt, giving the audience an indication that this is possibly a good character. Whilst Wayne is attired in dark sombre colours, black trousers and waistcoat with a navy blue shirt conveying to the audience that this is a dark and sinister character.

[Concluding paragraph]

After having meticulously studied the various ways in which mise-en-scene works to construct meaning in Red Rock West. It can be deduced that the very concept of mise en-scene withholds a significant amount of importance in clearly constructing and conveying meanings to the audience visually.

(Author's personal data)

Approaching language from a functional grammar perspective provides insights to support students as they engage with the formal, technical, impersonal genres that constitute academic discourse. Sometimes seen as unnecessarily alienating, these features of the discourse can also be seen as central to the work of academic study, in this case, determining whether a film-studies student is analysing a film or just expressing an opinion about it. Treating abstract entities (rather than humans) as subject is what distinguishes these two extracts from each other:

> <u>I</u> *think this shot was used to give you the idea that it's the middle of nowhere*
>
> <u>Costume worn by Wayne and Michael</u> *contributes significantly to the generic verisimilitude of the film.*

9.10 Stance, persona, and assumed degree of alignment with others

By means of the grammar of the interpersonal metafunction, speakers or writers align themselves with particular perspectives and values. In the process, they establish a persona with viewpoints and values, and acknowledge, to greater or lesser extent, the existence of others with similar or different viewpoints and values.

The next two activities explore how an international organisation exploits modality in constructing its institutional persona and competing for customers and market share in the global marketplace.

The genre that will be considered is an economic forecast. These are produced by investment banks to give their customers information about the world's economies on which they will base decisions about movements of large quantities of money around the world's money markets.

Economic forecasts are high-stakes documents and through them investment banks build relations with customers and establish an institutional persona. New economists at the bank develop the genre knowledge needed to create effective examples of the economic forecast genre and participate in this marketplace dialogue. As a genre, economic forecasts consist of two major stages: description of previous trends and prediction of future trends. Within each of these stages are a number of sub-stages, which are known as **phases**. As you will see in the next activity, there may be up to three phases in each stage. There is a generally sequential movement through these stages and phases, but the pattern is not rigidly adhered to for every forecast. Phases may be reversed or omitted as the economist or the editorial team sees fit. The activity below introduces this genre form.

Activity 9.10

The text below is a short example of an economic forecast.

(a)   Identify and label the Description and Prediction stages.

(b)   Use the mixed-up list below to identify and label the phases in each stage. Not all the phases are exemplified in this forecast. One clause in the text is bracketed as it performs a communicative function belonging to a different phase from the one it is in.

- explaining previous trends;
- setting the basis for predictions;
- describing previous trends;
- assessing risk to the forecast;
- predicting future trends;
- revising or confirming previous forecast.

(c)   Underline all examples of modalisation in the text.

Text 9.9 United States Second Quarter forecast

Stages and Phases	
Stage 1	
Phase 1	As the Spring quarter approaches, the optimism that we have expressed about a recovery in the US economy seems to be supported by the early data.
Phase 2	Political events have taken an unexpected twist, as plans for fiscal stimulus for FY92/93 have been completely quashed. In addition, President Bush's political popularity has plunged [and his re-election prospects are far from assured]. While the political drama unfolds . . .
Phase 3	

Stage 2	
Phase 1	the Federal Reserve Board should sit quietly on the sidelines until the economy is solidly back into real growth territory. Its surprising 9 April, 1% cut in the Federal Funds rate (to 3¼%) seems likely to be its last move for some time, unless the economy dives again. But, by late in the third quarter, we expect the growth outlook to be sufficiently strong that the Fed's attention will be re-directed toward dampening inflation expectations and we would not be surprised to see increases in short-term interest rates well before the US elections.
Phase 2	The result should be a flatter yield curve by the end of the year, with most of the movement in the short and intermediate term securities.
Phase 3	

(Summary section of United States forecast in *Natwest Treasury and Capital Markets, County Natwest, Global Economic Forecasts Second Quarter 1992*, p. 6)

As this example illustrates, modalisation is a defining grammatical feature of the prediction stage of an economic forecast. Such modalisation is sometimes regarded as a 'hedging' device. By predicting cautiously, economists avoid making mistakes that would damage the reputation of the bank.

However, in a comparison of UK and Dutch economic forecasts written in English, it became evident that Dutch economists almost exclusively used the modal *will*. Interviewed about this, the Dutch economists claimed that using weaker modal forms would show a lack of professional confidence. In view of the difference between their writing and that of economists speaking English as a first language, they looked for advice on what was appropriate. The next activity considers this.

379

Activity 9.11

In the forecast text below, written by a British economist, the modal forms originally used in the predictions have all been replaced by the modal, *will*.

(a) Read through the text to gain a general impression of the forecast.
(b) Then underline all the predictions with *will*.
(c) Experiment with alternatives to *will* by replacing it with any of the range of modalising language features listed in Table 9.5.
(d) On the basis of this experiment, what, in your opinion, is the function of modal forms in an economic forecast?

Text 9.10

United Kingdom

(1) The need for a political risk premium has disappeared, not just diminished. (2) This is the real election surprise. (3) The UK is now one of the few major economies to have a right-of-centre government solidly entrenched for the next 4–5 years. (4) The 21 seat majority achieved will be able to accommodate the 5–7 seat by-election losses suggested by the historic record for a normal Parliament. (5) If Mr Major has learnt anything from recent experience, it is the critical importance of synchronising the economic and political cycles. (6) With a safe majority and no need to pander to public opinion in the short-term, the authorities will decide that squeezing inflation is the first priority.

(7) The fact that the election result will boost sentiment and reinforce the recovery tendencies, which are beginning to emerge already, strengthens the case for this stance. (8) The implication is that the authorities will be reluctant to see short-term interest rates coming down too far, too fast. (9) A move to base rate below 10% will, therefore, come less rapidly than the market is currently assuming, though the fact is that, with Sterling strengthening to DM2.90, a first move (i.e. to 10%) will have occurred before the local authority elections on 7 May. (10) A move to narrow bands in the ERM, which again is high on the agenda of optimistic market expectations, will be an Autumn, rather than an imminent, decision. (11) As the intention is to moderate the interest rate decline, it does not make sense to aggravate the pressures by an additional confidence-boosting measure at this time of exaggerated bullishness.

(*Natwest Markets, Global Economic Forecasts, Second Quarter 1992, United Kingdom Report*, p.10)

The original version of this forecast can be seen in the Answer key. Closer investigation of British forecasts suggests that modals are not exclusively intended to express caution. Instead, through modalisation, British economists appear to be engaged in dialogue with other economists in the economics community, acknowledging other positions and talking their own version of the future into existence.

High commitment modality closes out other viewpoints and discourages contradiction. The Stern report on climate change (quoted in Text 9.5 in Chapter 5) uses high commitment modality to discourage opposition to its predictions and recommendations. However, even in such a strongly worded document, at the point where strong opposition can be expected, the modality is downgraded from *must* to *should*:

The response to climate change <u>must</u> be based on a shared vision

Adaptation efforts <u>should</u> be accelerated.

Persuasiveness depends on more than strength of opinion. We saw Blair adopt this approach in his use of the low probability proposition – *it may be that it's impossible* – to allow for a contrary view from Bush.

The issue is whether the writer or speaker adopts an **open stance**, and accepts the existence of alternative positions, or a **closed stance**, which may signal great confidence but equally may signal a narrow mind. The Dutch economists, recognising that it was likely to be more commercial to actively engage readers through their texts, decided to adopt a more dialogic open stance in their institutional documents.

To exploit modality for this purpose is more challenging than simply deciding if a particular proposal or proposition should be 'strong' or 'weak'. Modals cannot be graded precisely on a scale. The force of a particular modalised clause is dependent on its interrelationship with the rest of the text, particular the evaluative language of that text. The final prediction in Text 9.10, read on its own, looks very cautious.

(10) A move to narrow bands in the ERM, which again <u>may be high</u> on the agenda of optimistic market expectations, <u>could well be</u> an Autumn, rather than an imminent, decision.

However, seen in its textual context, as the culmination of a tightly argued accumulation of modalisation, this final prediction is stronger than it seems alone. Commitment and persuasiveness are woven into the patterning of the range of modal forms – both typical and non-typical ones – across the whole text, in combination with the social purposes of the genre in which they occur. The communicative functions of the modal system are highly sensitive to context and social purpose. Developing the skills to use modalising lexicogrammatical forms effectively can really only be achieved within a particular communicative context.

9.11 The expression of attitude: appraisal

This chapter has concentrated on the mood element. However, as indicated at the end of the previous section, <u>accumulation</u> of meaning is a characteristic of the grammar of interpersonal metafunction. Interpersonal meanings are spread throughout a clause, and evaluation accumulates through a text.

By means of a wide range of lexicogrammatical resources, referred to as **appraisal** resources (and including some we have already studied in this chapter), speakers or writers can:

- express **attitude** in terms of:

    (i)   **affect** or emotion

    (ii) **judgement** of people's behaviour

    (iii) **appreciation** of phenomena;

- grade **the degree of commitment** to the attitudes expressed;

- signal open or closed stance.

These meanings can be conveyed by choices of noun, adjective, adverb, or verb, and can appear in any of the SVOCA positions of a clause. The next activity traces the accumulation of meanings involved in persuading someone to change their point of view.

Activity 9.12

The transcript below is from a meeting of a book publishing company. Use different coloured pens for this activity.

(a)   Read the dialogue and underline in one colour all the lexicogrammatical items that express attitude or evaluation. These can be nouns, adjectives, adverbs, or verbs.

(b) Decide if the exchange deals primarily with affect, judgement, or appreciation (see the gloss on these above).

(c) Underline in a different colour any lexicogrammatical items that <u>grade</u> attitudes or evaluation.

(d) Is there an accumulation of evaluation across the text?

(e) What is the culmination of this accumulation?

Text 9.11 Deciding whether to replace a product

A: But I have to admit that [Name of book] now looks like an old book.

B: Do you think so?

A: Yes. It's got an old, it's got an old fashioned look and feel about it.

B: I think you only mean you've just done a four colour book and it's in black and white.

A: No, I don't just mean it's in black and white it's got an old feel about it.

B: Well, I hope you are wrong. In the sense that I hope it's not going to go down everywhere, its, its sales figures . . .

A: It's an old book, you think of the number of years it's been out.

B: I suppose I have.

A: You forget just how long some of our list has been out.

C: Is it eight?

D: No, nine.

B: Well, of course, the trouble is that something like [Name of different book] is a kind of perennial book and therefore you tend not to . . .

A: [Name of book] can you just remind us when it was published?

B: I can do that, it was published in 1991 . . . the original.

A: In other words, it is, to all intents and purposes, I mean, other publishers would see that as a . . .

> B: Seven years.
>
> A: ... a dead a book.
>
> B: seven years, is a ...
>
> A: Seven years. It's peaked, it's on the way out.
>
> B: In fact, he's exactly right because books that succeed, the life cycle is supposedly seven years before they decline into senility. They, they take like people, they take a few years to go through their geriatric period but they are basically dead after seven years.

(Extract from Nelson, M., The Business English Corpus (BEC) (details available at http://users.utu.fi/micnel/business_english_lexis_site.htm))
(Extract adapted by omission of identifying book titles)

The evaluative focus of this exchange is appreciation of a book. The strength of this evaluation is accumulated across the text through the following lexicogrammatical features:

- the amplifications of the adjectives and nouns used to describe the book:

  A   *old-old fashioned-old feel-dead*

  B   *senility-geriatric-basically dead*;

- graduation language used throughout the interaction to modify the evaluations: *only, just, in the sense that, a kind of, exactly, supposedly, basically*;

- material processes with evaluative connotations: *go down, succeed, decline*;

- mental processes used as grammatical metaphors expressing open stance: *I have to admit, think, hope, suppose, tend, mean*;

- adjuncts signalling that the speaker is taking a position: *of course, in fact*;

- there are two judgements of people's behaviour and these signal the main shift of attitude across the text: *I hope you are wrong; he's exactly right*.

By means of the negotiated accumulation of evaluation across the exchange, the two main participants come successfully to a shared position on the object of their evaluation.

Activity 9.13

Return to the string of emails in Activity 9.1. For each of the aspects of tenor below, what does the analysis tell you about the breakdown in the communication?

(a) Social roles and status: Focusing on the mood structure of clauses you consider important in each mail, and the evaluative language used, identify the social purpose of each mail in the exchange.

(b) Social distance: Select about three mails to focus on and identify features of social closeness or distance.

(c) Stance/alignment with others: Focusing particularly on the use of modalisation and the accumulation of evaluation through the emails, identify how each writer does or doesn't align themselves with the others' viewpoint.

9.12 Using interpersonal analysis to explore real world problems

The premise of systemic functional grammar presented in this chapter is that each time we use language to represent our experience of the world, we also intrude into the text and interact with our interlocutors.

Several of the activities in this chapter were derived from actual applications of this premise. These have included:

- Corporate communications training for economists and market analysts of international banks to enhance dialogue with clients through company publications.

- Communications training for corporate account managers and administrative staff in internal and external email correspondence.

- Presentation and negotiation skills development for international business staff.

- Academic literacy development for undergraduate and postgraduate students from both UK and overseas.

- Critical analysis of newspaper reports.

You might like to think whether there are practical issues in your own environment that would benefit from the approach adopted here of treating a wide range of lexicogrammatical resources as an extensive system developed to manage interpersonal relations in particular contexts.

9.13 Summary

Tenor refers to the identities, relationships, values, and perspectives of interactants in a particular context of communication. In this chapter, tenor has been described in terms of social roles and status, social distance, and stance or alignment with others' views. These aspects of tenor are realised primarily by the lexicogrammatical systems of mood and modality. Together they constitute the interpersonal metafunction of language and context.

Mood is realised by choices at subject-finite level and in turn realises a range of speech functions derived from the speech roles of giving and demanding and the items that are exchanged, goods and services, and information.

Modality intersects with mood and is exploited to adjust the commitment of the speaker to the proposition or proposal they are making. Modality is thus a clear signal of the speaker's intrusion into the text and plays a major role in establishing the speaker's stance. The delicacy of managing relationships means that, in addition to the grading of commitment that can be achieved by modal verbs, adjectives, and nouns, a number of material, mental, and verbal processes are manipulated to also adjust the commitment. Transferring grammatical forms from one metafunction to another like this is an example of interpersonal grammatical metaphor – that is, using a grammatical form to perform a non-typical function.

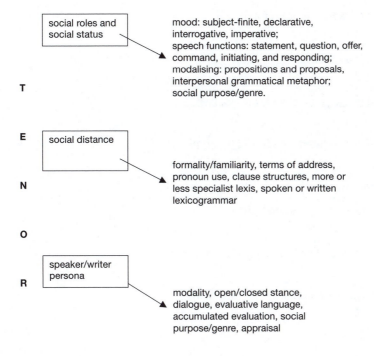

Figure 9.2

Resources for interacting and taking a position

social roles and social status

mood: subject-finite, declarative, interrogative, imperative;
speech functions: statement, question, offer, command, initiating, and responding;
modalising: propositions and proposals, interpersonal grammatical metaphor;
social purpose/genre.

social distance

formality/familiarity, terms of address, pronoun use, clause structures, more or less specialist lexis, spoken or written lexicogrammar

speaker/writer persona

modality, open/closed stance, dialogue, evaluative language, accumulated evaluation, social purpose/genre, appraisal

T E N O R

Answer key

Activity 9.3

Declarative:

(3) You're leaving?
    S F

(6) I told that to the man.
    S F

(10) I just want some movement.
    S   F

(12) Yesterday we didn't see much movement.
        S   F

(13) It may be that it's impossible
    S F

(14) I am prepared to say it
    S F

---

(22) It's awfully thoughtful of you
S F

---

(23) It's a pleasure
S F

---

(24) I know you picked it out yourself.
S F

---

(25) Oh absolutely – in fact I knitted it!
S F

Interrogative:

---

(1) How are you doing? (*wh-*)
F S

---

(7) Are you planning to say that here or not? (*polar*)
F S

---

(17) Who is introducing the trade? (*wh-*)
S F

Imperative:

---

(19) Tell her to call 'em.
F

---

(21) Tell her to put him on, them on the spot.
F

Activity 9.4

	Speech function	Bush	Blair
Initiating the exchange: giving information	Statement	10, 12, 23	5
Initiating the exchange: giving goods and services	Offer		
Initiating the exchange: demanding goods and services	Command	18, 20	
Initiating the exchange: demanding information	Question	1, 3, 16	7
Responding: supplying information	Answer/ disclaimer	6, 8, 14	2, 4, 9, 15, 17

Responding: supplying goods and services	Supply/ refuse supply		19
Responding: receiving goods and services	Acceptance/ rejection	21	
Responding: receiving information	Acknowledge/ contradict		11, 13, 22, 24

Activity 9.5

(2)	**Blair:**	I'm just . . . (interrupted declarative)
(4)	**Blair:**	No, no, no not yet. (ellipted declarative)
(6)	**Bush:**	Yeah, I told that to the man. (declarative)
(8)	**Bush:**	If you want me to. (ellipted declarative)
(11)	**Blair:**	Yeah. (minor)
(13)	**Blair:**	No, no, (minor clause) it may be that it's not, it may be that it's impossible. (modalised statement)
(15)	**Blair:**	But it's just I think that we need to be an opposition. (declarative)
(17)	**Blair:**	Angela [Merkel, the German Chancellor]. (ellipted declarative)
(19)	**Blair:**	Yes. (minor)
(22)	**Blair:**	It's a pleasure. (declarative)
(24)	**Blair:**	Oh absolutely (minor) – in fact I knitted it!!! (declarative)

Activity 9.6

A business meeting.

A and B appear to be work colleagues.

A appears to be getting advice from B, and so B can be seen as more powerful.

The exchange appears to be successful as it moves forward without breakdown and appears to reach a mutually accepted plan of action.

Clause types are predominantly declarative. A and B produce one interrogative each.

Activity 9.7

Negative interrogative	*Yeah, why don't we play it along the lines of*
Projecting mental process	*I think what we need first of all, are some more facts*
Projecting mental process	*so we need I think we, for you to have a list of questions*
Modalised verbal process	*what I would suggest is you, you try and say*

Activity 9.8

(b)

Contractions of the subject-finite mood element:
I'm, I'll, Let's, I don't, Here's, I'd

First and second person pronouns:
All pronouns are *I, you, we*

Ellipsis:
Doesn't matter, I know you don't

Colloquial language or dialect:
I went with a girl, damn chili, mom, will y'all, I'll kill you, Man

Vocatives:
honey, mom's, Chris, David, Dave, Man

Formulaic utterances:
give it a rest, Well, here we are.

Lexical and grammatical inaccuracies:
I mean I would rather do it <unclear> some other instance in my mind

Independent clauses with short nominal groups:
Nearly all the clauses are simple clauses.

Non-technical/non-specialist lexis:
Terminology is suited to a 'starting a meal' situation, so only 'specialist' terminology related to that: *chili, chips*

Activity 9.9

Essay 1 is written in a relatively informal, conversational style, whereas Essay 2 has the technical, objective, and more formal style that is conventional for university essays.

Essay 1	Essay 2
Contractions of the subject-finite mood element	
it's, you're, can't.	None
First and second person pronouns	
I, you, my	Absence of first and second person pronouns and reduced number of pronouns generally as a result of impersonal, passive forms; e.g., *it can be deduced.*
Ellipsis	
the next shot you see.	None
Colloquial language	
life can't be that good, kind (of) set the mood.	None
Independent clauses with short nominal groups	
Most of the sentences are short verb-based clauses with human subjects. The punctuation reinforces this similarity to spoken language. Where clauses are connected, this tends to be by means of coordinating conjunctions.	Long nominal groups: *Costume worn by Wayne and Michael; characters in contemporary American West settings wearing denim, cowboy boots and cowboy style shirts.*
	Non-finite dependent clauses used in establishing connections between clauses or for embedding information in nominal groups. *The protagonist is dressed in light serene colours, . . . giving the audience an indication; Wayne is attired in dark sombre colours . . . conveying to the audience . . .*
	[It could be noted that there is some lack of clarity in the writing about whether non-finite clauses are subordinated or embedded.]
Technical terminology	
There is limited use of the technical terminology of the field. There is also limited use of semi-technical academic language. The film is presented as a	Technical and semi-technical terminology is used extensively. The film is framed by technical or abstract terms which are used in subject position to organise a description

391

narrative sequence made up of material processes.

as opposed to a narrative. *Costume and props play an essential role. Their costumes also visually convey meanings.* Process types tend to be relational or at least function as relational: *Their costumes visually convey meaning.*

Lexical and grammatical accuracy

Speech-like changes of direction in the middle of some clauses and some inaccurate vocabulary use.
Mise-en-scene to me is important to all films but referring it to film noir mise-en-scene is important.
splits it up from

Generally accurate although it is evident that the technical terms are still being learned and the semi-technical style is not always accurately executed.

Essay 2 was judged the most successful.

Activity 9.10

Stages and phases

Stage 1 Description

Phase 1 **Revising or confirming** **previous forecast**	As the Spring quarter approaches, the optimism that we have expressed about a recovery in the US economy seems to be supported by the early data.
Phase 2 **Describing previous trends**	Political events have taken an unexpected twist, as plans for fiscal stimulus for FY92/93 have been completely quashed. In addition, President Bush's political popularity has plunged [and his re-election prospects are far from assured]. While the political drama unfolds, . . .

Phase 3
Explaining previous trends
There is not really an explicit explaining phase, but to some extent, the describing of phase 2 is explanatory as well.

Stage 2 Prediction

Phase 1
Setting the basis for predictions
This phase also contains predictions but they are predictions on which the central prediction of phase 2 is based.

the Federal Reserve Board <u>should sit</u> quietly on the sidelines until the economy is solidly back into real growth territory. Its surprising 9 April, 1% cut in the Federal Funds rate (to 3¼%) <u>seems likely to be</u> its last move for some time, unless the economy dives again. But, by late in the third quarter, <u>we expect</u> the growth outlook to be sufficiently strong that the Fed's attention <u>will be</u> re-directed toward dampening inflation expectations and <u>we would not be surprised to see</u> increases in short-term interest rates well before the US elections.

Phase 2
Predicting future trends

The result <u>should be</u> a flatter yield curve by the end of the year, with most of the movement in the short and intermediate term securities.

Phase 3
Assessing risk to the forecast
There is no risk assessment in this forecast.

Activity 9.11 Original text

(1) The need for a political risk premium has disappeared, not just diminished. (2) This is the real election surprise. (3) The UK is now one of the few major economies to have a right-of-centre government solidly entrenched for the next 4–5 years. (4) The 21 seat majority achieved **(i) should be well able to** accommodate the 5–7 seat by-election losses suggested by the historic record for a normal Parliament. (5) If Mr Major has learnt anything from recent experience, it is the critical importance of synchronising the economic and political cycles. (6) With a safe majority and no need to pander to public opinion in the

short-term, the authorities **(ii) may well decide** that squeezing inflation is the first priority.

(7) **(iii) The likelihood that** the election result **(iii) will boost** sentiment and reinforce the recovery tendencies, which are probably beginning to emerge already, strengthens the case for this stance. (8) The implication **(iv) would be that** the authorities **(v) may be** reluctant to see short-term interest rates coming down too far, too fast. (9) A move to base rate below 10% **(vi) may,** therefore, **come** less rapidly than the market is currently assuming, though **(vii) the likelihood is that**, with Sterling strengthening to DM2.90, a first move (i.e. to 10%) **(viii) will have occurred** before the local authority elections on 7 May. (10) A move to narrow bands in the ERM, which again **(xi) may be high** on the agenda of optimistic market expectations, **(x) could well be** an Autumn, rather than an imminent, decision. (11) If the intention is to moderate the interest rate decline, it hardly makes sense to aggravate the pressures by an additional confidence-boosting measure at this time of exaggerated bullishness.

Activity 9.13

Relative social status

Mail 1:	Offer of goods and service (a CV). Response to a request in earlier telephone call – so is, in fact, supply.
Mail 2:	Not an acceptance, but a demand for information.
Mail 3:	Disclaimer – shifting the item exchanged from information to one about a service – providing information. This then becomes an initiation statement – giving Daniel some advice, but not the information requested.
Mail 4:	A long, information-giving mail in response to Alan's statement, functioning as contradiction.
Mail 5:	A long, information-giving mail that contradicts the information in Mail 4.
Mail 6:	Primarily another information-giving mail that contradicts Mail 5. Ends with an offer.
Mail 7:	Contradicts statement in Mail 6 and rejects the offer.
Mail 8:	Contradicts statement in Mail 7, and ends the communication.

The two emailers are not cooperative. This is evident from the number of speech acts that are surprising or shift the exchange from one kind of interaction to a different one, and from the high level of contradiction in the exchange. It is unlikely that, after Mail 3, the two men are attempting to cooperate, but had they been trying to, they would need to mitigate the contradictions by exploiting less congruent lexicogrammar to perform speech functions

Distance

In the context of such oppositional correspondence, the direct and somewhat familiar language of Alan is likely to exacerbate the confrontation. Success would be more likely if participants increased the distance and reduced the degree of directness and familiarity.

Stance

There is clearly a serious misalignment of views. Although the communication is already seriously damaged after Mail 3, it is possible that each man was still seeking to convince the other of his position. There is very little openness of stance, however, and positions are simply reinforced by the accumulation of negative and unmodalised evaluations.

ten

Making a text flow

10.1 Introduction

You have seen in Chapters 8 and 9 how we use language to interact with others, as well as to represent our experience of the world, and that both representation and interaction occur simultaneously throughout the language we use. In particular, you have seen that, in order to understand the way a text simultaneously functions both as interaction and representation, you need to look at the same piece of language from different perspectives. To understand representation means looking at the grammatical resources associated with the ideational metafunction (Chapter 8), and to understand interaction means focusing on the grammatical resources associated with the interpersonal metafunction (Chapter 9). So, if we return to a clause we encountered in one of the texts in the first half of the book, we can now look at it not only from the perspective of its formal structure but also from the perspective of ideational and interpersonal meaning:

The Amazon has lost a vast extent of its rain-forest in the last forty years!
What has caused this great destruction?

The Amazon	*has lost*	*a vast extent of its rain-forest*	*in the last forty years!*	traditional formal perspective
subject	verb	object	adjunct	
Subject	finite			interpersonal perspective
declarative mood, statement				
agent	material process	affected	circumstance	ideational perspective

What	*has caused*	*this great destruction?*
subject	verb	object
subject	finite	
interrogative mood, question		
agent	material process	affected

In this chapter, we look at language from yet another viewpoint. This time we will see how the same clause or text can be explored, not only from an ideational and interpersonal perspective, but also from a textual perspective. Once again, the difference in perspective brings into focus different language items or different aspects of the same language items, as we explore the grammatical resources associated with the textual meta-function. Developing an awareness of how language helps to organise ideational and interpersonal meanings as coherent and cohesive text can be useful in addressing a wide range of real-world problems, for example, in areas such as education, translation, and speech disorder.

The textual metafunction was introduced in Chapter 6.

Scenario

The following notices appeared on the display board at the end of each carriage in a German Inter-City-Express train. Can you identify anything odd about the notices?

Text 10.1 Train notice

> At all seats you can listen to 3 ICE Programmes (classical, pop, fairy tales) over the headphones.
>
> Screens to watch the ICE video programme you will find in the backrests of the seats in the first class coaches.

(J. Bateman, unpublished)
(This notice was found by J. Bateman.)

Although it is not difficult to understand the information given in the notices, you may have been somewhat disconcerted by the order in which it unfolded. This is because the English translations have preserved the same meanings in initial position in each clause that were in the original German sentences:

At all seats . . .
Screens to watch . . .

However, English and German differ in terms of the kinds of meaning that are usually placed in first position in a clause. The literal translation thus results in two rather poorly worded notices. As you work through this chapter you will see that the meanings we place at the start of a clause (and also at the start of a paragraph and text) are significant in managing a smooth and coherent flow of meaning.

Chapter 6 explained that the textual metafunction relates to the contextual variable of mode. Mode is largely to do with how a text or interaction is produced (for example, as writing, speech, or email), and therefore how spontaneous and interactive it is. It also relates to communicative distance and the role of language (whether it constitutes the social activity, or accompanies it). These aspects of context affect how we use lexicogrammar to package information and to manage information flow. Figure 10.1 provides a review of the resources we have explored so far.

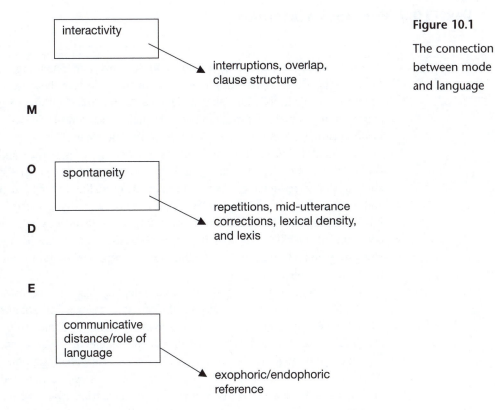

Figure 10.1

The connection
between mode
and language

10.2 Previewing and signposting: macro- and hyper-theme

Activity 10.1

In order to select candidates for university or college courses, personal statements (as opposed to interviews) are increasingly used by admissions officers in many parts of the world. In these statements applicants need to explain why they are interested in the courses they have applied for and make the case for why they should be selected. The real-world consequences of such a text not fulfilling its goal are obvious. Look at the following personal statement submitted by a student applying for a degree in law and French. We have taken out certain parts of the text. Can you identify what these might be?

Text 10.2 Personal statement

I love to read Le Monde every day and feel my understanding of French affairs and vocabulary grow. I wish to study Law because it encompasses a wholly enthralling subject that is embedded within every aspect of any social infrastructure, with French, a passion of mine that has intensified the more I have explored it over the years.

Critical Thinking has taught me how to be more analytical and furthered my ability to formulate and structure arguments; whilst the study of French has enabled me to communicate more fluently in French and increased my knowledge of French customs. In studying History, I have learnt how to extract key information while improving my communication skills through intensive debates. Maths was highly enjoyable and allowed me to become apt in problem solving and following complex reasoning.

In winning the vast majority of debates held against other schools, I was chosen to debate in the House of Commons against MP Dianne Abbott, where my team won. My desire to study Law was enhanced by the sheer exhilaration I felt in having to articulate my views into captivating my audience, while gaining the technical debating points. Attending a Law workshop with UCL allowed me to speak to Law and French undergraduates and participate in a mock trial, giving me a realistic approach to life as a Law student. The completion of work experience with Linklaters gave me the opportunity to speak to high-ranking solicitors, which drove me to Law studies. Furthermore, during a school visit to KPMG offices, I engaged in conversation with a founding partner of KPMG Forensic department. As a result he contacted my school praising my 'confidence and direct questioning' and offered me a position within his division. As I return there every summer, I relish the challenge of speaking French with others, building rapport with useful contacts and working in teams on different Projects, which augment my teamwork abilities. I am a part-time librarian and frequently have to encounter the public and speak French and some Spanish to those who can only speak these languages.

I committed myself to spending a year tutoring a GCSE maths student; although this was a huge test of my ability to speak, explain and teach clearly, it was incredibly rewarding as the student progressed from a U grade to a B grade, and I gained a good friend. I am a Senior Member of our Justice and Peace organisation, assuming prominent roles of responsibility and problem solving and helping to raise over

£1000 for an African school. I am a passionate member of my Sixth Form Gospel Choir and have always enjoyed singing, reading in mass and performing.

I look forward to applying what I have gained and contributing my personality to university life, studying Law with French.

(http://www.studential.com/bio/getps.asp?ps=905&view=subject)

While recognising the strengths of the personal statement above, did you feel from the start somewhat disoriented – not quite sure of where the text was going? And as you read further did you wonder what the writer's 'point' was? It would not be surprising if you did since we had removed several pieces of information from the statement and, in so doing, erased from view the overall 'architecture' of the text. If you compare Text 10.2 with the original text in the Answer key you will see that the missing sections were located at the beginning of the text and at the beginning of each paragraph.

Since it was in these sections that the writer provided the higher-order meanings of her statement (ones that she went on to elaborate in the remainder of the text and each paragraph), the modified text does not come across as a smoothly flowing, cohesive argument. In SFL, the departure point for a text is called the **macro-theme**, and the departure point for a paragraph (or section of information) is called the **hyper-theme**.[1] Both macro- and hyper-themes provide an orientation as to what is to come: they establish expectations about how the text or paragraph will unfold.

Activity 10.2

Look at the following (abridged) letter of complaint to a hospital.

(a) Highlight the initial section of the text that sets up the overall message of the text (the macro-theme).

(b) Then, highlight each of the starting points for paragraphs 2–4 that set up the main messages for each of the sections (the hyper-themes). Consider their role in contributing to the organisation and flow of information.

(c) Observe any patterns in the use of nominal groups and appraisal in the macro- and hyper-themes.

Text 10.3 Hospital complaint

Dear X

My family and I recently witnessed what we regard as unacceptable treatment of patients by your hospital staff, caused in part by poor supervision and communication systems on the ward. We are writing this letter in order to alert you to the problems as detailed below and to urge that you rectify as a matter of priority a situation which is putting patients at risk.

On Sunday, October 12th, 2008, my mother Helene Xanthou was admitted to Brook Ward having suffered a bad fall. Since she suffers from Alzheimer's, and seemed very agitated by her situation, my brother, sister-in-law and I spent much of the subsequent week in the ward. During this time we encountered a number of concerned nursing staff who were helpful and kind. However, our overall experience, showed that there is a significant absence of the care and attention one would expect in a hospital. Indeed we would go so far as to say that a low level bullying culture has developed amongst some of your staff. We identified three major problems.

One major problem was an absence of basic patient care and kindness. The calibre of the 'bank' staff was depressingly low. Many were rude, unbelievably unhelpful and did not seem properly qualified. It is not an exaggeration to say that we were scared to leave our mother in their 'care' overnight. What an indictment.

[. . .]

A second major problem that we identified was a lack of any clear supervisory system. Apparently because Brook ward is an 'overflow' ward there is no ward manager or overall supervisor. Given that they have no permanent staffing, this seems to be a particularly dangerous situation. Certainly during our time we saw no monitoring or checking of even basic, routine tasks. As a result the following incidents occurred. In many cases they occurred routinely.

1. The taking of medication was not supervised. On one occasion, for example, we found what we believe to be one of my mother's warfarin tablets on the floor and two unidentified tablets floating in her glass of water.

    [. . .]

Finally, there was often a complete lack of information about patients and their situation. A standard response to questions by concerned family and visitors was for a nurse to say that they would go and find out and then simply not return. We felt we had entered an Alice in Wonderland world where everyone told you something different and it was impossible to get any rational answers

[. . .]

The problems outlined above are jeopardizing the wellbeing of many of your patients, particularly those who do not have family or friends to act as advocates. We therefore urgently request that action be taken:

1. Most importantly, all wards to have a supervisor who checks standards of care and has the power to discipline lapses of care.
2. Agency staff to be replaced by permanent staff or a balance of permanent and agency staff be organized. Too often our requests for information and help were greeted by a shrug of the shoulders and the excuse that they were just 'bank'.

[. . .]

We understand that your hospital is under pressure. We were in fact impressed by the doctors in both casualty and on the ward. They are let down by the poor care and organisation on Brook Ward.

We very much look forward to hearing your response. We feel very strongly about this, and are ready to take matters further if we do not receive an adequate response.

Sincerely,

cc   PALS Queen Elizabeth Hospital
     Keith Corrigan MP
     Councillor June Szeben, Brunely

(Author's personal data)

Activity 10.1 and Activity 10.2 demonstrate the significance of how we set up and frame a text, and the way this is often done at key points in a text, namely the start of a whole text and the start of each paragraph or sub-section of information. In Text 10.2, for example, you will have seen that at the level of whole text the writer uses the opening paragraphs (the macro-theme) to set out the overall aim of the letter (to prevent further unacceptable treatment of hospital patients) and the general nature of the problems (concerning the poor treatment of patients), which she will go on to elaborate in the body of the letter. This opening section (the macro-theme) ends by indicating that there are three main problems (*We identified three major problems*), and in this way foreshadows that the body of the letter will flesh out these three problems.

In written and spoken texts that are of a reasonable length and are at the non-interactive, non-spontaneous end of the mode continuum, opening paragraphs are usually crucial in providing the overarching, higher-order message of the text. By highlighting the key ideas, areas, or arguments that the writer or speaker will go on to elaborate, they help the reader to make sense of the ensuing text.

At the level of paragraph, the letter writer makes use of the initial sentences in a similar way to the initial paragraph: she previews the main focus of the ensuing section. Thus in paragraphs 3–5 the hyper-themes function to introduce the main problems, which link back and provide justification for the need to complain. In paragraph 6 the hyper-theme looks back to the previous problems and forwards to the recommended actions. The thematic structuring of Text 10.3 can be made clear using the following visuals:

Dear X

My family and I recently witnessed what we regard as unacceptable treatment of patients by your hospital staff, caused in part by poor supervision and communication systems on the ward. We are writing this letter in order to alert you to the problems as detailed below and to urge that you rectify as a matter of priority a situation which is putting patients at risk.

First two paragraphs are macro-theme

On Sunday, October 12th, 2008, my mother Helene Xanthou was admitted to Brook Ward having suffered a bad fall. Since she suffers from Alzheimer's, and seemed very agitated by her situation, my brother, sister-in-law and I spent much of the subsequent week in the ward. During this time we encountered a number of concerned nursing staff who were helpful and kind. However, our overall experience, showed that there is a significant absence of the care and attention one would expect in a hospital. Indeed we would go so far as to say that a low level bullying culture has developed amongst some of your staff. We identified three major problems.

1. One major problem was an absence of basic patient care and kindness. The calibre of the 'bank' staff was depressingly low . . .

2. A second major problem that we identified was a lack of any clear supervisory system. Apparently because Brook ward is an 'overflow' ward . . .

3. Finally, there was often a complete lack of information about patients and their situation. A standard response . . .

The problems outlined (above) are jeopardizing the wellbeing of many of your patients, particularly those who do not have family or friends to act as advocates. We therefore urgently request that action be taken:

1. Most importantly, all wards to have a supervisor who checks standards of care and has the power to discipline lapses of care . . .

One of the lexicogrammatical patterns that characterised the macro- and hyper-themes in Text 10.3 was the use of dense nominal groups, often with heads that represent abstract phenomena; e.g.

a lack of any clear supervisory <u>system</u>

a significant <u>absence</u> of the care and attention one would expect in a hospital.

a low level bullying <u>culture</u>

three major <u>problems</u>

A second pattern is the degree of appraisal present. For example:

<u>unacceptable</u> *treatment*

<u>*a lack of any clear*</u> *supervisory system*

<u>concerned</u> *nursing staff who were* <u>helpful and kind</u>.

<u>significant absence of the care and attention</u> *one would expect in a hospital.*

a <u>low level bullying</u> *culture*

You came across the use of appraisal for expressing different types of attitude in Chapter 9.

405

The use of appraisal sets up an interpersonal frame for how we are to interpret the writer's position on the issue.

Both these patterns are common in texts across many registers and genres. In the narrative genre, for example, the use of appraisal in hyper-themes can help to build momentum as the story moves from one stage to another. In argument and discussion genres, appraisal serves to punctuate the text with judgements on the issue at key points.

Activity 10.3

The text below was written by a secondary school history student (aged 13 years) and is an example of a discussion genre written in response to the following question:

> *Hitler's leadership was the main reason Nazis came to power in 1933.*
> *Do you agree?*

While the student has developed a reasonable sense of how to organize the overall stages of a discussion genre, the meanings do not fit together or flow as well as they might. (There are also problems with the clause structure and the tenor realisations, but they are not the focus of this activity.)

(a)   Identify the macro-theme. Does it help the reader to predict how the text will unfold overall?

(b)   Identify the hyper-theme for the second paragraph. Can it be improved?

(c)   A hyper-theme is needed to introduce the 'against' arguments that appear in paragraphs 5 and 6. Can you suggest one?

(d)   Observe any patterns in the use of nominal groups and appraisal in our revised macro- and hyper-themes (see Answer key).

Text 10.4 Why Hitler came to power

Mi essay is about ...
why hitler and the nazis were in power. was it because
of the wall st crash was it not ...??? why and how he
became cancelor ??? why he was a good speacker and
why people of germany listerned to him !!!

1

why I agree !!!!
well i agree in some aspects that hitlers leadership was
the main reason nazis came to power in 1933 because hitler
was a very powerful speaker he could manipulate people
in to getting them to think how he thinks his point of
views and his opinons. he may not have used his special
talent to and for the right purpose but because he was
turned down for work he used his talent to make sure
he got what he wanted which you have to admitt is very
very clever because he blamed the jew for getting turned
down jobs.

2

I think the people listened to him because they
wanted someone to blame and with Hitler's manipulative
words they blamed the Jews.

3

i disagree because ...
Hitler just wanted to rule germany so he could take over
england and have everything his way!!!! the more people
joined him the more power he had the more he wanted.
and because of the wall st crash they needed a back up
plan and hitler promised alot of things.!!.

4

conclusion: i think it was a mix between desperation for
help with the wall st crash and because of hitlers
leadership.

5

(Author's personal data)

The initial unfinished clause – *Mi essay is about . . .* – together with the first paragraph sets up some of the aspects that are relevant to the essay question. However, several of these (e.g. *why and how he became chancellor*) are not developed in the essay, and conversely the 'arguments against' (why

I disagree) are not mentioned. To be effective in helping the reader to predict the direction that the discussion will take, it would need to preview both arguments for and arguments against.

A more effective hyper-theme for the second paragraph would also come at a higher level of abstraction and would need to link back to the macro-theme. For example:

> *Further evidence that Hitler's leadership was the main reason Nazis came to power was his ability to make people listen to him.*

Similarly, a hyper-theme is needed to introduce the 'against' arguments (although in a more effective macro-theme they might have already been previewed). One possible rewrite is as follows:

> *Although there are a number of reasons why Hitler's leadership can be seen as the main factor in the Nazis coming to power in 1933, it can also be argued that there are several other important reasons for their ascendance. These include Hitler's obsession with power and territory, and the Wall St. Crash.*

In our reworkings of the hyper-themes, the main message and meanings of the student's essay become more prominent. Notice that, to achieve this, the nominal groups become more abstract and more dense; e.g.

> <u>*Further evidence that Hitler's leadership was the main reason Nazis came to power*</u> *was* <u>*his ability to make people listen to him.*</u>

Note, too, the use of modality in making the writer's position more open to negotiation:

> *Hitler's leadership <u>can</u> be seen as the main factor*

> *it <u>can</u> also be argued that there are several other important reasons*

Clearly, one of the problems facing the writer of Text 10.4 is his lack of experience as a writer. It is only through ongoing exposure to, and practice in, writing such texts that young writers learn to write in more textually sophisticated ways. Nevertheless, it is probably true to say that, regardless of how old, educated, or experienced we are as writers, there are often occasions when we have problems in making a text 'flow'. This may arise in a professional context (for example, when giving a presentation, writing a report, or making a case for promotion) or a personal context (for example, writing a letter of complaint, posting a message to a blog debate, or raising an issue with a local residents' committee). Reworking the macro- and hyper-theme structure is often helpful in tightening the connections between the different parts of the text. In the next section, you will see that choices in the starting point at the level of clause are equally important.

10.3 Providing a frame: clause themes

Activity 10.4

Take the following clause and see how many ways you can rearrange the wording without changing the sense. Take note of which (if any) words have to stay together as a group:

> We had a delicious ice-cream at the café on our way back to Joe's flat from school last week.

(Hint – there are at least ten possible variations!)

You will have seen that if we move around individual words we produce nonsense, such as:

> delicious at Joe's flat week last had a café on ice-cream school from week the back

However, if we keep some words together and move chunks around, then we can produce a number of variations, as illustrated in the Answer key. While some of these may be more likely than others, all are quite acceptable clauses. This gives us some insight into the flexibility of English clauses – it is possible to rearrange certain chunks of a clause and still end up with something meaningful. These chunks correspond to grammatical structures – nominal groups, verbal groups, and prepositional phrases – which in turn generally correspond to functional elements – participants, processes, and circumstances. (Note, however, that, although all the prepositional phrases correspond to circumstances, *last week*, which is a nominal group, is also a circumstance.) You may have noticed that, although these different orderings create different patterns, they do not in any obvious way transform the meaning of the reality they represent. Because the types of process, participant, and circumstance remain the same, the interpretation of the world (the ideational meaning) stays reasonably constant.

Nevertheless, the clauses do differ in subtle ways: they differ as 'packages of information'. Therefore their textual meanings differ. In English, what we put at the beginning and end of a clause is significant. As with choices in macro- and hyper-themes, the meanings we choose to highlight at the start of a clause are generally purposeful and functional. While in theory it is possible to rearrange chunks of a clause, paragraph, or text almost randomly and still end up with something that makes some kind of sense, the coherence may be badly affected. To illustrate this point, compare the following short texts (one is taken from a book on philosophy):

A philosopher is indeed what?

Like the moon, imagine a grey and striated surface. We realise it is less like rock than skin, panning back a little. We understand, further back still, it is the skin of an animal. Is it a rhino? or a hippopotamus? – retreating further reveals it is a large animal.

What, indeed, is a philosopher?

Imagine a surface, grey and striated, like the moon. Panning back a little we realise it is less like rock than skin. Further back still, we understand it is the skin of an animal. Retreating further reveals it is a large animal – is it a rhino? or a hippopotamus?

The second short text is the one that appears in Christopher Ross's *Tunnel Visions* (2002, p. 12). The ideas unfold smoothly, coherently, and effectively, illustrating how things are perceptually modified by proximity and perspective. In the first paragraph, the ideas do not link together so effectively.

Given that there is a reasonable amount of choice concerning which element we begin a clause with, the question arises as to why we make the choices we do and how this affects the information flow and overall coherence of a text. To answer this you need to look at clauses in context and consider what elements come first in each one. This is the focus of Activity 10.5.

Activity 10.5

Read the following short extracts from texts.

(a)   Divide the texts into clauses.

(b)   What kinds of element occur at the beginning of each clause – participants, processes, or circumstances?

(c)   Are there different patterns and principles at work in each of the different texts?

(d)   Are there any functional reasons for this?

Text 10.5 Preheat the oven . . .

1.   Preheat the oven to 170C/325F/Gas3. Line a tin with lightly buttered greaseproof paper or foil.

2.   Put the plain chocolate and butter in a large bowl, place over a pan of simmering water and allow to melt.

(Author's personal data)

Text 10.6 The League of Nations

The League of Nations was also quite successful. It did a lot of work to get the world back on its feet after the crippling effects of the World War. The League worked with refugees and prisoners of war and helped them get back to their motherlands. When a refugee crisis struck in Turkey, the League acted smoothly and successfully to prevent all types of diseases that usually strike in the camps. This was a major achievement from the League's point of view as it proved that the countries could all work together to achieve what they wanted.

(Author's personal data)

Text 10.7 I'm not going out with her

A1: I'm not going out with her at the moment

B1: Ah!

A2: But I should be by around Tuesday night

B2: You said by Monday last time.

A3: Did I? Well I lied.

B3: Yeah, you did.

(Biber *et al.* 1999, p. 1106)

In each text there are different patterns of what comes first in the clauses. There are two main reasons for this – genre (and therefore the overall social purpose of the writer or speaker) and mode (how interactive or planned the language is). In writing, for example, where text is generally planned and edited, usually a great deal of thought goes into organising the text and making clear its overall direction and the key meanings. This is partly because there is no opportunity to use voice or gesture to help structure the information. Neither is there an opportunity for the addressees to interrupt and ask for clarification if they find it difficult to understand. Nor is there any contextual information available to help 'fill out' the meaning. Writers therefore have to be careful to make their meanings 'flow'. In Text 10.5, for example, the use of reference words (*it, this*) in the first part of the clause serves to summarise and link aspects of the preceding historical evidence with the overall claim that the League of Nations was successful.

In SFL, the technical term for the first element or departure point at the level of clause is theme. **Theme** is formally defined as stretching as far as, and including, the first ideational element in a clause – that is, the first participant, process, or circumstance. The remainder of the clause is called the **rheme**. For example:

The League of Nations was also quite successful.

Theme = *The League of Nations*

This is a participant and, hence, an ideational element – and therefore satisfies the definition of theme above.

Rheme = *was also quite successful.*

This is the remaining part of the clause and is therefore the rheme.

Activity 10.6

Practise identifying clause themes by:

(a)   breaking up Text 10.8 (which is an extract from *Great Expectations* by Charles Dickens) into clauses;

(b)   identifying the theme and rheme.

Text 10.8 *Great Expectations*

The marshes were just a long black horizontal line then, as I stopped to look after him; and the river was just another horizontal line, not nearly so broad nor yet so black; and the sky was just a row of long angry red lines and dense black lines intermixed. On the edge of the river, I could faintly make out the only two black things in all the prospect that seemed to be standing upright; one of these was the beacon by which the sailors steered – like an unhooped cask upon a pole – an ugly thing when you were near it; the other a gibbet, with some chains hanging to it which had once held a pirate. The man was limping on towards this latter
. . .

(C. Dickens (1980) *Great Expectations*, Penguin Books, p. 39)

Although the themes in Text 10.8 were relatively straightforward to analyse (in that generally they mapped onto the grammatical subject of each clause), when conducting theme analysis there are several questions that emerge. These are the most common. Here are the responses with illustrations:

1 What happens when there are elements such as finite auxiliaries in interrogatives?

Polar interrogatives were introduced in Chapter 1.

Finite auxiliaries in polar interrogatives (e.g. *does*, *did*, *have*, *has*, etc.) are not ideational elements and therefore do not comprise the whole theme. In polar interrogatives, the theme comprises both the finite and the subject.

<u>Did we</u> see much movement yesterday?

2 What happens when there are question words such as *where* or *how*?

A *wh*-word used in a question (e.g. *what*, *why*, *where*, *when*, and *how*) often functions as a circumstance or participant and therefore counts as an ideational element:

<u>Where</u> did they film that?
Circumstance

<u>Who</u> framed Roger Rabbit?
Participant

3 What about other elements that often come before ideational elements, for instance, vocatives (e.g. *Russell*, *Darling*), modal adjuncts (e.g. *perhaps*, *maybe*), conjunctions, and connectors (e.g. *and*, *but*, *then*, *after*, *when*, *where*) or relativisers (*which*, *that*)?

As in the case of finites, these elements are not ideational and therefore do not comprise the whole theme. The first ideational element also needs to be included in the theme:

<u>Sweetheart you</u> are sadly mistaken

<u>Darling Russell you</u> shouldn't have gone to so much trouble

<u>Perhaps he</u>'s just having a laugh

<u>Maybe he</u>'ll raise his game at the G8?

<u>But it</u>'s just I think that we need to be an opposition . . .

<u>And then she</u> was gone.

<u>A lorry last week</u> pulled into a layby to let us past, || <u>which was</u> nice of him

Non-finite verbs and clauses were examined in Chapters 1–3.

4 What happens where there is a non-finite verb in initial position in the clause?

414

There is no theme, as in the second clause below:

He became a 'bedroom DJ' || learning to mix and beat match.

5   What happens in cases where the subject has been ellipted?

There are different views on this, but the simplest answer is that there is no ideational theme.

She stumbled backwards || and <ellipted subject> shook her head.

6   What happens with minor clauses?

There is no ideational theme in a minor clause, as in the second clause below:

When are you coming? On Monday.

10.4 Shifting focus: marked themes

As previously noted, in writing that is planned, writers are often careful to signpost the direction their text is taking. In the following activity, you will see how they signal to the reader when there is some change in the organisation of information or a shift to a new angle.

Activity 10.7

Read Text 10.9 (an extract from some teaching materials) and Text 10.10 (which was produced by a 12-year-old schoolgirl as an electronically constructed text).

(a)   Decide which genre each is an example of and identify the generic stages.

(b)   Break the text up into ranking clauses, ignoring any embedded clauses or minor clauses.

(c)   Underline the themes of each independent and dependent clause. Note that one theme has already been underlined.

(d)   Look for any overall patterns, and consider where and why the patterns change. What might be the functional reason?

Text 10.9 A woman in white

A woman in white was standing just behind the car, not moving. He could not see her legs, he could not see her head or face. Because of where she was standing[2] he could only see part of her in the rear-view mirror. He did not want to turn around and look at her. He was afraid. He looked into the side mirror and could see a little more. Yes, a woman. It was definitely a woman. But he could not see the head, nor the face. He felt even colder inside now. His stomach suddenly felt very empty. His hands felt as if they were stuck to the steering-wheel. He could not move and she did not move. And then suddenly she too took a step forward and John watched her disappear from the rear-view mirror. He looked at the side mirror and she took another step forward.

(http://www.cambridge.org/elt/readers/pdfs/LP_4_Ladyinwhite.pdf (accessed 14 April 2008))

Text 10.10 Leonardo Da Vinci

Leonardo Da Vinci was an architect, musician, engineer, scientist and inventor. He sketched the first parachute, first helicopter, first aeroplane, first tank, first repeating rifle, first motor car, as well as a swinging bridge and paddle boat. He was one of the first artists to sketch outdoor portraits. Leonardo was a sculptor and designer of costumes. He was also a mathematician and a botanist.

Leonardo was born on the 15th April, 1452, and was brought up by his father who did not marry his mother.

In 1466, at the age of 15, Leonardo joined the studio of Andrea del Verrocchio in Florence, where he spent most of his time painting. Five years later he became a member of St Luke, a painters' society in Florence, and then after 4 years, he worked as an independent artist in Florence where he had his own studio. He differed from other artists because he painted things realistically.

On the 5th August 1473, the first known work of Leonardo came out. It is a pen and ink drawing of a valley, by the river Arno.

Another painting by Leonardo is the *St Jerome*. It was painted around 1481. However, this painting, like many others, is unfinished. If it had been completed it would be as well known as the *Mona Lisa*.

The *Mona Lisa* is Leonardo's most famous painting. In fact, it's thought of as the most famous painting in the history of art. Leonardo started his work in 1503, when Mona Lisa was 24 years old. There is no certainty of who she was, or why he painted her. It has even been suggested that it is a self portrait! He worked on the portrait for the next 4 years.

Leonardo died on the 2nd May 1519, at the age of 67.

You will have seen from the text analysis that the dominant pattern in Text 10.9 (an extract from a narrative genre) is for participants to be in theme position in both the orientation and complication stages:

Orientation:
A woman in white
He
he
Because of where she was standing
he
He

Complication:
He
He
It
But he
He
His stomach

417

His hands
He
and she
And then suddenly
and John
He
and she

Generally speaking, in declarative mood, clause themes in English are participants in the subject role. In the clause beginning *And then suddenly she took a step forward*, however, there is a sudden switch to a circumstance of manner – *suddenly*. This use of the circumstance *suddenly* signals an important shift. Through the unexpected action, the suspense is ratcheted up. It is a signal that the complication of the story is reaching a peak. Where a theme and subject in a declarative clause are not the same, as illustrated here, we call the theme **marked**. This is because, with a marked theme, less typical meanings gain textual prominence. (As a linguistic term, 'marked' means atypical or unusual).

In Text 10.10, which is a biographical recount, a different pattern is established. The initial stage (the orientation) orients the reader to key features of Leonardo Da Vinci's life. In this stage, the themes are predictably the participant (*Leonardo*, *he*), and there is a conflation of theme and (grammatical) subject. In the main record of events stage, however, and in the text overall, the pattern is for themes to be circumstances of location in time or place, providing the departure point of each clause:

Orientation:
Leonardo Da Vinci
He
He
Leonardo
He

Record of events:
Leonardo
In 1466
where he
Five years later
and then after 4 years

where he
He
because he
On the 5th august 1473
It

In the record of events stage, where theme does not conflate with subject, there is a functional reason for such a break in the typical pattern: by foregrounding dates and intervals of time, the writer provides a 'backbone' of relevant historical meaning all the way through the text. Given that the overall social purpose of a biographical recount genre is to record events in a chronological order, this is an appropriate organising principle for such a text.

In biographical recounts there is an optional 'evaluation of person' generic stage, and in this text the young writer moves through such a stage (albeit not as developed as it could be). Within this generic stage, the writer switches theme choice again – the departure point becomes Leonardo's work – the pen and ink drawing, *St Jerome*, and the *Mona Lisa*. Interestingly, the multimodal resources available to the writer (in an electronically constructed text) are also exploited at this stage, with reproductions of the paintings integrated into the text through the use of arrows. You may also have noticed that, in the evaluation of person, another switch occurs. The movement is from past tense (in the record of events stage) to present tense. Present tense is used to express timeless and contemporary views on the significance of the artwork.

10.5 Compressing and packaging: the role of nominalisation

So far, we have primarily considered the problem of text flow from the perspective of writers and readers. For writers, the (potential) problem concerns the successful communication of their ideas and meanings – their message. For readers, the (potential) problem is whether they understand the writer's message without having to work unnecessarily hard to unravel it. In this section, we will continue to consider the linguistic reasons why texts may flow more, or less, smoothly and effectively and cause more, or less, strain, not only for readers but for listeners too.

Activity 10.8

The two texts that follow are the opening sections of two academic lectures. Text 10.11 is from an economics lecture. Text 10.12 is from a lecture given by Daniel Dennett, a prominent American philosopher who specialises in philosophy of the mind. Figure 10.2 represents the speech bubble which accompanies Dennett's lecture and to which he makes several references.

(a)   Read the transcripts of the two lecture extracts.
(b)   Consider which one might be more difficult to follow and process, from the point of view of a 'lay' listener (i.e. a person without specialist field knowledge). What are the reasons for your decision? Provide as much linguistic evidence as you can.

Figure 10.2

Mock-up of speech bubble accompanying Dennett's lecture

Text 10.11 Elasticity

Let me begin by resuming where we finished yesterday we're talking about the concept of elasticity in particular we were looking at the price elasticity of demand we've looked at a number of applications and seen the empirical relevance of this but everything we've done before last time was to talk ra-, in rather vague imprecise terms about the elasticity being a measure of the responsiveness of for example demand to change in price towards the end of last time we started making this concept of ena-, elasticity a more precise quantitative measure and where we got to at the end of last time was to this point here we said we can define the price elasticity of demand as being the proportional change in quantity demanded divided by the prop-, proportional change in price and we can see that easily in terms of the demand curve we start off at some point A we said initial price is P-zero price falls to P-one so delta-P is the change in price and that induces a movement down the demand curve to point B the quantity demanded increasing from Q-zero to Q-one so delta-Q measures the increase in quantity.

(Base Corpus: http://www2.warwick.ac.uk/fac/soc/al/research/projects/resources/base/lecturetranscripts/ps/pslct016_nopause.txt (accessed 30th October 2008))

Text 10.12 Consciousness

Consciousness is both the most familiar thing to all of us and one of the most mysterious. What could be more familiar to you than your own stream of consciousness? And yet how on earth could it fit inside your brain? How on earth could what goes on in your brain actually account for what goes on? What we see here is the cartoonist's wonderful convention, the thought balloon, or thought bubble, and I think everybody understands immediately what's going on here, what appears in the balloon is the stream of consciousness as it were of the person that you see, from whom it is emanating. My favourite example of a thought balloon is this brilliant one from Saul Steinberg, this was a *New Yorker* cover of many years ago, and what we see is that the gentleman over here on the left is looking at a painting in the museum and he is identifying it as a painting by George Braque, and the word Braque reminds him of the word baroque which reminds him of the word barrack and then bark and then poodle, and then we're off to the races and we get his stream of consciousness unfolding with all of its associations. And it's not just words it's colours and shapes and uh even the genius of Steinberg wasn't able to represent recalled odours, aromas and music but we can imagine them being in there too. Now then, what's the problem . . .

(transcribed from Youtube video: http://www.youtube.com/watch?v=wIdxbJyvfNw (no longer available))

For most audiences, Text 10.11 (*Elasticity*) would be more difficult to process than Text 10.12 (*Consciousness*), one reason being the degree of specialist lexis. There are a number of terms used here that are likely to have meaning only within the field of economics (for example, *price elasticity of demand, demand curve, P-zero*). Dennett (at least in the introduction to his lecture) does not make the same assumptions about audience familiarity with technicality.

A second, and perhaps the most significant, reason for why Text 10.11 (*Elasticity*) might be difficult to process is the degree of abstraction in the nominal groups and density of information packed into them; e.g.

the proportional change in quantity demanded divided by the prop-, proportional change in price

In Chapter 6 you saw how the lexical density of a text can be calculated by dividing the number of lexical items or content-carrying words by the number of ranking clauses.

Dennett, on the other hand, uses fewer densely packed nominal groups. Information density is also reduced through greater use of interactivity, resulting from his constant use of rhetorical questioning.

Similarly, while there are a number of examples of **nominalisation** in the economics lecture (e.g. *elasticity, relevance*), there are fewer in Dennett's philosophy one. Nominalisation is a type of grammatical metaphor. In formal written English there is a tendency to represent events, qualities of objects and events, and logical connections, not in their most 'natural' or congruent form as verbs, adjectives, adverbs, and conjunctions, but as nouns. This is particularly the case in academic, technical, and specialised uses of English. Table 10.1 illustrates the shift from congruent to nominalised forms:

You were introduced to interpersonal grammatical metaphor in Chapter 9.

Table 10.1: Nominalisation

Meaning	congruent form	nominalised form
event/process	verb, e.g. *move, demand*	*movement, demand*
quality of object	adjective, e.g. *elastic*	*elasticity*
or event	adverb, e.g. *cruelly*	*cruelty*
logical relationship	connector e.g. *because, therefore*	*cause, reason consequence, result*

The use of nominalisation increases dramatically in topics that are based on abstract concepts, properties, and theories. Arguably, without the ability to nominalise, it would be difficult to develop many scientific notions (e.g. *evaporation*, *radiation*, etc.)

In some cases, nominal groups containing nominalisations are used to condense meanings that would otherwise be spread across more than one clause. Take as an example:

I came back early	*because my father died*
clause 1	clause 2

This can be reworked as one clause with two dense nominal groups. This compression of information has been enabled by the nominalisations *reason*, *return*, and *death*.

The reason for my early return	*was*	*the death of my father*
nominal group 1	process	nominal group 1

From the previous activities, you may have decided that nominalisation, rather than aiding text flow, causes problems. Certainly it often makes texts more dense, which can create problems for processing meaning (particularly if one is listening to a lecture). However, there are a number of reasons why packaging meanings into nominalisations and nominal groups can help the organisation and flow of a text. The next two sections explain these.

10.6 How is nominalisation used?

There are a number of functional reasons why people use nominalisation. These are explained and illustrated below.

1   Nominalisation allows the formation of technical terms that stand for complex but commonly occurring – and commonly understood

423

– phenomena. A simple example is the water cycle, where processes are turned into 'things': see Figure 10.3.

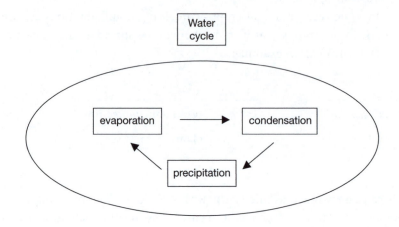

Figure 10.3

Technical terms associated with the water cycle

2   It allows the development of abstract concepts and properties.

Many areas of knowledge deal not with 'real', tangible objects but with abstract concepts (for example, *progress, dysfunction, diffusion, degeneration*).

3   It allows us to bring into relationship one 'thing' with another, often in terms of a causal relationship. For example:

These shaded words are examples of nominalisation

Government oppression	*caused*	*revolution*
agent	process	affected

The loss of neurons	*leads to*	*alterations in the activity of the neural circuits within the basal ganglia that regulate movement*
agent	process	affected

4   It allows for the measurement, comparison, classification, evaluation, and ordering of events.

Once something (such as an event or quality) has been nominalised and turned into a noun we open up the possibility for it to be measured, described, compared, evaluated, ordered, and classified in a way that a verb or adjective cannot be. This is because English has more resources for building up the description of a thing (a noun) than it does for other grammatical phenomena. In technical and scientific fields, in particular, measuring, comparing, and ordering are crucial for the development of the field. Compare for example:

It rained a lot yesterday.

Twenty-five mm of rain fell yesterday – the second heaviest rainfall this century.

You will find that no matter how hard you try, it would be difficult to reach the same kind of precision in the second example if you were restricted to using the verb 'rained'.

5   Nominalisation allows us to organise texts in terms of abstract ideas, reasons, causes, etc.; e.g. *the first significant reason for the Second World War, the second argument in favour of public transport . . .*

Activity 10.9

Using the points above, find examples of different ways in which nominalisation is used in the lecture transcripts (Texts 10.11 and 10.12).

As we have already discussed, macro- and hyper-themes tend to package ideas in fairly abstract language. This pattern is explored in Activity 10.10.

Activity 10.10

Without looking back at Text 10.2 (Personal statement) at the beginning of this chapter, try to work out what nominalisations might fit into the following sections of the text. When you have finished, check how far your answer matches the original version.

Paragraph 1 – macro-theme:

It is always challenging, attempting to remain impartial and attentive to detail in a murder trial over a relative. My _____ to do so was tested greatly during the trial over the _____ of my cousin, Christopher Alaneme. He was stabbed to death in April 2006 by men who were said to be intoxicated with cocaine, and therefore claimed not to have intended to murder him. Such a trial succeeded in consolidating my strong _____ towards Law and justice; not only from the obvious vested _____ I have in the case, but from the incredible _____ to consider every single detail involved.

Paragraph 2 – hyper-theme:

The _____ of French is a huge _____ of my life and fortunately, a very exciting part too.

Paragraph 3 – hyper-theme:

My _____ during my A level course have enabled me to better develop my _____ and skills towards legal studies and French culture.

Paragraph 4 – hyper-theme:

My _____ for Law was first induced by the emotional and practical _____ I gained through avid debating as the Captain of my school debate team.

Paragraph 5 – hyper-theme:

My _____ in the Sixth Form has been spent as a Year 9 form mentor, a Sixth Form prefect and member of the Student Council, which has meant discussing strategies and mediating between the students and teachers.

This activity has shown how packaging meanings into nominalisations in macro- and hyper-themes helps the organisation and flow of a text. One further aspect of nominalisation that we will investigate is related to transitivity patterns and how language users represent events, an area you explored in Chapter 8.

10.7 Nominalisation and the problem of agency

In detective work, a major challenge is to work out who the actors or agents of a crime are. Such a challenge, indeed problem, may also apply to various representations of events we read or hear about. At times it may be difficult to work out who is responsible for what. At other times the question of responsibility may not even occur to us.

There are two main grammatical reasons for this, one of which is connected to nominalisation. Both are linked to patterns of transitivity, so let's briefly recap.

In Chapter 8 we identified patterns by which a text represents particular individuals or groups as initiating or causing actions and events and, hence, as the agents of those actions. For example:

Police	*shot*	*the Brazilian*	*eight times*
agent	process	affected	circumstance

In some transitivity patterns, however, the agent (the initiator or cause) of some action can go unmentioned. This occurs, for example, in **short passive** structures, where there is no *by-phrase*):

Passive voice was introduced in Chapter 2.

Brazilian Jean Charles de Menezes, 27,	*was shot*	*seven times in the head and once in the shoulder*
affected	process	circumstance

Clearly, the kind of formulation in the second example has the potential to obscure or at least de-emphasise the role or involvement of the unmentioned agent. If that action is likely to be viewed negatively by the reader/listener, then such a formulation can act to deflect criticism from those responsible for the action. For example, in the second example above, the use of the short passive means those responsible for the shooting of de Menezes are not brought into the picture (at least in this clause) and, hence, are less likely to be negatively assessed. Short passives, then, may be used to present an agent in a more positive light, or at least to mitigate any negative evaluations of them. (There is considerable work using this type of analysis, referred to as 'critical linguistics' or 'critical discourse analysis'.)

Anther mechanism by which the role of those responsible for an action may be obscured or suppressed is the use of nominal groups and nominalisations. For example, in the following sentence, the act of shooting is buried within an embedded clause, within a nominal group:

The man [[shot dead in Stockwell tube station yesterday]]	*was not connected to*	*the attempted bombings of London on July 21*
participant	relational process	participant

In the next example, too, the action of shooting is buried within the nominal group, but in this case, it is also nominalised.

None of the cameras at the scene of the shooting of Jean Charles de Menezes at Stockwell Tube station on 22 July	*were working*
agent	material process

The use of nominal groups and nominalisations has a similar positioning power to that of the short passive: once again, the reader's attention can be drawn away from those who initiated the action, thereby, at least potentially, deflecting criticism from them. Arguably, the use of nominalisations and nominal groups as illustrated here is more effective rhetorically than the use of short passives, which leave an information gap that may be noted by the reader. Thus, in the case of:

> *Brazilian Jean Charles de Menezes, 27, was shot seven times in the head and once in the shoulder.*

it is possible that the short passive structure itself may provoke the reader to ask who shot him, since the sentence so obviously lacks a by-phrase agent that would provide this information. In contrast, no 'gap' is quite so obviously present in a formulation such as *the shooting of de Menezes*.

Of course, it must be stressed that the use of nominalisations or nominal groups, such as passives, by no means always acts to suppress or obscure agency. Nor are they necessarily deliberately manipulated. Nominalisation often occurs for textual reasons because, through the packaging of meaning, texts may flow more smoothly. In addition, instances of nominalisation vary in the degree to which the responsible agent is retrievable from the context or from elsewhere in the text. For example, in many of the news articles from which the sentences above were taken, it was quite clear that the police were responsible. And, of course, agent suppression is not a necessary feature of nominalisation, since there are various options within nominalisation by which the agent can be explicitly stated; for example:

the shooting of de Menezes <u>by the police</u>

Nevertheless, there are consequences of using nominalisation for the angle of representation, and it is important to bear this in mind when conducting analysis of certain types of text (such as media reports).

10.8 Weaving a text together: the role of cohesive devices

This section briefly explores two types of cohesive device – the use of reference and lexis. Cohesion is an area of the lexicogrammar that is particularly affected by the contextual variable of mode. For example, depending on whether speakers share the same physical context or not, there are likely to be different patterns in the use of anaphoric and exophoric reference.

Activity 10.11

Read the following transcript of a spoken interaction between two people.

(a)   Consider what the context for the text might be.
(b)   Underline any parts of the text where the referents are not clear (i.e. where it is not clear who *they* or *that* etc. is referring to).

Reference and referents were introduced in Chapter 3.

Text 10.13 Did someone bring you?

I: . . . did someone bring you [here]?

P: did someone bring me . . . no nobody brought me . . . I flew in my very own plane . . . I wouldn't trust anybody down at the airport to bring me anywhere

I: why not?

P: why not . . . why not . . . for the very simple fact that I don't think that they can really handle a plane . . . unless they are going to lay me down as a little rose and put me back in the box and they can fly me around because there's a million people out there that can meet the same world . . . it's just world after world after a world right

I: yea

P: and there's no need to be worried about that and if you want them you can go down and get them and if you figure you need plastic ones or other ones if they figure they need those things and they want those things it's entirely up to them

---

(Fine, J. (2006) *Language in Psychiatry*, London: Continuum.)

The encounter above is between an interviewer (I) and a patient (P) who is suffering from mental illness. In the interaction it is difficult to follow the meaning of what P is saying, not only because of the unusualness of the ideational representation, but also because many of the reference words do not clearly link with referents elsewhere in the text (endophoric reference) or in the social context (exophoric reference).

Another aspect of the text that is challenging is the constant switching from one unrelated lexical set to another (*plane, airport*, then *rose*, then *box*, then *same world*). These fast shifts in topic, together with a lack of clear referents, may be found in a range of acquired or developmental communication disorders. Some relatively recent research suggests that more emphasis needs to be placed on training communication partners to develop creative strategies to assist joint meaning-making.

Although this section only touches on aspects of cohesion in relation to reference and lexis, you should be aware that these are lexicogrammatical features that are particularly affected by the role language plays in a particular context, namely the degree to which language is accompanying or constituting a social process.

10.9 Using textual analysis to explore real world problems

The premise of systemic functional grammar presented in this chapter is that each time we use language to represent our experience of the world and to interact with our interlocutors, we are also making choices as to how to organise and package our messages. These choices have implications for the effectiveness of our communication. In this chapter we have seen several examples of problematic as well as effective texts.

Returning now to the scenario that opened the chapter, we can see that the problem with the translated train notices is that they each have a marked theme but that this is not functionally motivated – rather it is the result of a direct translation:

At all seats	_you can listen to 3 ICE Programmes (classical, pop, fairy tales) over the headphones._
marked theme (_at all seats_ is not subject)	

Screens to watch the ICE video programme	_you will find in the backrests of the seats in the first class coaches._
marked theme (_screens to watch the ICE video programme_ is not subject)	

You might like to consider whether there are practical issues in your own environment that would benefit from the approach adopted here of viewing a diversity of lexicogrammatical resources as an extensive system developed to manage information flow in particular contexts.

10.10 Summary

In this chapter we have considered the relationship between lexicogrammar and the textual metafunction, as summarised in Figure 10.4. We have examined the way clause themes and hyper- and macro-themes function in texts and have explored how nominalisation and cohesive devices contribute to textual meaning by organising and linking together the different parts of a text. We have also seen how textual resources can have ideational consequences through obscuring the agents responsible for actions.

In the course of our exploration we have considered the impact of the register variable of mode. We have seen that the more interactive, spontaneous, and therefore more 'spoken-like' a text is, the more likely that it presents experience congruently. Spoken language favours the use of clauses and clause chaining, where processes take place one after the other. It is more in agreement with how reality actually unfolds, i.e. nouns are used to represent people and things; verbs are used to express doings and happenings; conjunctions are used to express logical connections.

We looked at clause chaining in Raeesha's letter to an MP – Text 6.1.

The less interactive, spontaneous, and therefore more 'written-like' a text is, the more likely it is that representations are less directly related to the categories of our experience. In other words, written language tends to be more abstract, with processes often being compressed into 'things' through nominalisation. This suggests that being literate is likely to affect our perceptions of what the world is like.

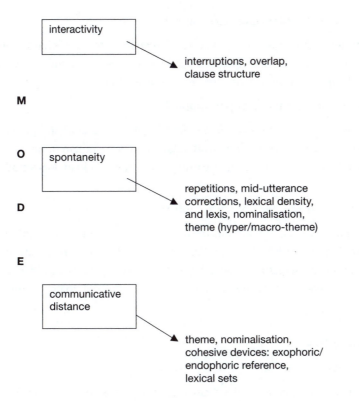

Figure 10.4

Resources for
text flow

Answer key

Activity 10.1

Missing initial paragraph:

It is always challenging, attempting to remain impartial and attentive to detail in a murder trial over a relative. My ability to do so was tested greatly during the trial over the killing of my cousin, Christopher Alaneme. He was stabbed to death in April 2006 by men who were said to be intoxicated with cocaine, and therefore claimed not to have intended to murder him. Such a trial succeeded in consolidating my strong inclination towards Law and justice; not only from the obvious vested interest I have in the case, but from the incredible necessity to consider every single detail involved.

Missing first sentence of paragraph 2:

The study of French is a huge part of my life and fortunately, a very exciting part too. I love to read Le Monde every day . . .

Missing first sentence of paragraph 3:

My studies during my A level course have enabled me to better develop my perceptions and skills towards legal studies and French culture. Critical Thinking has taught me how to be more analytical . . .

Missing first sentence of paragraph 4:

My enthusiasm for Law was first induced by the emotional and practical experiences I gained through avid debating as the Captain of my school debate team. In winning the vast majority of debates held against other schools . . .

Missing first sentence of paragraph 5:

My time in the Sixth Form has been spent as a Year 9 form mentor, a Sixth Form prefect and member of the Student Council, which has meant discussing strategies and mediating between the students and teachers. I committed myself to spending a year tutoring a GCSE maths student . . .

Activity 10.4

Variations:

At the café we had a delicious ice-cream on our way back to Joe's flat from school last week.

On our way back to Joe's flat from school last week we had a delicious ice-cream at the café.

On our way back to Joe's flat from school we had a delicious ice-cream at the café last week.

Last week we had a delicious ice-cream at the café on our way back to Joe's flat from school.

Last week on our way back to Joe's flat from school we had a delicious ice-cream at the café.

Last week at the café on our way back to Joe's flat from school we had a delicious ice-cream.

We had a delicious ice-cream last week at the café on our way back to Joe's flat from school.

We had a delicious ice-cream at the café last week on our way back to Joe's flat from school.

We had a delicious ice-cream at the café on our way back to Joe's flat from school last week.

Activity 10.5

Clause theme pattern	Functional reason for theme patterns
Text 10.5 Preheat Line Put place and allow	Text 10.5 is an extract from a procedure genre (a recipe) and therefore the focus is on the material processes to be carried out (as realised by the imperative verbs in a series of commands).
Text 10.6 The League of Nations It The League When a refugee crisis the League This as it	Text 10.6 is an extract from a discussion genre (*Was the League of Nations doomed from the start?*), and therefore the focus is on the historical participants under discussion (realised through nominal groups and pronouns). Reference words (such as *this*) can serve to summarise a previous stretch of text. Because the text is not interactive, there are no question words (the only speech function deployed is the statement, realised through declaratives).
Text 10.7 I But I You Did Well I Yeah, you	Text 10.7 is an extract from a casual conversation and therefore both interactive and spontaneous. Not surprisingly the starting points for each clause are generally the participants in the dialogue – *I* and *you*. The finite operator *did* also appears since questions are deployed as well as statements.

Notice that in Text 10.6 the connector *when* has been included in the theme, together with the participant *a refugee crisis,* and the connector *as* has been included in the theme together with the participant *it.* This is explained later in the section.

Activity 10.6

The themes are underlined; the remainder of each clause is the rheme.

<u>The marshes</u> were just a long black horizontal line then

<u>as I</u> stopped to look after him

and the river was just another horizontal line, not nearly so broad nor yet so black

and the sky was just a row of long angry red lines and dense black lines intermixed

On the edge of the river, I could faintly make out the only two black things in all the prospect that seemed to be standing upright;

one of these was the beacon by which the sailors steered – like an unhooped cask upon a pole –

<it was> an ugly thing

when you were near it

the other <was> a gibbet, with some chains hanging to it which had once held a pirate

The man was limping on towards this latter . . .

Activity 10.7

Genre

Narrative – because the text is incomplete we only have the stages orientation and complication. We have identified the complication as beginning at *He was afraid* because typically, in a narrative, suspense and emotion (realised through the appraisal system of attitude) become prominent in this stage.

Orientation

|| A woman in white was standing just behind the car, not moving. || ||| He could not see her legs, || he could not see her head or face. ||| Because of where she was standing || he could only see part of her in the rear-view mirror. ||| He did not want || to turn around and look at her. |||

Complication

|| He was afraid. || ||| He looked into the side mirror || and could see a little more. ||| Yes, a woman. || It was definitely a woman. || But he could not see the head, nor the face. || He felt even colder inside now. || His stomach suddenly felt very empty. || His hands felt || as if they were stuck to the steering-wheel. ||| He could not move || and she did not move. ||| And then suddenly she too took a step forward || and John watched || her disappear from the rear-view mirror. ||| He looked at the side mirror || and she took another step forward. |||

Genre

Biographical recount with the three stages: orientation, record of events, and evaluation of person. (Themes underlined.)

Orientation

|| <u>Leonardo Da Vinci</u> was an architect, musician, engineer, scientist and inventor. || <u>He</u> sketched the first parachute, first helicopter, first aeroplane, first tank, first repeating rifle, first motor car, as well as a swinging bridge and paddle boat. || <u>He</u> was one of the first artists to sketch outdoor portraits. || <u>Leonardo</u> was a sculptor and designer of costumes. || <u>He</u> was also a mathematician and a botanist. ||

Record of events

||| <u>Leonardo</u> was born on the 15th April, 1452, || and was brought up by his father who did not marry his mother. |||

||| <u>In 1466</u>, at the age of 15, Leonardo joined the studio of Andrea del Verrocchio in Florence || <u>where he</u> spent most of his time painting. ||| <u>Five years later</u> he became a member of St Luke, a painters' society in Florence, || <u>and then after 4 years</u>, he worked as an independent artist in Florence || <u>where he</u> had his own studio. ||| <u>He</u> differed from other artists || <u>because he</u> painted things realistically. |||

|| <u>On the 5th August 1473</u>, the first known work of Leonardo came out. || <u>It</u> is a pen and ink drawing of a valley, by the river Arno ||.

Evaluation of person

|| <u>Another painting by Leonardo</u> is the *St Jerome*. || <u>It</u> was painted around 1481. || <u>However, this painting</u> like many others is unfinished. || ||| <u>If it</u> had been completed || <u>it</u> would be as well known as the *Mona Lisa*. |||

|| <u>The *Mona Lisa*</u> is Leonardo's most famous painting. || <u>In fact, it</u>'s thought of as the most famous painting in the history of art. || ||| <u>Leonardo</u> started his work in 1503, || <u>when Mona Lisa</u> was 24 years old. ||| || <u>There</u> is no certainty of who she was, or why he painted her. ||| <u>It</u> has even been suggested || <u>that it</u> is a self portrait! ||| || <u>He</u> worked on the portrait for the next 4 years. ||

|| <u>Leonardo</u> died on the 2nd May 1519, at the age of 67. ||

Activity 10.9

These are just some examples:

- Consciousness;

- Elasticity;

- delta-P is *the change in price* and that induces *a movement down the demand curve to point B* (nominalisation allows relationships, including causal ones);

- the price elasticity of demand.

Activity 10.11

P: why not . . . why not . . . for the very simple fact that I don't think that they can really handle a plane . . . unless they are going to lay me down as a little rose and put me back in the box and they can fly me around because there's a million people out there that can meet the same world . . . it's just world after world after a world right

I: yea

P: and there's no need to be worried about that and if you want them you can go down and get them and if you figure you need plastic ones or other ones if they figure they need those things and they want those things it's entirely up to them.

Notes

1   The use of the term 'theme' in functional grammar needs to be distinguished from its more general (often literary) use, which refers to the most important or general messages in a work of art, film, public talk, etc.

2   Notice that this is a prepositional phrase (*because of* . . .) although it has an embedded clause within it (*because of [[where she was standing]]*).

Bookend: further reading

As we proposed in Chapter 1, the purpose of *Exploring English Grammar* is to present an account of a grammar that is useful. We have sought to do this by means of activities that relate the insights of formal grammar to those of functional grammar. In the process, we have introduced new terms to handle concepts that were not a part of traditional formal grammar but come into view when a language observer looks at what language users do through a functional lens. Now that you have completed this journey from formal to functional grammar, you may be wondering how to apply and perhaps extend the knowledge and skills you have developed so far.

It should, first, be recognised that functional grammar is still an emerging approach to the description of language. Traditional formal grammar has had a much longer history in which to both establish itself, and also alienate people from the study of grammar. For those excited by the prospects for revitalisation and growth that functional grammar promises, its originality is appealing. However, originality may be seen differently by those who are committed to formal accounts on the one hand, or those who have lost faith and interest in grammar entirely on the other.

If the model of grammar favoured by your institution or colleagues is not functional in orientation, you may perhaps feel constrained in using your new knowledge in your professional context. If you are a teacher, for example, institutional policies, testing practices, curricula, and textbooks may be a barrier. Decisions will therefore need to be made as to how to apply your new tools – in deciding, for example, what concepts and terms will be useful to you as a professional/teacher and what may be useful to your clients/students/colleagues. Your new analytical skills may be useful, for example, in conducting needs analyses or diagnostic tests, in selecting and creating texts and resources, in carrying out professional research, or in enhancing the communicative effectiveness of your organisation, your colleagues, or yourself.

Whatever you decide, you may wish to extend the basic introduction to systemic functional grammar that this book has provided. Below, we therefore make some suggestions for further reading and study.

If you want to develop your general understanding of SFG we recommend the following:

Bloor and Bloor (2004) *The Functional Analysis of English*, second edition, Arnold.

This is a comprehensive and thorough introduction to SFG aimed in particular at English language teachers. There is a mixture of explanation and exercises, and the authors deal with ambiguities, complexities, and problems.

Butt, Fahey, Spinks, and Yallop (2000) *Using Functional Grammar: An explorer's guide*. NCELTR, Macquarie.

This provides a combination of explanatory text with some exercises and is aimed at university students, teachers, and others interested in language discourse. There are sections and exercises designed specifically for English language teachers.

Downing and Locke (2006) *English Grammar: A university course*, second edition, Routledge.

This is a reference grammar and workbook that uses terminology consistent with *Exploring English Grammar* and develops the grammatical concepts presented here to a more advanced level.

Eggins (2005) *An Introduction to Systemic Functional Linguistics,* second edition, Continuum.

This is a lucid and comprehensive introduction to systemic functional grammar seen from a genre perspective.

Martin and Rose (2003) *Working with Discourse*, Continuum.

This book shows how tools developed in systemic functional linguistics and register and genre theory can be used in a range of disciplines. It requires no prior knowledge of functional linguistics and avoids academic complexity wherever possible.

Thompson, G. (2004) *Introducing Functional Grammar*, second edition, Arnold.

This introduction to SFG is aimed at university students and teachers. There is a mixture of clear and accessible explanation and exercises.

If you want to develop your understanding of SFG and see some of the connections with corpus linguistics, we recommend the following introductory textbooks produced by the Open University:

O'Halloran, K.A. and Coffin, C. (eds.) (2006) *Getting Started: Describing the grammar of speech and writing*, Milton Keynes: The Open University.
O'Halloran, K.A. (ed.) (2006) *Getting Inside English: Interpreting texts*, Milton Keynes: The Open University.
Coffin, C. (ed.) (2006) *Getting Practical: Evaluating everyday texts*, Milton Keynes: The Open University.
Hewings, A. (ed.) (2006) *Getting Down To It: Undertaking research*, Milton Keynes: The Open University.
Mayor, B. (ed.) (2006) *Applications: Putting grammar into professional practice*, Milton Keynes: The Open University.
English Grammar in Context (http://www.ouw.co.uk/classifications/Languages.shtm)

If you are working in first, second, or foreign language teaching contexts, we recommend the following:

Lock (1996) *Functional English Grammar*, Cambridge University Press.

This book is designed for teacher educators and second language teachers with a number of examples being taken from languages other than English. The following workbooks are primarily aimed at teachers:

Gerot and Wignell (1994) *Making Sense of Functional Grammar*, Queensland: Gerd Stabler.
Gerot (1995) *Making Sense of Text*, Queensland: Gerd Stabler.

Droga and Humphrey (2002) *A Workbook for Getting Started with Functional Grammar*, NSW: Target Texts.

If you want to sharpen up your analytical skills and practise working on texts that raise interesting analytical issues, we recommend:

Martin, Matthiessen, and Painter (1997) *Working with Functional Grammar*, Arnold (new edition forthcoming).

This is partly designed to work in tandem with Halliday's *Introduction to Functional Grammar*. It has a series of trouble-shooting sections that are excellent for dealing with typical problems/misunderstandings.

If you want to understand more about the theoretical underpinnings of SFG, we recommend the following. Please note, however, that they do not provide any activities to develop analytical skills.

Halliday, M.A.K. and Mathiessen, C.M.I.M. (2004) *An Introduction to Functional Grammar*, London: Arnold.

This is the latest edition of the book that presents the grammar on which all the other recommended books in this list are based.

Halliday, M.A.K. and Hasan, R. (1976) *Cohesion in English*, London and New York: Longman.

This seminal account by Halliday and Hasan is based on a systemic functional approach to language and focuses on how language items within clauses work to unite clauses into cohesive text.

Martin, J.R. (1992) *English Text: System and structure*, Philadelphia: John Benjamins.

In this, Martin outlines an approach to discourse analysis based on systemic functional linguistics. This influential book assumes prior knowledge of *An Introduction to Functional Grammar*, so is not an introductory text.

If you are interested in using the tools of SFG to look critically at language we recommend:

Young and Fitzgerald (2006) *The Power of Language: How discourse influences society*, Equinox.

This provides an introduction to discourse analysis aimed at undergraduate and postgraduate students of SFG and critical discourse analysis.

If you are interested in genre and different types of genre, as well as the relations between them, we recommend:

Derewianka (1991) *Exploring How Texts Work*, NSW: PETA.

This provides a basic introduction to genre and is aimed at primary school teachers.

Christie, F. and Martin, J.R. (1997) *Genre and Institutions. Social Processes in the Workplace and School*, London: Cassell.

This edited collection discusses the different genres identified in a range of school subjects and workplace settings.

Martin, J.R. and Rose, D. (2008) *Genre Relations: Mapping culture*, London: Equinox.

This book introduces the SFL approach to genre analysis and provides a set of tools for thinking about genres and genre relations. In particularly it considers 'families' of genres, including stories, reports, and explanations, and procedural and associated genres.

References

Chapter 2

OED Online (1989) *The Oxford English Dictionary*, second edition, Oxford University Press (available from: http://dictionary.oed.com/cgi/entry/ 50189128 (accessed 10 January 2008)).

Chapter 3

Angela Downing and Philip Locke (2002) *A University Course in English Grammar*, London: Routledge.

Carter, R. and McCarthy, M. (1997) *Exploring Spoken English*, Cambridge: Cambridge University Press.

Chapter 5

Pinker, Steven (1999) *Words and Rules: The ingredients of language*, London: Weidenfeld and Nicolson.

Yule, George (1998) *Explaining English Grammar*, Oxford: Oxford University Press.

Chapter 7

Halliday, M.A.K. (2004) *An Introduction to Functional Grammar* (revised by Christian M.I.M. Matthiessen), London: Arnold.

Martin, J.R. (1992) *English Text: System and structure*, Amsterdam: John Benjamins.

Martin, J.R. and Rose, D. (2007) *Working with Discourse: Meaning beyond the clause*, second edition, London: Continuum.

Martin, J.R. and Rose, D. (2008) *Genre Relations: Mapping culture*, London: Equinox.

Chapter 8

Al-Ali, Mohammed N. (2004) 'How to get yourself on the door of a job: A Cross-cultural Contrastive Study of Arabic and English Job Application Letters', in *Journal Of Multilingual And Multicultural Development*, 25(1): 1–23 (reprinted with permission of Taylor & Francis Journals UK).

Armstrong, E. (2001) 'Connecting lexical patterns of verb usage with discourse meanings in aphasia', *Aphasilogy*, 15: 1029–46.

Halliday, M., (1994) *An Introduction to Functional Grammar*, London: Edward Arnold.

Chapter 10

Ross, R. (2002) *Tunnel Visions*, London: Fourth Estate.

Index

446

www.routledge.com/textbooks/9780415478168

Visit the *Exploring English Grammar* **website** and discover a range of online resources designed to test and support your understanding of formal and functional grammar.

The ideal extra resource, this website will enhance your learning experience through:

- additional activities
- interactive quizzes
- further passages for analysis and discussion
- links to relevant websites
- more information on related Routledge titles for further study